ACPL ITEM
DISCARDED

D1601290

DO NOT REMOVE
CARDS FROM POCKET

DEMCO

A Naturalist in
NEW GUINEA

Number Seventeen
The Corrie Herring Hooks Series

A Naturalist in
NEW GUINEA

Bruce M. Beehler

Illustrated by John Anderton
Photographs by the author

University of Texas Press, Austin

Copyright © 1991
by the University of Texas Press
All rights reserved
Printed in the United States of America

First Edition, 1991

Requests for permission to reproduce
material from this work should be sent to
Permissions, University of Texas Press,
Box 7819, Austin, Texas 78713-7819.

Jacket / Cover: View of Mt. Victoria from
Mambare River
Title Page: Palm trees and beach, near
Vanimo, West Sepik Province

∞ The paper used in this publication
meets the minimum requirements of
American National Standard for Information Sciences—Permanence of Paper
for Printed Library Materials, ANSI
Z39.48-1984.

Library of Congress
Cataloging-in-Publication Data
Beehler, Bruce McP.
    A naturalist in New Guinea / by
Bruce M. Beehler ; illustrations by John
Anderton. — 1st ed.
        p.   cm. — (The Corrie
Herring Hooks series ; no.17)
    Includes bibliographical references
and index.
    ISBN 0-292-75541-4 (alk. paper).—
ISBN 0-292-75544-9 (pbk. : alk. paper)
    1. Birds—New Guinea. 2. Beehler,
Bruce McP. 3. Ornithologists—United
States—Biography. I. Anderton, John.
II. Title. III. Series.
QL691.N48B45   1991
508.95'092—dc20   90-44280
                                  CIP

Contents

To my mother,
a self-taught naturalist who encouraged my explorations

Preface

In 1974, as a senior in college, I was awarded a fellowship for a year of postgraduate study abroad. My winning application outlined a plan to study the courtship behavior of birds of paradise in Papua New Guinea, then an Australian dependency in the southwest Pacific. At that time, I knew little of New Guinea or of birds of paradise, but I was ready for an adventure.

What, exactly, led me to attempt that initial, year-long stay in New Guinea? Why would I leave my familiar surroundings in the eastern United States to fly across the Pacific in order to become an unpaid, novice staff member of the Wau Ecology Institute? It can only be explained by my passionate interest in birds that developed when I was a schoolboy.

My parents encouraged my interest in birds and the outdoors. Several times a year my mother drove me to the big public library in downtown Baltimore to search through its considerable collection of ornithological books. On weekends, my father took my brother and me on various outings that allowed us to see birds not generally found in our neighborhood. My father spoke frequently of his boyhood adventures in the countryside north of Baltimore. He had spent many a summer day hunting for birds' nests with neighbors and school chums E. Thomas Gilliard and Brooke Meanley. Meanley went on to become a wildlife biologist with the U.S. Fish and Wildlife Service, specializing on birds of marshlands and southern swamps. Gilliard, on the other hand, became a curator of ornithology at the American Museum of Natural History, in New York, and devoted years to studying the birds of New Guinea, especially the birds of paradise. As a youngster I had pored over the *National Geographic* articles Gilliard wrote about his expeditions to the South Pacific.

My interest in birds and the outdoors grew during my school years. For a dozen summers I visited the Adirondack Mountains in upstate New York, and there I frequently stalked birds with the tiny opera glasses loaned to me by my grandfather. During these Adirondack summers I learned the ways of the woods: camping out under a canvas tarp; surviving a long hike in the chill mountain rain; or reveling in the challenge of climbing a mountain that had no trail to its summit.

———

Getting to New Guinea that first time was more a product of luck and chance than of conscious design. First, I decided I wanted to win a Thomas J. Watson Fellowship, a no-strings-attached grant to travel overseas for independent study, although I remained uncertain about where, exactly, to go. New Guinea was not the most obvious choice.

I visited Professor Nathaniel Lawrence at his home, a few minutes' walk from my dormitory. While I walked there, my mind raced with schemes of overseas adventure. I knew I wanted to study birds, but where? I myself had never *been* overseas. Lawrence did not let me down. Within two minutes of my arriving at his house we were upstairs with an open atlas, scanning the continents for inspiration. One of his first suggestions was the vast marshland of the Camargue in southwestern France, famed for its waterbird populations. I shied away from this because I did not speak French and lacked a strong interest in waterbirds. Lawrence's hand moved across the page and settled on the island of New Guinea, perched like some deformed bird atop the Cape York Peninsula of northernmost Australia. Birds of paradise, jungle, headhunters, and the missing Michael Rockefeller were about all I could conjure up at that point. When birds of paradise caught my imagination, I thought of my father's friend Tom Gilliard, and I made my decision.

New Guinea! To visit that mountainous, jungle-clad tropical island just once is a naturalist's dream. To spend nearly five years there over eight separate visits has been the dominating experience of my life. For this, I owe many persons and organizations generous thanks.

Professors Nathaniel Lawrence and C. Frederick Rudolph, of Williams College, advised and supported me in my successful application for a Watson Fellowship. The Thomas J. Watson Foundation supported my first year in the field. During that time, and on several subsequent stays, I was based at the Wau Ecology Institute, New Guinea's first biological field station. These various visits were made possible by the financial assistance of the Smithsonian Institution, Princeton University, National Geographic Society, New York Zoological Society, Society of Sigma Xi, and the Frank M. Chapman Fund of the American Museum of Natural History.

My Papuan research was carried out with the permission of Papua New Guinea's Department of Environment and Conservation, headed by Karol Kisokau. Success of the fieldwork often depended on the efficient help of my New Guinean field technicians, especially Ninga Kawa (now deceased), Michael Yamapao, Amat Titi, Timis Surrey, Michael Lucas, and Rodney Goga.

Various researchers and staff members of the Wau Ecology Institute (WEI) helped me in many ways. The late Dr. J. L. Gressitt, founder and director of WEI, initially invited me to use the station as a base of operations and continually encouraged me in my studies. Allen Allison, Agnes Safford, Paul Kores, Abid beg Mirza, Betsy and Wayne Gagné, Steve and Melinda Pruett-Jones, Harry Sakulas, Martin Simon, Ellen Fitzpatrick, and Yael Lubin were especially generous with their friendship, advice, and assistance. Research volunteers Andy Hare, Lee Rocke, Pauline Duncan, Jim Grant, John Woinarski, Maria McCoy, and Karen Kool provided valuable field help on several aspects of my work in Papua New Guinea.

Residents in New Guinea who provided all sorts of support were: Ian Fraser, Roy and Margaret Mackay, Brian Finch, Helen and Michael Hopkins, Ian and Barbara Burrows, Roger and Jennie Hicks, Jim and Jennie Croft, Karin Malim, and Chris and Pacquita Boston. My wife, Carol, accompanied me on expeditions to New Guinea in 1982 and

1984. I thank her for helping me in the field and sharing my love of that island, its people, and its natural history.

As my doctoral supervisor at Princeton University, John Terborgh encouraged me to choose a dissertation field project in New Guinea. He, along with Henry Horn, Robert M. May, and S. Dillon Ripley, oversaw my doctoral research. Dillon Ripley has unfailingly encouraged my studies of New Guinea since 1975, and to him I owe a great debt of gratitude.

Finally, I thank Roger Pasquier and David Wilcove for their advice and comments on an earlier draft. John Anderton produced the evocative scratchboard sketches that add so much to this book. This work became a family effort when my wife cheerfully agreed to design the book for publication.

Introduction

*I*n 1982, my wife and I spent our honeymoon on the Si River, in the Kunamaipa lowlands of Central Province, Papua New Guinea. Spending a honeymoon in the jungle was not my idea of a sadistic prank—it just so happened that this ornithological field trip had been planned in advance of our brief engagement and subsequent marriage, and we agreed that the expedition should go forward as planned. Carol's willingness to accompany me to New Guinea made it possible for us to combine honeymoon, jungle camping, and ecological field study.

This was Carol's first visit to the tropical rainforest, and I wanted to share with her, first hand, an environment that is as awe inspiring and complex as any on earth. Carol, a graphic designer, was fascinated by the forest and the experience of camping in a spot so isolated from the world she had previously known. She marveled at the profusion of small but colorful butterflies that swarmed in the gravel of the river's shallows on sunny days. She was swept away by the sight of a Great-billed Heron slowly gliding up the river's course, each wingbeat a ponderous achievement seemingly in defiance of laws of flight. The tiny leeches that crept, inchwormlike, onto her wet boots and socks made her blood run cold. I watched her reaction to the novelty of it all and then and there decided that I would write a book describing the New Guinea I knew as a naturalist. This might serve as a lay introduction to the island's natural history and a sort of catalog of the things naturalists do when out in the forest.

I decided the best format for such a book was a more-or-less chronological narrative based on my own experiences. I arrived on the island in early 1975, a recent college graduate on my first overseas travel. I stayed in Papua New Guinea for fifteen months, based at the Wau Ecology Institute, but also traveling extensively. In 1976 I left Papua New Guinea to return to graduate school in biology. I did two years of courses and independent study before returning to do my doctoral field research. I spent twenty-nine months studying the behavior and ecology of birds of paradise. During that sojourn I again traveled about the region, visiting western New Guinea (Irian Jaya), Bougainville and Goodenough islands, and various parts of mainland Papua New Guinea. Since joining the Smithsonian Institution in 1981, I have visited New Guinea an additional six times as part of my continuing ecological studies of birds of paradise.

This book describes a number of these field trips, from my ascent into the Saruwaged Range with Paul Kores in 1975 to our frustrating efforts to study Macgregor's Bird of Paradise in the alpine woodlands of the English Peaks in 1986 and 1987.

I have embellished this generally linear sequence of events with additional brief narratives on important facets of Papuan history and natural history. In some instances, as with World War II and a number of complex ecological phenomena, I have appended discrete sections that describe these separate from my own story.

In chapters 1 through 3, I focus on my first experiences on the island and my initial tentative attempts to study birds in New Guinea's forbidding mountain forests. Here I highlight the sights and experiences most remarkable to a novice's eye. I begin my initiation on the grounds of the Wau Ecology Institute, in a pleasant, heavily settled valley in the mountains of eastern New Guinea. I then shift to Mount Kaindi and Bulldog Road, in the hills above Wau, where I establish my first field-study camps for learning the birdlife.

In chapter 4 I describe two expeditions I made to Goodenough Island, in the Milne Bay section of southeastern Papua New Guinea.

Here I encounter an environment and culture quite distinct from what I have grown accustomed to in the mountainous Wau area.

Chapters 5 and 6 focus on field studies related to my doctoral work on birds of paradise. The bulk of this work I did on Mount Missim, outlined in chapter 5, supplemented by brief field studies made in Papua New Guinea's highlands area, northwest of Wau and Mount Missim.

In chapter 7 I take a first-hand look at Irian Jaya, Indonesia's easternmost province, comprising the western half of New Guinea. Culturally, the contrasts with Papua New Guinea are striking, and the natural history is just more and better of what I have come to know from Papua New Guinea. Irian Jaya remains one of the great unstudied wildernesses of the Old World tropics.

All of my initial field experiences in New Guinea focused on the mountains. I held a lingering fear of the humid lowland forests that dominate in many coastal areas and river basins. In chapter 8 I speak of experiences from expeditions to Papua New Guinea's rich lowland jungles in the southeast and northwest, respectively. Today, the lowlands hold a fascination for me equal to that of the Papuan montane forest.

In the final chapter I describe two trips to Lake Omha, the tiny alpine tarn high in the English Peaks, in search of the elusive and little-known Macgregor's Bird of Paradise. I describe New Guinea's alpine and subalpine environments and delve into the mystery of the bird of paradise known to the local people as Mo, the island's most specialized fruit-eating bird.

The events in the book span a period of more than a decade. During that period, Papua New Guinea achieved political independence from Australia (on September 16, 1975) and has changed in a multitude of ways. The Papua New Guinea I saw in July 1989 is not the same country I knew in 1975. The new nation is more sophisticated and more westernized. The Papua New Guinea of 1975, I believe, is of greater interest to the reader, and I have stressed the old and the traditional over the new and the Western. The old and the traditional are still present, but for a visitor to see them today requires more effort and travel further into the interior, where the trappings of modern civilization have failed to make their impression.

A note about hardships. Throughout the narrative I have high-lighted the "difficulties" of doing fieldwork in the Papuan forest. I personally think these challenging moments are more interesting to the reader than the "fun" or "leisure" times that, in most cases, are indistinguishable from such times back in the United States. I would not trade the hardships I experienced in New Guinea for anything—they today comprise some of the clearest (and often most amusing) memories of my thirty-eight year existence. Working in the field in New Guinea is all about testing one's inventiveness and spirit. This, in fact, is the real "fun." The reader should thus refrain from interpreting my more graphic descriptions of tough experiences as complaints. For biologists working in the Papuan rainforest, the highs and lows are inextricably linked, and that is what makes these experiences so memorable and worthy.

This is not a book of headhunters and cannibals. Both phenomena were commonplace in the days long prior to my first visit. These two topics have continued to fascinate western minds, and yet I hope to prove, in the following pages, that there is much more to New Guinea that can waken the imagination and please the mind.

Opposite: Rainbow Lorikeets

1 First Impressions

On an afternoon in early April 1975, a Qantas jet carried me northward from Brisbane, Australia, toward Port Moresby, Papua New Guinea. We were high over the Coral Sea when the pilot announced that we could see our destination. From my window I could make out little more than thick stacks of clouds—a typical Papuan vista, especially in April, the end of the rainy season.

The huge, mountainous bulk of New Guinea, surrounded by warm tropical waters, generates clouds and rain in abundance. Warm, water-logged winds sweep off the sea to form clouds that grow and settle on the foothills and higher ranges. The rain from these cloud banks produces the rich rainforests I had come to study.

When the Papuan coast appeared, dark against the white of the waterline and reef, the main impression was one of heavy atmosphere. It was clear and bright out over the sea, in strong contrast to the somber shades of dull green and gray inland from the coast. Low, thin clouds reached out to the coastline but ended abruptly there.

Landing at Jackson's Field, Port Moresby, I found the sun shining. As I was to learn on my first flight into the interior, the real stuff—the thick weather—sat atop the higher mountain ranges. The coastal area around Port Moresby was under thin overcast, but here the rain rarely fell, and the sun usually broke through for much of each day. Clouds dominate the Papuan environment, even in the drier parts of the island.

———

I now had arrived on an equatorial island of near-continental proportions. Fifteen hundred miles long and 450 miles wide at its broadest, New Guinea is larger than Borneo or Madagascar and second only to ice-bound Greenland. New Guinea lies at the heart of the islands of the southwestern Pacific. So many islands! The Bismarck Archipelago stretches to the northeast; the Solomons to the east; the Trobriand, D'Entrecasteaux, and Louisiade islands to the southeast; Torres Strait Islands to the south; Aru and Kai islands to the southwest; Moluccan Islands to the west; and Palau (Belau) Islands to the northwest. Only the great, isolated continent of Australia, immediately to the south, outsizes New Guinea in this Pacific realm.

So much salt water! New Guinea is ringed by seas with exotic names: Coral, Arafura, Banda, Seram, Bismarck, and Solomon—not to mention the vast South Pacific. In general, the seas to the south of the island are shallow and warm, whereas those to the north are deep and cool. The Solomon Sea, on the northern side of the island, is the site of the Planet Deep, a 26,000-foot oceanic trench. By contrast, the

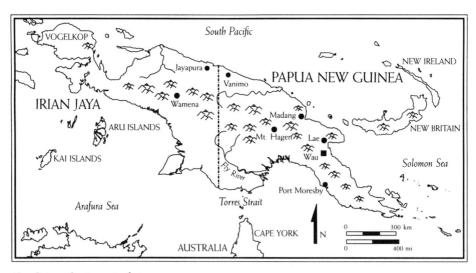

New Guinea, showing major features

Torres Strait, separating New Guinea from Australia, is littered with reefs and atolls and is nowhere deeper than 600 feet. Many of the shallower sections were dry land during the last Ice Age, some ten thousand years ago.

Mountains, however, define New Guinea. Much of the geological history of the island has involved mountain building processes in competition with the ever-working actions of erosion, producing deep gorges, vast alluvial plains, swamps, steep scarps, and highland plateaus. In April 1975, it was the montane environment that attracted me, but first I had to negotiate coastal Port Moresby, with its bureaucrats nestled in musty government offices, its hilly brown savannas, and its curiously old-fashioned city center.

Port Moresby

Disembarking onto the black tarmac of Jackson's Field, I was hit by the sun's furious glare and the thick, heated air. These forever seem to hang about tropical airports. Never again would I step off a plane in the tropics dressed in coat, tie, and long pants, unless in the relative cool of the night.

I had arrived in Port Moresby with no reservations for lodging, no foreign currency, no local residents to meet me, not even a list of available hotels. The last of these I did find posted on a wall of the open airport, a simple concrete structure cooled by banks of slowly rotating overhead fans. I jotted down several names and then hailed a taxi. I failed to convince the Pidgin-speaking driver that I preferred cheap lodgings. After being turned away from the oldest and most expensive resort hotel on Ela Beach (no vacancy), I was dropped by the cabby at the town's newest hotel in the inland suburb of Boroko. My large, spotlessly clean room cost forty-two dollars a night—to me a king's ransom. Meals were tasty but outrageously expensive. At these rates, my cash would be gone in a week's time. Since I had forwarded most of my grant money directly to Wau, I needed to do my city business quickly and move on. In two hectic days I visited the Wildlife Department, the university, and a local amateur ornithologist, Bill Peckover, with whom I had corresponded before my departure. These various efforts proved informative, but as with nearly anyone who arrives in Port Moresby with the ultimate objective of getting into the interior, I was eager to escape from my expensive hotel, the crowds, and the dust of the largest city on the island.

Port Moresby is nonetheless a marvel to the first-time visitor to the tropics. The vistas of sea and harbor are superb; the water is many hues of green and blue. The sharp, conical hills that define the coast and harbor have the look of extinct volcanoes, although they are not. The few birds I saw around town seemed wonderfully exotic. I loved the chattering flocks of Rainbow Lorikeets that raced overhead and hid in the coconut palms along Ela Beach. These multicolored parrots excited senses trained to the likes of Robins, Wood Thrushes, and Myrtle Warblers. The Black-faced Cuckoo-shrikes that inhabited the eucalypts in the savanna behind my hotel were unlike any birds I had known from my bird-watching in North America. Small flocks of the cuckoo-shrikes sailed gracefully from tree to tree with an almost hawklike flight. They had a distinctive habit of stiffly flicking their wings after perching.

In 1975, Port Moresby was a sleepy colonial capital, small and undeveloped. Whereas the coastline was quite beautiful, the hilly savanna that surrounded the town was drab. Squatters regularly burned the roadside grasslands, and large black swaths of burn scarred the hillsides. I was to find that this casual roadside pyromania is a national pastime. In the dry season the fires sweep the countryside, and the smoke fills the sky day after day. At the time, this seemed like nothing more than an unsightly nuisance. Today, with threat of the Greenhouse Effect, the Papuan pyromania is one more contribution to the excess of atmospheric carbon dioxide. Unfortunately, in spite of the local authorities' increased environmental awareness, roadside burning continues.

The city was a shopper's nightmare. The two competing all-purpose stores, Steamships and Burns Philp (not Philip), provided little more than the most basic supplies and foods. I wondered what I would be eating for the next year. In any event, I wanted to get to Wau (pronounced "wow"), the mountain town where I was to be stationed, although I had no reason to expect conditions there to be any better.

The night before leaving Port Moresby I dined with Bill Peckover, who lived in a small bungalow on a hill overlooking the air field. He served as an official in the post and telecommunications department, but his love was bird photography. While having coffee in his living room I heard the chirps of a House Gecko, which I initially took to be the call of some nocturnal bird. These diminutive lizards, nearly transparent white, commonly live in houses in coastal New Guinea and on many neighboring islands. The geckos spend most nights clinging either on vertical walls or on ceilings, near a light fixture. They prey on the insects that are attracted to the light. The *chk chk chk chk* sounds are synonymous with evening in the lowlands of New Guinea.

After we discussed the relative merits of painting versus photography for illustration of field guides, I boldly told Bill that one of my planned field projects was to solve the ecological and identification riddles of New Guinea's yellow-eared *Meliphaga* honeyeaters—six nearly identical species of nondescript forest songbirds. He laughed at my cockiness and wished me good luck.

Over the Ranges

I was the only passenger on the day's flight from Jackson's Field to Wau. Operating a sleek Cessna 402, the cheerful, red-haired Australian pilot was probably just a few years my senior, but that did not worry me as much as did the weather. A cottony wall of cumulonimbus clouds sat atop the high central cordillera of the Owen Stanley Mountains. These clouds build on the hills nearly every morning and reach enormous size by early afternoon. My destination, Wau, lay to the north of the mountain wall. The plane sat at the end of the runway, waiting for clearance to take off, and although the pilot opened his hatch for a breeze, the small cabin became unbearably hot. After clearance, we lifted off effortlessly and began climbing. In a short time I was shivering in my damp clothing.

The flight from Port Moresby to Wau, which I have taken a dozen times since then, offers a quick lesson in the island's natural features. As we swept up off the airfield, the vista was a jumble of tree-dotted, brown coastal hills that led back to the steep scarp of the Sogeri Plateau. Housing tracts, winding dirt roads, and savanna gave way to the green of forest verging the Laloki River. Before long, we were scudding over swamp forest of the lower Brown River. This habitat, flat, sparsely populated, and with a forest canopy broken by sinuous bends of river and tributary, was not at all inviting. After passing north of the tangled mangrove estuaries of Redscar Bay, we turned inland (northwestward) and headed toward the base of the foothills of the main ranges. Here the coastal plain is fifteen or twenty miles wide, giving way to rough hills of some considerable relief. April is the end of the region's rainy season, and to the south lay a mosaic of savanna country and flooded grassland. To the north I looked out at the rough ridgelines leading up into the clouds and the central divide.

As we ascended, approaching the main cordillera, the topography was drained of color by the thick overcast. I could see sharp ridge crests dropping away to deep ravines; a flank of a ridge side scoured bare by a recent landslip; a sinuous thread of white water deep in the recesses of a rugged gorge. I saw no sign of human habitation. Typical flights in New Guinea provide long, unbroken vistas of uninhabited, jungle-clad expanses.

We circled for a few ear-crackling minutes before leveling out above the clouds. In New Guinea, a safe pilot always flies over, or around, but never through, a cloud. The pilots have a saying: "Beware of clouds, for they may have a granite lining." We climbed to 15,000 feet in the unpressurized little plane. Grinning, the pilot put on his supplemental oxygen mask, the only one in the cabin. It took a moment for my eyes to adjust to the deep blue of sky and dazzling white mat of clouds underneath. A few blackish mountain crests poking up through the clouds, and the irregularity of the cloud surfaces, were the only indication that we were traversing the central divide. I wondered about how I was going to clear my ears on the descent to Wau, only 3,800 feet above sea level.

After flying for about forty minutes, a combination of compass, timing, and intuition led the pilot to decide that we were in the vicinity of the Wau valley. He made for a hole in the clouds, and we reentered the dull gloom of overcast. The plane moved over the irregular forested topography, and I had my first close views of montane forest. The canopy included a variety of crown shapes. In openings grew cascades of scrambling bamboo and the antediluvian-looking, stilt-rooted but palm-headed *Pandanus* or screw pine. The country looked rough, and it looked wild. I couldn't help wondering what it would be like to put down into that tangle and then have to make one's way to the nearest settlement. Dozens of American airmen had to do just that during World War II, when their bombers ran out of fuel after long runs from Port Moresby to targets far to the north. Not many of those who went down made it to safety. Today it's not entirely different. Each year, several small bush planes find final resting places in the rugged mountain forests.

We raced along, above the forest and below the layer of low cloud, skimming frighteningly close to the ridgetops. Suddenly, the land dropped away and we were in the Wau valley. Here, grassland dominated the valley floor, with forest on the upper ridges and in the protected ravines. I could make out footpaths of orange earth and a dirt road. Here and there I saw gardens, in most cases placed near a cluster of rough dwellings—a village.

We passed over the sloping grass airstrip at Wau. As the plane banked for its final circle in, I saw corrugated tin roofs, prominent rows of tall *Auracaria* "pines," and dark green expanses of planted coffee, one of the area's cash crops. Mountains rose up at the valley's verges. The town lay at the base of 7,500-foot-high Mount Kaindi, whose summit hid in the gray overcast.

=====

Wau is a district headquarters of the Morobe Province, one of the political subdivisions of what was then an insular dependency of Australia. On the verge of becoming an independent sovereign state and a full-fledged member of the British Commonwealth, Papua New Guinea encompassed the eastern half of the great island of New Guinea as well as a number of islands to the north and east. The western half of New Guinea was long a part of the Dutch East Indies and more recently had been named Irian Jaya, "victorious Irian," the easternmost and largest province of Indonesia. For more than a century, the map of New Guinea has featured a precise political boundary that forms an arbitrary slash across the island's broad midsection. Since 1828, New Guinea has been bisected at 141° east longitude, when the Netherlands laid claim to all of the lands west of this line. In 1884, the eastern half of the island was divided between Germany, which took the northeast, and

Great Britain, which took the southeast. During World War I, Germany lost its colony, and slightly later (1920) Australia was given charge of the entire eastern portion of the island. Because of the influences of colonial rulers, the eastern half has tended to look southward to Australia for ideas, while the western portion has looked westward, to Java. Today, although the colonial system has gone, the contrasts between east and west continue.

A cool breeze greeted me when I clambered out of the snug cockpit of the Cessna. The Wau airstrip is hot on a sunny day, but temperatures remain pleasant on cloudy days, often below seventy degrees Fahrenheit. Because of the altitude and the grass runway, this landing field does not bake like Jackson's Field in coastal Port Moresby.

Several short Papuan men, dressed in torn shorts and dirt-stained T-shirts, approached the plane and opened the cargo bays in order to remove the mail sacks and luggage. On my way to the tiny terminal, I stopped and looked upward to the steep, forest-covered slopes of a looming Mount Kaindi. I hoped to get up there sometime soon!

Small knots of people, apparently family groups, squatted outside the tin-roofed terminal. They spoke rapidly in some unintelligible tongue. I was in a land where English was not spoken by the average villager. In Port Moresby I had bought a tiny handguide to Neomelanesian Pidgin—the lingua franca here. I had to start studying it.

The Institute

Deaf-eared from my maiden flight to Wau, I was met at the airport by Linsley Gressitt, director of the Wau Ecology Institute, and his wife, Margaret. The Gressitts, both Americans raised in Japan by missionary parents, were the eccentric pioneers of the young field station and knowledgeable experts on Wau, New Guinea, and the Pacific. The Gressitts had founded the Ecology Institute in 1971. I was to be their newest staff member, and they made me feel welcome, although they could not allay my feeling of disorientation. On the way to the institute we stopped at the post office for the afternoon's mail. I soon learned that incoming mail was a major preoccupation of many of Wau's inhabitants, especially of Dr. Gressitt.

As I sat in the back of the Gressitt's tiny pickup, a New Guinean woman passed close by, bent over with the heavy load she carried in a colorful woven string bag, a *bilum*. She was walking downtown to the Friday afternoon market. Her heavy bag was carried on her back, held in place by a long, braided handle that was looped over her forehead. Thus, the burden of her load was borne by her head and neck, the pressure of this weight padded by a small, grimy towel placed between the braided handle and her forehead. I noticed that the men I saw loafing about the post-office environs all carried miniature versions of the *bilum*, only large enough for a pack of cigarettes and a wallet.

The broad-canopied shade trees that sheltered us from the afternoon sun were like no others I had seen. They were Rain Trees (*Samanea saman*), native to South America but introduced and planted for shade in communities throughout the tropics. The knots of men who waited on the lawn below the post office conferred in low voices. They punctuated their exchanges with explosive expectorations of a milky red effluvium, juice from the concoction of betel nut, lime, and pepper vine. Betel nut is New Guinea's version of smokeless tobacco, and like the Rain Tree, it originated in South America; what looks like a macadamia nut is, in fact, the seed of an arecoid palm. This graceful palm species is now planted in villages throughout New Guinea, its fruit an important trade item and commodity for sale at markets and roadsides. The panicles of fruit hang on a stem below the leafy head of the palm, and the green fruit turns yellow or orange when ripe.

We drove up the rough dirt road that ultimately leads to the summit of Mount Kaindi. The Ecology Institute is situated on that mountain's lower slopes, about a mile from the post office. The Gressitts left me at the institute's hostel, then in the final stages of completion. I dropped my bags in my little room, put on my binoculars, and began to look about my new surroundings. I now stood near the geographic center of Papua New Guinea, relieved to be at my destination after a week's travel.

The hostel sat on a small knoll that looked northward to the forested slopes of Mount Missim, the nine-thousand-foot mountain that, along with its sister peak, Mossy Knoll, forms the eastern wall of this midmountain valley. The hostel's large, screened living room opened onto a broad, covered porch. The thick green foliage of the regenerat-

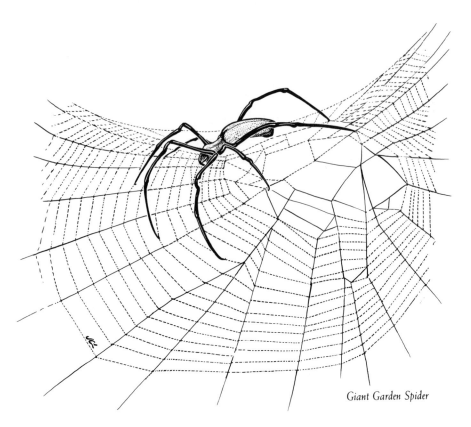

Giant Garden Spider

ing forest trees framed this vista. I could hear several distinct bird calls and itched to get a research project going. But first, I needed to get my bearings, learn a new bird community, and come to grips with this new environment.

The last point became clear the moment I focused on the very large web hanging under one of the eaves of the hostel. The web was at least two-and-a-half feet across, made of yellow silk. In the center of the web clung a garden spider (*Nephila maculata*) almost the size of my hand. Although the beast is not burly like a tarantula, its spindly legs are as long. It is quite handsome, with a silvery green abdomen, black-and-orange legs, and black back and head. These giant garden spiders were common about the grounds of the institute. I was soon to learn to accept the species as a showy, harmless member of the Wau valley fauna. The big brutes that hung motionless in their webs were the adult females, whereas the tiny males, which share the web with the female as well as a host of other unrelated ("free-loader") spiders, were easily overlooked by all but arachnologists. An advantage of working at the institute was that a variety of expert biologists passed through each year, some remaining for months at a time in order to do research. I was to learn a great deal from them.

Leaving the spider in peace, I turned my attention to the vociferous bird life. A group of grackle-sized, scruffy, gray-brown birds chased each other about and called raucously from the tall trees in front of the hostel. They were Helmeted Friarbirds, one of the conspicuous garden birds of New Guinea. Largest of the island's honeyeaters, they are pugnacious and aggressive. Their endlessly repeated morning chorus in the first few minutes of dawn wakes light sleepers in most of New Guinea's lowland and hill towns. I grew fond of these birds, mainly because of the apparent complexity of their social lives. Groups regularly congregate, with lots of chasing and singing—interactions that are either of a sexual nature or meant to establish dominance relationships. Although the precise nature of the friarbird's social behavior is still unknown, its belligerence with regard to other species is legendary. When foraging in a fruiting or flowering tree, the friarbird often expends much effort in physically expelling other feeding birds, even fellow friarbirds, from the tree. This is a common trait in honeyeaters, the diverse Pacific family that is New Guinea's most characteristic bird group. This belligerence is carried to an extreme in the Helmeted Friarbird.

The single species of Old World oriole that inhabits New Guinea's interior looks remarkably like the friarbird and often shared the groves of trees surrounding the hostel. This oriole's plumage would not be remarkable except that most orioles are brightly colored and distinctively patterned. Biologists generally agree that the Brown Oriole has evolved to look like the friarbird, a case of interspecific mimicry. The best explanation for this mimicry is that the oriole is mistaken for a friarbird by other bird species and thus avoided. This presumably gives the oriole foraging advantages at favored feeding sites.

The oriole-friarbird relationship was first delineated by Alfred Russel Wallace in *The Malay Archipelago*, his treatise on the natural history of the East Indies, published in 1869. Wallace, cofounder with Charles Darwin of the theory of evolution, was one of the Nineteenth Century's great field naturalists, whose biological insights were inspired, in part, by a visit to western New Guinea. Wallace showed that this mimicry phenomenon is repeated on several Indonesian islands to

Brown Oriole and Helmeted Friarbird

the west of New Guinea, with several different pairings of oriole and friarbird species. More than a century after its discovery, the behavioral function of this remarkable convergence is still no more than a matter of scientific speculation. No field tests have been performed on any of these examples pointed out by Wallace.

I gradually expanded my horizons from the front porch of the hostel out to the nooks and crannies of the institute grounds and, finally, to brief forays into the surrounding countryside. Near the institute's main office stood the Sedlacek Arboretum, a thick stand of trees that served as my introduction to the Papuan forest. None of the young trees stood more than fifty feet high at the time, and their trunk diameters did not exceed eight inches. This was a good place to watch birds and try to learn some of the common plants, because most of the latter bore identification labels. I tried to associate the scientific names with some physical characteristic, but it was next to impossible for someone who did not know the meaning of many of the Latin and Greek words. Some of the common open-country trees, like *Macaranga aleuritoides* and *Homalanthus novoguineensis*, had the large and distinctly shaped leaves typical of forest-edge or successional species, but many others had small leaves that looked alike. In the same manner, the trunks of most were alike—smooth and unmarked.

During my first fifteen months in New Guinea I learned no more than a handful of the more distinctive trees in the valley. My focus was on the birds, which kept me amply busy. Nonetheless, I was aware of and often amazed by the vegetation. The epiphytic staghorn fern that grew on the trunk of one of the trees beside the hostel was more like a hothouse plant than anything I knew from the woodlands back home in Maryland. Its leathery, gray-green leaves formed a protected niche in which I imagined all sorts of little creatures made their homes. I was even more taken by what must have been the largest of ground ferns, which grew in a damp spot in the shady forest patch on the slope below the institute's office. Each mature frond was more than eight feet long, and the stem had a diameter of an inch or more. This giant looked quite like a typical fern except for its enormous size.

The most abundant woody plant on the institute grounds was *Coffea arabica*, the coffee bush, planted in monoculture to provide cash to pay the ever-growing costs of the impecunious research station. I was living on a coffee plantation! The largest part of the indigenous staff cared for and harvested the coffee. A coffee plant, when tended in a plantation, is a man-high bush with a thick batch of shiny, dark green leaves and, in season, a heavy load of deep red berries. In Wau, the coffee bloomed in the early months of the year, usually in April. At this time, the rich white blossoms produce a lovely, gardenialike fragrance that becomes most pungent at night, one of the most pleasing sensory experiences of the Wau valley. Coffee, a plant native to Ethiopia, was brought to New Guinea by the Germans in the last century but became economically important only after World War II. It is now one of Papua New Guinea's important export cash crops.

Another of the remarkable botanical phenomena of the valley is the blooming of the Molasses Grass. It is so named because of the resinous exudate produced by the plant, evident when one attempts to walk through a waist-high stand of the stuff. It is awful to handle, but its mild, toasted-grain fragrance is another of the long-lasting memories of Wau. The flowering grass gives a pinkish glow on the grassy slopes around the valley. This, too, often appears in abundance at the end of the rainy season, in April or May.

In my initial days at the institute, virtually everything around me was unfamiliar. What vines or leaves were poisonous? Were the mosquitoes that swarmed up from the grass at dusk vectors of malaria or other tropical diseases? What were the intentions of the Pidgin-speaking local people I passed on the dirt paths of my daily walks? Fellow hostelers helped me overcome my initial fears. I shared the communal kitchen with three or four staff members. My first Papuan acquaintance was Tola Gulaga, the institute's bright young assistant manager, who was from the south coast. Tola spoke perfect English, so he was not much help with my Pidgin studies. However, he patiently answered dozens of my questions about Wau, about New Guinea, and about local customs. Visiting researchers used the hostel as a base of operations for short visits to the area, either for research or for vacation. They assured me that once I was out working, I soon would be communicating fluently with the local populace.

One afternoon, while sitting in the living room of the hostel, my ears picked up a steady, low, background sound that gradually grew in volume as the sky darkened. I walked to the porch and looked out over the valley to see a dense wall of rain obscuring the view of Mount Missim and the town below. The low sound grew to a loud and staccato rushing as hundreds, then thousands, of heavy raindrops began striking the vegetation on the slope below. In the next few moments a wave of cool, damp air struck my face, and my ears roared as the torrent of rain fell onto the corrugated iron roof over my head. The sound of that volume of rain! It was to become an oft-heard warning to take cover.

Many of the sights and sounds of Wau continued to surprise me. When I lay in bed at night, I was startled by a strange sound in the garden outside my screened window: first some rustling, then the rapid clapping that slowed and suddenly stopped, only to be repeated a minute later. It was clearly not human in origin. A few days later, Dr. Gressitt crossed his arms, laughed lightly, and told me that I had been hearing a large fruit-bat, *Dobsonia moluccensis*, leaving its perch and taking flight. These fruit-bats visited the garden near the hostel to take large figs that grew in untidy bunches on the trunk of one of the trees not far from my window. When foraging, a bat would snatch a fig from the bunch while hovering, then carry it to a perch, mash the fruit with its teeth, swallow the sugary juices, and spit out the pulp.

Wau

From April 1975 through July 1976, Wau would be my home. Nestled in the upper Bulolo watershed, Wau was a fifty-year-old frontier town that still survived on the bounty brought to light in the gold rush of the 1920s. Shark-eye Park's 1922 strike on the lower part of Koranga Creek was still, in 1975, the site of active extraction. Wau was a gold town. The original gold rush attracted men with gold fever from far and wide. In his autobiography, *My Wicked, Wicked Ways*, Errol Flynn described joining the rush and making his way over the mountains from Salamaua to Wau. Most, Flynn included, failed to make good on their dreams. The gold was there, but never was it an easy path to riches. Flynn departed Wau penniless and tried his luck as a plantation manager on the islands to the north before he made his way to Hollywood, fame, and scandal. In New Guinea, today's boom depends on high-tech extraction methods and the high market prices for the precious metal.

To me the gold was irrelevant, but because of it Wau was an interesting place to live, a little enclave of civilization tucked into the bosom of the New Guinea mountains. Wau was a mix of goldminers, gold company administrators, Christian missionaries, government officials, and planters. The staff of the institute was a new and, to the town's folk, unknown quantity. The institute was called *Haus Binitang*, "the bug house," by the New Guineans as well as by the long-term expatriate inhabitants who understood Pidgin. The name devolved from the original establishment of the field station by collections-oriented entomologists, who offered the local populace ten-cent pieces for interesting insects. New Guinea Goldfields Company was the largest employer in town. Government offices also provided employment for quite a few, including the assistant district commissioner, who oversaw this section of the Morobe Province. The lower portions of the valley were occupied by plantations of varying sizes, operated by expatriates. These produced coffee, vegetables, beef, milk, and pork. Various missionary groups were represented in the valley, most prominently the Lutherans, who supported a large boarding school for the children of missionaries posted in Papua New Guinea. Morobe Province was a patch of territory long held under Lutheran domination, but Roman

Catholic, Anglican, and various evangelical protestant faiths also worshiped and proselytized here. Christianity was alive and well here in Wau, at least among the New Guineans.

In 1975, Wau was primarily an expatriate community, dominated in all ways by what were known as "Europeans." Certainly, however, the population of the valley then, as now, was 95 percent New Guinean. The traditional landowners, the Biangai, inhabited several villages outside of Wau, the largest of which were Wandumi and Kaisenik. This tribe was much outnumbered by a varied mix of groups who have migrated to the valley in search of employment in the gold fields. Squatters occupied patches of ground in many parts of the valley. The problems caused by squatters were a sore point with both expatriate and Biangai landowners. The squatters dug gardens where they didn't belong and pilfered clothing hung to dry in backyards. However, these were minor affairs. Aside from the power that devolved from tribal land ownership, confined to the Biangais, the New Guineans owned few business enterprises except for some small-scale gold prospecting and coffee plots. Thus, a relatively tiny white population controlled the economy of the valley.

———

As a newcomer to Wau, my contact with the town community was limited. Hitching a ride with the Gressitts each Saturday morning, I visited town to shop. We browsed for frozen, baked, and canned goods at the two European food stores, Hardings and Burns Philp. These were remarkably poorly stocked in comparison to the same establishments a decade later, but I was happy with the fare, and I suppose everyone else was, too, because no one expected any better. We also visited the bustling, open-air market, whose main day of commerce was Saturday. There we were able to buy a range of fresh vegetables: tomatoes, lettuce, carrots, tiny white potatoes, sweet potatoes (kaukau), various forms of cabbage, string beans, bananas, papayas (here called pawpaw), oranges in season, pineapples from Bulolo, and a variety of other fruits. The local hunters occasionally sold slabs of fire-roasted pig and Dwarf Cassowary. The cassowary, one of New Guinea's large, ostrichlike, flightless birds, is the most popular "big game" animal among the native fauna of the valley. The roasted cassowary and pig I did not venture near, although on future field trips I was glad to share these delicacies with local hunters who brought them into our forest camps.

The town market is an important institution in Papua New Guinea. Here, the local gardeners hawk their tubers, fruits, and greens for the excess cash of the town workers. The dominant component of the local diet is *kaukau*, available in a variety of delicious cultivars of the common sweet potato, yet another plant of South American origin. I had always disliked sweet potatoes at home, but I soon grew fond of these, especially when roasted in the coals of a camp fire.

Another important staple dispensed in the market was *buai*—the betel nut. Betel nut vendors commonly outnumbered all other types at the market, which attests to the nut's great popularity. The nut, when chewed in combination with powdered lime (ground clam shell) and a leaf, root, or fruit of a pepper vine (*Piper* sp.), produces an alkaloid that gives the chewer a mild high, supposedly not unlike that produced by cocaine. The most obvious physical byproduct is the reddish expectorate that stains walls, garbage cans, and verges of town markets—spitting in the market proper is forbidden. Along with tobacco and beer, betel nut is used by many New Guineans of both sexes and most ages.

In 1975, expatriate inhabitants of Wau had the choice of two social clubs. The Wau Club, in the heart of the town, had a reputation for strong drinking and offered for entertainment lawn bowling, darts, and snooker, a complicated and difficult version of pocket billiards. For those more family oriented, the Golf Club, situated at the top of the town, provided its membership with a tennis court, nine holes of golf, a swimming pool, and ping pong, snooker, and darts (and a well-stocked bar for those who appreciated lifting an occasional social glass). Institute staff members joined the Golf Club. The Gressitts took me to the Friday night buffet on my first evening in the valley. There I met many of the town's prominent citizens.

The Golf Club in 1975 was, in spite of its family atmosphere, a true Australian male's domain. The bar was reserved for men only. Women were to sit in the chairs provided in the adjacent section reserved for them. Men could be "Members" but women joined as mere "Associates." Men had preferential access to the golf course, and I suppose the list of discriminatory rules went on and on. I joined the Club but only visited infrequently during my first year in the valley. There I was able to observe, at close hand, the now-endangered race known as the "True Australian Man": politically reactionary, deprecating of women, tinged with feelings of superiority over the local populace, and often garrulous from excessive drinking. Luckily, a good number of Golf Club members did not belong to this subspecies, and I befriended these more open-minded souls.

One of the social conventions that always kept me leery of the bar was called "standing." If, for instance, one were to approach the bar with a party of four friends, it was accepted that one of the five would order and pay for the first round. Once one of the five finished his first beer, one of the group would then "stand" the second round, and so on. The cycle would be repeated until all five men had each bought rounds. Slow drinkers, light drinkers, and stingy drinkers suffered. The slow drinker ended the night with a line of full bottles of beer to be finished (otherwise offense would be taken). Light drinkers were likewise forced to consume five drinks whether wanted or not. Stingy drinkers had to pay for five drinks, no matter what their budget.

Whereas it is the people who define a community, it was the climate that made the Wau valley a paradise. I never heard a resident complain of the weather. I continue, today, to think of Wau's weather as the best I have known. The coldest nights bring temperatures down to sixty degrees Fahrenheit, whereas the hottest days rarely exceed eighty-five. Seasonal shifts in temperature are slight but noticeable. The coldest mornings generally come during the clear weather of the austral winter (July). The warmest days occur between October and March.

By New Guinea's standards, Wau lies in a rain shadow, protected from the heavy precipitation of the north coast by the high wall of the Kuper Range. Still, the strongest climatic changes involve the rains. There is a distinct, but unpredictable, dry season from June to October. Most rain falls between December and March. I mention unpredictable because each year brings a new cycle of weather that may differ remarkably from the preceding. Whereas the mean rainfall in Wau is seventy-one inches, it has ranged from a low of fifty inches to a high of ninety-eight inches.

One can expect rain in any season, but during the dry season the rain usually appears in short afternoon showers, or else after dark. During the height of the wet season heavy clouds and rain may persist for several days. There were times in February or March when the continuous, heavy gray overcast made life a bit gloomy. These times were more than outweighed by the wondrous days of August and September, when the nights were chilled by the black, star-filled skies and the days began with a sharp bite but warmed to perfection by lunchtime.

Another marvel of Wau in 1975 was its peaceful isolation. For fifteen months I lived without a television, VCR, radio, or newspaper. The latter two were readily available but easily forsaken. I had my hands full with local pursuits and concerns: learning a new language, new fauna, and new culture.

Mount Kaindi

The Wau Ecology Institute sits at the foot of the imposing northwestern flank of Mount Kaindi, whose ridges rise steeply to the summit, 3,500 feet above. The institute owned a small field camp atop Mount Kaindi. In 1975, staff members visited the summit camp once a week in order to check the weather instruments there. The day after my arrival in Wau, I accompanied the Gressitts to the summit camp. We loaded the big Land Cruiser with gear and drove up the rutted dirt road that leads to Mount Kaindi's south summit and the rich goldfields at Edie Creek, just a few miles further to the south.

For the first ten minutes we moved steadily up across the steep face of the mountain, through areas heavily disturbed by gardening, fire, coffee plantings, and mining. At one point we turned into a deep, protected glen filled with giant forest trees. This humid ravine of Kunai Creek had not been logged because of the difficulty of removing the timber. Several towering Klinkii Pines, *Araucaria hunsteinii*, rose above all other vegetation. The limbs of these sparsely leafed conifers were draped with wisps of pale yellow bearded lichen. Their trunks, though not more than three feet in diameter, were perfectly formed and straight throughout, more than 140 feet tall.

As we rose steadily, the succession of views down into the Wau valley grew in scale and beauty. It opened up more and more, but not a single guardrail marked the clifflike drops on the road's downhill lip.

We could see the rugged ridges that tumbled down from the flat-crested summit of Mount Missim. On either side, the view gave way to more rough, thick-forested country of the Kuper Range. The valley bottom was hazy with smoke, but one could plainly see the patterned products of man's hand—geometric blocks of coffee, orange earth-works marking the Koranga and Nami goldpits, the pale pasture lands of the various plantations, and the regimented greens of reforestation. Much of this valley floor had been grand forest before the discovery of gold in 1922.

After this all-encompassing vista, the road turned sharply to the left and followed a fissure in the side of a slope that dropped away into a huge breach in the mountain, a gorge that dwarfed the one we had earlier navigated. Gloomy gray clouds hung a few hundred feet above the road, and, when we gained an unimpeded view, I was able to see the great, gaping landslide that marked what is called Blue Point. A gigantic patch of bare soil and rock scarred the opposite side of the ravine, near where turbulent Edie Creek poured out into a waterfall, dropping off into the depths of the gorge. We stopped here to check an institute rain gauge. I stared at the gorge as Gressitt made his readings and dumped the water from the stoutly set apparatus. He told me that one of the problems he faced in this monitoring program was that occasionally a passerby would urinate into the collecting container. He wasn't certain whether this was meant as a practical joke or a protest against the perceived meddling of the institute in the local people's traditional domain.

It was cool here at six thousand feet. Greater Wood-swallows wheeled gracefully in the clouds overhead. Several woodsmen, their arms wrapped about themselves for warmth, made their way by the car, nodding to us as they passed.

It took about forty minutes to reach the road's summit. We arrived at the camp in a light, misting rain. Clouds enveloped the summit, and there was little to do but take shelter in the small, prefabricated house and let the Gressitts take charge. They built a warm fire in the wood stove, and Margaret Gressitt prepared hot tea and then cooked a simple supper.

The next morning, birds were calling everywhere from the damp vegetation. Last night's rain had given way to a crisp dawn, cold and bright. We shared the clearing with a microwave repeater station, a telephone link between Wau and other major communities in Papua New Guinea and the reason this summit was accessible by road. The repeater station was unstaffed, so we were up here on our own.

To help me become oriented, Dr. Gressitt pointed out the most prominent topographic features then visible: Mount Amungwiwa and its brown, grassy alpine cap to the southwest; the great, bluish massifs of the Owen Stanley Range to the south, and the jagged summits of the Saruwaged Mountains to the north. From this point it was obvious that Mount Kaindi was indeed insignificant—nothing but a small bump on a long ridge that branches off the high central divide. I breakfasted with the Gressitts and then, leaving them to their entomological and botanical work, went out in search of birds.

I moved along the edge of the summit clearing until I found a small trace leading into the forest. I carefully picked my way down the slick clay path, and again, I wondered if the plants I brushed against were poisonous. It was nearly 9 A.M. Thick mists were appearing, lifting up from the valley floor and obscuring the sun. More often than not, the montane forest is still, especially so between midmorning and late afternoon, though on damp, overcast days, the tiny, moss-dwelling microhylid frogs beat out a monotonous, high-pitched series of musical notes. But where were the birds? The strains of the remarkable dawn chorus were long gone.

Dampness was the pervading influence in this mountain forest. Water shaken from overhanging vegetation had drenched my clothing, and my binoculars clouded with condensation. I wanted to see some of those marvelous birds of the cloud-forest interior—the Stephanie's Astrapia, Belford's Melidectes, the Blue-capped Ifrita, or Loria's Bird of Paradise—birds that I had studied, whose names I had memorized in preparation for this moment. I now wished to see the real, living counterparts to the stiff museum study skins that I had pored over in the ancient cabinets at Harvard, filled with the pungent, antiseptic aroma of moth flakes.

I made the *spishing* sound that is used to attract birds in North American woodlands. A small bird with a fanned tail flitted up into the low vegetation a few feet from me. It jerked back and forth on its perch, dropped its wings while cocking its tail, and delivered a few sweet notes. Aptly named "Friendly Fantail"—a bird I remembered well from my museum crash course—it is one of the few truly unwary forest birds of New Guinea. A slight, nondescript little flycatcher weighing only ten grams, it is probably too small to present much of a meal to any predator.

I heard a more substantial, musical song in the distance. Continued *spishing* had no effect, so I began to edge toward the voice. After another five minutes, my tennis shoes thick with mud from the forest path, I found a male Regent Whistler. This is a stolid but handsome member of the whistler family, the Pachycephalidae, which, like the fantails, inhabits tropical climes from southeast Asia to Australia and the Pacific islands. The Regent Whistler spends most of its time searching for arthropods among small branches below the canopy vegetation. It peers about for stationary prey, and it periodically hops short distances to a new perch. To me this bird was a glorious find: richly patterned with a black cowl, white chin, yellow nape, green back and tail, and a stunning yellow and burnt orange breast and belly. I could, at that moment, imagine how the first western naturalist to encounter this bird might have felt.

Here everything was green. The forest floor was a tangle of shrubs, ferns, and vines. The trunks of trees were overgrown with mosses and other small epiphytes. Spindly saplings with large leaves reached up in search of sunlight from open spots in the canopy. In the uppermost vegetation, I could see all sorts of strange-looking plants. Some were clumps of orchids, identifiable by their distinctive leaves and bulbous stem bases. A small, pink-flowered rhododendron sprouted from high in a crotch formed by an upper branch. Thick mats of moss and dead plant material piled up on the larger horizontal limbs. A red-flowered vine (a *Dimorphanthera*) hung from one tree. There I saw a big, jay-sized honeyeater with a long, pale bill and a whitish eye patch, probing the flowers. This bird, Belford's Melidectes, clambered about nimbly and hung inverted to reach the less-accessible flowers. Before long, this species would be known to me as the bully of the montane forest, a common, vocal, and aggressive brute that is characteristic of this forest habitat.

Light rain began to fall. The wisps of low-hanging clouds crept into the higher parts of the forest vegetation. I took shelter under the leaning trunk of an old tree that had fallen into a tangle of canopy vines and limbs of neighboring trees. Insufficiently clothed in cotton pants and a thin cotton shirt, I was, nonetheless, elated. This was the New Guinea of my dreams.

Following page: Raggiana Bird of Paradise, male in display

2   *Venturing Out*

One day, shortly after my arrival, I rose at dawn, took my binoculars and notebook, and made my way along several damp institute footpaths to the Allison property. This small tract of old forest formed the westernmost portion of the grounds. It was also the site of a display tree of Raggiana Birds of Paradise, and I wanted to see for myself why these birds and their displays were so special.

The Raggiana Bird of Paradise is notable for its courtship behavior, in which a number of adult males congregate in a favored tree, the lek, where they sing and display, day after day, attracting and mating with visiting females. Each male owns a specific perch in the tree. Apparently, males compete for these perches, and perch ownership is the first stage in gaining access to females. Successful lek males may mate with dozens of females in a single season, whereas unsuccessful birds (mostly nonperch holders) probably do not mate at all. It's not an equitable system of reproduction, but "fairness" is a rare trait in nature. The words *despotism, cheating,* and *domination* are terms frequently used by students of animal behavior.

As I approached the tract, I could hear the loud, insistent cries of the male birds of paradise: *wau wau wau wau Wau Wau Wau WAU WAU*

WAUUAGH WAAUAGH! I knew this call already. Although plumed adult males are rare, the equally vocal immature males, wearing the cryptic brown female plumage, were common throughout the valley. Several of these young birds regularly loitered about in the trees near the institute's office, calling with annoying frequency during the late afternoon.

By the time I found the small track into the patch of forest, several birds were calling in unison: *kwa kwa kwa kwa kwa kwa kwee kwee kwee kwee kwee kwee kwee*, a series that rose with a surging, swelling quality. The vocalizations resonated with excitement. I could hear flapping sounds in the canopy. Weak sunlight, in misty rays, slipped into the tops of the trees. Below this, in the gloom, I could see birds moving about. Suddenly, I fixed my binoculars on the brilliant flashing orange of display plumes—a male Raggiana!

I could make out a single plumed male, perched on a high branch just below the green roof of the canopy. He was about the size of a small crow, with a pale gold crown, emerald chin and throat, a velvety chocolate brown breast cushion, and a long train of silky orange pectoral plumes. The thick thatch of plumes, some fifteen inches in length, initially appears to be tail feathers but in fact originates on the sides of the breast, under the bend of the wing. In older males, these plumes stretch out far beyond the dull-colored tail.

In display, the male erects his orange plumes into a radiant cascade. He crouches over, lowers his wings, and lifts the long display feathers into a fiery arch. He will hold this pose, motionless, for examination by the visiting females being wooed.

I saw only a single plumed male, but many unplumed individuals were also present. Some were young males and others were certainly females. The obvious excitement generated by this congregation was evident in the vocalizations and movements of the different players in the tree. The calling, posturing, and aggression were electric. More than a decade after seeing this sight for the first time, I am still overwhelmed by its beauty and the remarkable tension created by the cluster of males in rivalry for the favors of the females. There is a delicate tension, too, in the interaction between the skittish female and the eager male.

The various forest habitats surrounding the Wau valley were home to as many as fifteen species of birds of paradise. To see more of them, I needed to establish camps at several sites. My brief experience on Mount Kaindi tempted me to think of that tract of mountain forest as a first possibility.

Kaindi Camp

I did make my first camp on Mount Kaindi. This made sense, because the road was well traveled by gold miners and the institute's Kaindi weather stations were checked once a week. I could rely on these options, among others, to get up and down the mountain. In addition, it was close—only six miles' drive.

One problem was habitat disturbance. Activity on Mount Kaindi increased each year, mainly because of the growing influx of gold miners. I wished to establish a forest camp that was relatively free of traffic—especially hunters.

In early May, Gressitt dropped me off at a point below the summit ridge so I could scout for a good research site. I reasoned that the least disturbed site would be the most inaccessible one, so I decided to hack a small, disguised trail off the side of a steep landslide area. From the road, I clambered forty feet down the steep open face of gravel and dirt to the forest's edge. There, I met a wall of raspberry vines and

Morobe Province and detail of Wau and environs (left)

bamboo. If I could make it through this barrier, I knew I would be on my way. I had a small bush knife (machete), and I began flailing at the thick vegetation. It was like trying to cut through barbed wire with a bread knife.

However, that was the worst of it. After negotiating the first fifty feet, I made my way into the heavily shaded forest, damp and slippery underfoot but an improvement over the previous dense thicket. I continued to pick my way, hacking at vines and saplings. I also needed to mark my means of escape. I was leery of simply moving cross-country on Mount Kaindi. If I became disoriented, I might have to spend a very uncomfortable night in the forest.

I fought my way about half a mile in from the road and came upon a small gorge through which water cascaded. I wanted to make it past this barrier, which I thought would make my study plot safer from intruders. Climbing up over the far lip of the muddy bank, I found myself on a relatively level, undisturbed patch of montane forest. Big trees loomed overhead, and the undergrowth was fairly sparse because of the thick shade cast by the tall canopy: my first study site.

=====

I had chosen a patch of forest that straddled the cloud line on the northern shoulder of the summit ridge. This exposed ridge caught the clouds as they floated southward from the Bulolo valley. The clouds that bumped the ridge and settled onto the tall trees of the plot were, at 7,100 feet above sea level, chilly and wet, and I was chilly and wet for much of the time I spent in this forest. However, the constant humidity produced a lush montane habitat, rich in highland bird and plant life.

I visited the Kaindi forest site dozens of times during 1975 and 1976, often for the day, and more frequently for periods of three or four days. I wanted to learn as much as possible about the composition of the bird community on this twenty-acre tract.

The highest temperature that I recorded in the forest on Mount Kaindi was sixty-six degrees Fahrenheit. The low reached forty-eight. Overcast dominated, even when I could gaze down on the valley and see the town bathed in bright sun. This was the price I had to pay to study a fascinating community of more than eighty species of birds, most of which I saw for the first time there. My first few days were spent simply trying to keep up with the novelties. For many birds, I was forced to make detailed notations in my field book of the size, shape, and coloration for later identification. I still knew so little, it was not unusual for me to see a bird I could not place to family. At a later time I would read through my notes and compare my descriptions with those in the *Handbook of New Guinea Birds*, by Austin Rand and E. Thomas Gilliard. In most cases I was able to use this method to identify correctly the birds I saw.

I trapped birds using mist nets. A mist net looks like a greatly over-sized badminton net, manufactured of fine black nylon thread. When strung between two tall poles in the forest, it is practically invisible, and birds flying into it are trapped in the loose mesh. I wanted to capture birds to weigh and measure them and, more importantly, to attach a single, numbered aluminum band on the leg. Mist netting is a productive (but not always easy) means of documenting a poorly known tropical avifauna. In a tropical forest, the nets have a way of attracting all manner of entangling objects, mostly vegetation. On breezy days, falling leaves can fill the nets in a few hours. The leaves make the nets easily visible to any birds, so the catch drops markedly; also, the leaves themselves are difficult to remove. Near the ground, the bottom lines of the net are continually becoming tangled with roots, vines, and pieces of vegetation cut to prepare a pathway for the net. This can be destructive to the net, because the netting catches firmly and one false step can create a big rent. Breezes also push the loose upper netting into swaying branches from neighboring saplings. Most importantly, in many instances the birds themselves can be exceedingly difficult to extract, especially if they have been allowed to remain in the net any length of time.

Perhaps there is nothing more psychologically trying to a novice bird bander in New Guinea than the extraction of a Belford's Melidectes that has been badly entangled in a net. One rarely has a big enough reserve of patience to escape from such an ordeal unflustered—this honeyeater is mean and aggressive, doubly so because of the situation. The bird has every right to be angry and vengeful with its captor.

The first time I naively reached for a honeyeater it struck with lightning-fast, needle-sharp claws drawing blood from the soft flesh at the base of my thumb. Next, it shrieked in my ear as I sought to remove the twined nylon from its legs and wings. Once I had freed the body, I found that a single piece of nylon had twisted itself around the twin, barblike projections at the base of its long tongue. Steady hands and the patience of Job were required to remove this final strand without injuring the bird.

Once the bird was out, still more trials followed. It was placed in a cloth bag for holding while I removed other birds from other nets. On returning to my rough "office" in the forest—no more than a small rain shelter—I had to extricate the honeyeater from its holding bag to measure, band, and eventually release it. This meant more painful wounds to the most tender portions of the hands. After my first week of cutting trails, clearing brush for nets, and bird banding, my hands were a mass of puncture wounds, some of them threatening infection. Later I did try using gloves but found I lost the dexterity needed to manipulate the tangled net and the small aluminum bands.

In spite of difficulties, the results of netting were wonderful. Loping up to a net that held some big bird dangling in one of its pockets was exciting, especially when the bird was something new, something I couldn't immediately identify. Could this be a species new to science? The thought was naive, but it went through my head at least once the first few months at the study area. After all, hadn't the mysterious Black-and-Green Scrubwren been discovered in 1962 only a few miles away, at Edie Creek?

On one day in June I netted twelve species of birds. Three were new to me. The first was a real mystery—a small, brownish, non-descript songbird looking unlike anything I had studied in the collections at Harvard. I began to think it might be something new and un-described. Only a long search through the keys of Rand and Gilliard's *Handbook* showed my hope to be in vain. This was my first and last encounter with the Lesser Ground-Robin on Kaindi.

The Wattled Ploughbill, an aggressive little brute, punished my fingers as I extracted it from the net. This is one of New Guinea's oddities of the montane forest. Inhabiting bamboo thickets, the plough-bill male is generally army green, patterned with a black breast patch, and outfitted with a powerful, stout bill and two incongruous-looking pink cheek wattles.

I was standing nearby when a pair of pygmy-parrots popped into one of the ridge nets. They were so small, at three-and-a-half inches, that I was surprised the birds did not pass through the mesh. These two were little gems—the male weighing thirteen grams, the female fourteen. Their attempts to break the skin of my hands with their tiny, weak bills were persistent, but endearingly ineffectual. This species is another of the natural wonders of the Papuan montane forest: wee, gentle creatures, with legs so short that no band could safely be applied. I released them unmarked and have never since caught another individual of that species. Here, in a single day, I netted two species that I would never net again.

———

In my ramblings on my Kaindi study area, I came upon my first bowerbird "bower," the terrestrial dance ground of Macgregor's Bowerbird. What a sight: a four-foot-tall vertical spire of stacked sticks set into a neatly groomed circular base of moss four feet in diameter. I have tried several times without success to capture the natural beauty and detail of this structure on film.

The bower is a courtship ground to which a polygynous male seeks to attract females for mating. Each bower is owned by a single male, and rival males actually attack each other's bowers and try to steal decorations or tear down portions of the construction of sticks. Since most male bowerbirds are relatively drably plumed, one can think of the bower as the male's adornment, a behavioral equivalent to the colorful display plumes of the male birds of paradise. Just as a male bird of paradise will be unable to attract females without his plumes, it is evident that the male bowerbird cannot attract mates without his bower. Even though some think the bower looks like an oversized nest, in fact, the bower has nothing whatsoever to do with nests or nesting but is solely related to a male's attempt to attract females for mating.

Each of the eighteen species of bowerbird builds its own distinct type of bower. The "maypole" type of bower made by Macgregor's Bowerbird is one of the simplest. By contrast, the Fawn-breasted Bowerbird, a common species in the scrub of the Ecology Institute, builds an "avenue" bower—two thick vertical walls made of bunched sticks set atop a larger mound of recumbent twigs, sticks, and assembled detritus. This bower is then adorned with green fruit and

Bower of Streaked Bowerbird

"painted" with a blackish substance that appears to be a mixture of the bird's saliva and charcoal. The Streaked Bowerbird, a little-studied species of southeastern Papua New Guinea, constructs what looks like a complex three-foot-high tepee, set atop a mossy base. There are two remarkable things about this tepee construction. First, there is a semicircular tunnel through the tepee (winding around the center pole). Second, on the base of the center pole the bird creates a neat wall of matted moss onto which it places an array of colorful bits of natural articles: blue-black wasp wings, yellow flower petals, red berries, black beetle elytra, and the like. Each type of embellishment is sequestered onto its own section of the wall, and the effect is quite artistic and very beautiful.

Some biologists believe that the remarkable construction of the male bowerbirds is evidence of an esthetic sense. Others prefer to believe that this spin-off of mating behavior is the product of the remarkable sexual competition among males to mate with females—a process that Charles Darwin named "sexual selection." What is it about these montane forests that has promoted the development of this bower-building behavior in the bowerbirds and the evolution of the wonderful plumes and displays of the male birds of paradise?

====

I have said that my Kaindi study plot was level forest, but this is a relative assessment. One of my strongest memories is of the trail system I cut there. Nearly every track either followed the contour of a ridge side or climbed up or down a steep hill. Within a few weeks of use, the trails were slippery and muddy. This never improved, and the tracks only got worse. My ankles ached from the continual strain. I got sick and tired of having to grip continually at the slick, sloping tracks with the uphill sides of my feet, and still I always slipped.

However, this first study area was lovely, mossy forest at one of New Guinea's most interesting altitudinal zones. The continual high humidity fosters a profusion of lush growth, and the distinct climate and flora have promoted a montane fauna quite different from that of the lower altitudes. The birdlife on my Kaindi site was almost entirely "montane." Very few of the species in that patch of forest also inhabited the wooded areas a few miles down the road at the Wau Ecology Institute. The two sites supported a combined total of more than 150 species of birds, and yet fewer than 15 were shared between them. Probably the same could be said for the plant life. Certainly the forest habitat was entirely different between Wau and Kaindi. At the institute the remnants of native forest were dominated by laurels, mahoganies, myrtles, figs, and araucarias. At the Kaindi camp the most common trees were oaks, antarctic beeches, podocarps, and pandans. Orchids and rhododendrons were common as epiphytes on Kaindi and rare or absent at the institute.

In 1975, I was aware of these structural differences, but I learned very little of the plant life except for the most common and most striking forms. The *Pandanus* screw pine is a small tree that abounded in the forest on Kaindi. It had a head of long, spiny, palmlike leaves and odd stilt roots protected by thorns. A multitude of ferns were present. The canopy trees, however, left me staring in incomprehension. How does one collect samples for identification? Fresh plant material is required for making botanical specimens. Ideally, one clips a branch that includes mature leaves and either fruit or flowers—both if possible—but for two reasons this isn't easy. First, how does one clip a sample if the leafy branches are confined to the canopy, seventy-five or a hundred feet overhead? Second, collecting fertile material depends on the vagaries of reproduction in these tropical plants, in which most trees at any point are not reproductively active; many of these plants, in fact, flower only once every few years.

Saruwaged Expedition

I was thrilled when, in July 1975, Paul Kores invited me to join him on a two-week field trip to the high mountains of the Huon Peninsula, eighty miles northeast of Wau. My first expedition! Here was my chance to visit a little-known wilderness in search of birds. Paul's plan was to find and collect a number of species of rhododendrons endemic to that isolated mountain region. I would go along to make ecological observations of the habitats and birdlife and to make a representative collection for the National Museum of Natural History of the Smithsonian Institution, in Washington, D.C. I had little difficulty deciding to temporarily abandon my study on Mount Kaindi for a trip into the great unknown.

My feet barely touched the ground in the days in advance of our departure from Wau. There was so much to do that I had little time to fret about how ill-prepared I was for my first journey into New Guinea's wild hinterlands. On July 18, Paul loaded our equipment and four Papuan staff assistants into his Land Rover, and the six of us rattled down to Lae. The next morning we were to fly to the mountain village of Derim, on the northern slopes of the Saruwaged Mountains—the highest of New Guinea's system of northern coastal ranges. One of the reasons Paul had chosen Derim as a starting point was that one of our staff assistants, Timis Suri, was born there and so knew the territory, the local language, and the culture.

Timis had assured Paul that there was a well-used walking track that passed through Derim and continued up to the alpine heights and down the southern scarp to Lae. We were amazed to hear that the local people regularly walked the grueling journey over a thirteen-thousand-foot pass to Lae, where they bought the modern conveniences of village life—aluminum cooking pots, bush knives, steel ax heads, blankets, assorted second-hand clothing, and the like. These rugged people go over the top because this is the shortest path between the two points. Throughout the mountain regions of New Guinea, the people are not afraid to expend some considerable energy in getting where they want to go. A stiff walk for two or three days is not uncommon for villagers in the hinterlands who wish to visit the nearest town.

As dawn broke, we boarded a tiny, single-engine bush plane for the twenty-minute flight to Derim. The plane rose off the Lae landing ground and out over the Huon Gulf. Amelia Earhart and her navigator had made the same take-off here thirty-eight years before—the last take-off of their fatal round-the-world attempt. Whereas Earhart had continued eastward over the open ocean, we circled and gained altitude to pass over the heights of the nearby mountain wall formed by the Saruwaged Range. Within minutes we could see our ultimate destination—Mount Bangeta, at fourteen thousand feet, the highest in the range. Our pilot flew us between Bangeta and Salawaket peaks over the barren gray-brown grasslands and alpine tarns.

Derim, ten thousand feet lower in altitude and twenty-five miles to the north, was in another world. As we circled the rough limestone landing ground, the high wall of the Bangeta Range loomed to the south. Derim was in karst country—with limestone sugarloaves poking up all about to the north. We were to head southward, away from the devilish karst, but it would be rough going, limestone or no.

The village inhabitants had effectively removed the native vegetation, and birds were few. I recorded three garden-dwelling species in my notebook that day: Pied Chat, Long-tailed Shrike, and Mountain Swiftlet. I was more concerned with the village environment than the scanty birdlife. Here, things were a far cry from conditions in Wau. Although the villagers seemed healthy and robust, they were all barefoot, and what clothing they wore was dingy and threadbare in the extreme. They were literally wearing worn-out cast-offs from Australia, sold in the secondhand shops of Lae. Although the village itself was tidily laid out, the general material poverty was a shock. A family's essentials consisted of some aluminum pots, a bush knife or two, digging sticks, string bags, sleeping mats, blankets and towels, some Chinese-made enamelware cups and plates, and perhaps, if particularly fortunate, a transistor radio. No wonder these villagers were so excited by our party of outsiders, bearing crates of exotic foods and supplies!

The people here had few material possessions, and yet I saw no evidence of hunger or true need. There was plenty of land for gardens and food staples for all. In addition, for the cash economy, Derim had productive groves of oranges and small stands of coffee. These the villagers sold to wholesalers who freighted them by plane to Lae. Most of our pilot's flights carried loads of these valuable trade crops.

We spent the night in Derim, allowing Timis to organize a crew of porters to carry our mountain of supplies. That night, the rest house was jammed with visiting "big men" (akin to village elders). We all squatted on the woven mat floor, raised about four feet above the ground. How that thin matting held the weight of all these people I don't know. The men built a large fire in the middle of the floor, and, miraculously to me, a bit of sand and ash allowed this fire to crackle and flame without burning through. Everyone chattered incomprehensibly while I sat in a corner and wondered how I would fare over the next fortnight.

The next morning, there was no sign of the sun when the first eager carriers began peering into our lodging. Most villagers rise before dawn, and this day the people were anxious to get going. We stumbled up in the misty gloom, arranged for pots of water to be boiled for tea and porridge, and began our final packing. Dawn in a mountain village is often cold, damp, and gray—showing little promise for the day ahead. A strong mug of tea, served in one of the scalding-hot enameled metal cups, is the necessary antidote for the inevitable early-morning depression that precedes the first day of a field trip.

The first stage of the trek was through a heavily settled zone, occupied by a series of clan groups. At 10 A.M., we came to our first clan boundary, and our twelve porters dropped their loads and demanded payment. These porters insisted that it would be inappropriate to trespass across their neighbors' lands. We wrestled with this issue for nearly an hour and finally won a partial victory. Our porters agreed to carry the entire day, but after that we would have to find replacements from the village where we were to spend the night.

Although we gained only a few hundred feet of altitude, the day's hike was a killer. Much of the walking was in the open, under an unforgiving sun. Nowhere was the track level. It either rose or dropped sharply. We passed through at least three deep river gorges, the worst torture of all. For each, we would begin by standing at the northern lip of the ravine, looking across the short distance to the southern lip. Then came the sharp, slippery descent, with the heavily loaded porters heaving and sliding. At the river we dropped to our knees and doused ourselves in the cool water. The climb back up was, of course, the worst, as we strained tired muscles to regain the ground we had surrendered on the way down.

The highlight of the day was a plumed male Superb Bird of Paradise, one of the common birds in the regenerating forest along the track. My attention was drawn by the male's conspicuous vocalization, a coarse, rasping *shh shhh shhhhh shhhh sshhhh shhhhh*. The black male perched in a small tree, excitedly flipping his wings at a female, in what appeared to be the beginning of a display. The female, with her black cap, brown back, and black-barred and dull buff underparts, is typically cryptic for members of her sex in this family. The male, on the other hand, is a wonder to behold: the stiff, iridescent feathers of the blue breast shield form a pair of pointed triangles, each of which project out from the sides of his body like false wings. The head plume, while more difficult to see, is even more fantastic—a thick mass of soft dark feathers that originates from the back of the crown and projects down the back when the bird perches upright. In display, the head plumes are raised and opened like an oriental fan.

We reached Kimbe, our day's destination, by midafternoon. This was the last of the settlements before the track turned up into the uninhabited forest. By day's end, the clouds had settled on the slope above, and small children in ragged clothing swarmed around our rest house, giggling, gawking, and hiding behind one another in embarrassment. Both the girls and boys had close-cropped hair. Clothing was much the same, but the girls often wore a towel, like a shawl, over their shoulders. This could be raised into a hood to hide their faces in a moment of shyness. My intruding camera caused the flock to flee a few yards, and then regroup, a writhing, laughing mass. The children are the life of these isolated villages.

We ate supper and then headed directly for sleeping bags. In what seemed like a blink of an eye, we were awoken in the predawn by the inquisitive crowd, who once again surrounded our rest house in the thick, cool mist. My body ached from the uncomfortable floor and from the rigors of the preceding day's hike. However, my adrenalin began to flow before long, for I knew that this was the big day, the ascent.

=====

After breakfast, Paul began hiring porters and found that the men demanded well above the market rate for their services. At that time, two Australian dollars was a good day's pay. They wanted five. Paul argued to no avail. The two of us decided to depart with those who agreed to help, leaving Timis to sort out the labor wrangle. In our absence, he solved the problem by hiring nine women, who were eager for the cash and would work for less. This proved an act of managerial genius, for the women never complained, carried the heavy loads, and were in most ways superior to our male help.

The day's trek required an ascent of 6,000 feet, from Kimbe at 5,500 feet above sea level to our high camp at 11,500 feet. Our group of nineteen toiled up the track, which led us into the luxuriant forest and followed a ridge that ascended steadily. After we set off, rain began to fall. While the women sang and laughed to pass the time, we grew cold, wet, tired, and cranky. The path led upward, seemingly without end.

I carried a small day pack that held my binoculars and camera. My load was tiny compared to those of the porters, yet I struggled to keep up with their pace. The climb brought back boyhood memories of tough ascents in the Adirondack Mountains, but the comparison was ill fitting (no Adirondack peak exceeded 5,500 feet!).

On a long climb the key is to try to "zone out." Get your mind away from the physically demanding task at hand; go into autopilot. One can do this by focusing on the memory of past delights now out of reach: savoring a hot bag of french fries from a boardwalk vendor at a beach resort visited in childhood, or the image of a particular moment in an early summer evening when the scent of honeysuckle and the promise of the night to come made the blood race. These fantasies help one drift away while the feet keep slogging on.

I was not totally uninterested in the climb, but a trail in the forest offers little to the hiker who is unable to stop and dally, and we were in a hurry to get up the ridge. Dark shapes darting in the wet vegetation were all I saw of the birdlife that day.

The vegetation changed from tall forest, to mossy montane forest, to elfin woodland. By late afternoon we broke out of the subalpine shrubbery into our first patches of grassland. Rain pelted us. The air thinned. The temperature dropped. Two of our pack-bearing assistants from the institute collapsed from exhaustion. Paul and I picked up their loads and continued to stagger through the tall, wet grass. The going was difficult because of the water-logged ground. The "grassland" was nothing but a marsh in disguise. Before long, I fell and gasped for air. The weight of the pack and the altitude were too much. I dumped the heavy load to rest for a minute, and one of the women, carrying a heavy *bilum* full of *kaukau*, picked up the pack, balanced it on her head, and walked on.

In the icy rain, we made for a huge limestone cliff. Our guide had told us of a cave where we could set our camp. As we approached the cliff, it grew larger and larger. Our hopes about the cave at the base of this mighty wall grew, but it was nothing more than a slight concavity in the rough rock. On a dry twig that protruded from a crack in the rock face hung a small decaying *bilum*. We were told this was the string bag of a man who had died here from exposure. He had been passing over the top on his way to Lae but never made it. At dusk at eleven thousand feet, it is either cold and wet or cold and dry—but it is always cold. So much for a cheering arrival at our top camp.

We needed sapling poles to fashion a shelter against the cliff, water for cooking and washing, and firewood for warmth. Paul and I huddled against the rock, where one of the men had started a small fire from a few pieces of wood that had been left at the overhang. We could barely move from the cold and our fatigue. A headache roared in my brain. Gradually an organization of sorts began to materialize. Rough poles were set against the rock and our long sheets of plastic were unfolded over these. Our chief guide ordered two fires built under this roof, and within an hour a large pot of water was boiling for tea.

The nineteen who jammed under the plastic tarp that night all craved warmth. Paul and I had sleeping bags, but the remainder of the crew had, at most, thin woolen blankets, poor protection from the alpine cold and damp. Both ends of our shelter were open to the elements. The Papuan answer to this dilemma, as it has been for millennia, is fire. Our group kept two fires burning through the night, which would have been fine except for the dubious quality of the wood and limited ventilation. It was green wood, covered in wet moss, and it smoked terribly. Whereas our Papuan comrades did not seem affected, Paul and I were forced to keep our heads near ground level, below the clouds of thick smog that hung below the roof. Our shelter remained a virtual smokehouse throughout our stay at this camp.

The living arrangements were awful, but the new environment was fantastic. I was in alpine tundra, at an isolated spot on a little-known island in a remote part of the Pacific. I spent every rain-free daylight hour out observing birds and the environment. The habitat, which looked so pastoral and inviting from the airplane, was devilish for the fieldworker. It so happened that nearly all of the grassland in the area of the camp was boggy and dominated by tussock grass. Although picturesque, it was very difficult to move through, because one had either to wade in the muck between the tussocks or else attempt to step from tussock to tussock. Either way, the going was tough—wet or wobbly. Add to this the difficult adjustment to the thin air and deceptively scaled landscape, and any adjacent destination was always much farther than imagined.

One afternoon, Paul pointed to a small knoll south of the camp and suggested we walk up there for a view. We clambered and puffed for nearly two hours before we arrived on the undulating plateau that stood above the great limestone cliff. Up here, it was like a moonscape, colored in grays and browns, small tufts of grass interspersed with barren rocky soil, broken here and there by a treacherous sinkhole. The overcast sky added to this somberness. I observed only one bird on this deserted plain—the chocolate brown Island Thrush. It was not difficult to tell that this bird is a close relative of the American Robin. Both have a nearly identical shrill alarm note, and both have the conspicuous yellow legs and bill. Up on this stark plateau, the few of these birds we encountered were remarkably shy. They skittered off at our approach, and I wondered why a bird that lives in this uninhabited region was so wary.

Titi, Timis, and I spent most of our time looking for birds in the grasslands and tiny patches of alpine forest. The small stands of trees and shrubs were a world apart, with stunted, gnarled vegetation encrusted with thick mattings of green, brown, and golden orange mosses. Rhododendrons and other shrubs formed thickets at the copse edges, and a few brave songbirds made this harsh woodland environment a home.

During our stay at this high camp, we listed a mere eight species of birds: swiftlet, thrush, fantail, two whistlers, pipit, warbler, and berrypecker. Although that list was probably incomplete, it indicates the very impoverished nature of the bird community atop the higher peaks of New Guinea. As the air thins with greater altitude, so do the plant and animal communities. One of the remarkable aspects of that camp was that I could stand at a spot not far from the shelter and look northward off the range to the Vitiaz Strait, the passage of salt water that separates New Britain from New Guinea. There the sun was beating down on distant Umboi Island, and with binoculars I could make out a white strip of coral beach. How I fantasized about that beach, the sun, the warm salt water!

I was, in fact, standing on an old reef bed—the limestone that capped this high range. This remnant of a tropical coral reef had ridden the sediments uplifted by the collision of the Pacific, Bismarck, and Australian tectonic plates. The Saruwaged Range is reputed to be one of the fastest-rising pieces of ground on earth—with an uplift of about a foot per hundred years. The speed of this process is most evident along the coast, where one can see the giant coral "stairsteps" of reef and sediment that have been lifted, in stages, by these ongoing earth forces.

━━━━

It turned out that the rhododendrons were fairly sparse this high up, so Paul decided we should retreat to a more habitable altitude. In the rain, we packed up and trudged down to a protected site beside a small forest pond on the ridge we had ascended from Kimbe. This site was a great improvement: easy access to water, firewood, and slightly warmer temperatures—and lots of birds and rhododendrons.

In subalpine forest at ten thousand feet above sea level, the lakeside camp nestled in the band of vegetation that lies directly below the timberline. This is low-statured, closed forest that is characterized by being heavily stunted and encrusted by thick mats of mosses. The trunks and low branches intertwine to form a maze of moss-cloaked vegetation. The slim trunks of the canopy trees are forced to bend and turn in their growth toward the sunlight. As a result, it can be very difficult for the naturalist to explore at will. Luckily, the low spot on the ridge, where the pond stood, supported forest that was taller, rather more upright, and less tangled than the forest in the more exposed sites. Nonetheless, ground, trunks, and limbs were layered with masses of colorful but soggy moss.

The entire expedition party was relieved by the change of scenery. We suffered from two problems, though. First, there were too many hungry mouths to feed. The Kimbe men prevailed upon the women to return to their gardens and children. The women promised to return in seven days to help us hike down. The second, more serious, problem related to the insects. As soon as we began settling into the camp, anyone who sat quietly and bared skin to the elements was pestered by bloodsucking simuliid flies—small, but voracious, blackflies, infamous in boreal zones in northern North America and elsewhere.

The blackfly became the camp's unwanted mascot. Everyone who had "careful work" to do suffered. Skinning a bird specimen was an unholy torture, punctuated by bouts of violent thrashing and cursing. While one delicately attempted to prepare the study skin, small clouds of blackflies took this motionless repose as an invitation to hover, land, and pierce skin in search of a capillary. More often than not, they were successful, and thus the outburst. Blackfly bites swell, then begin to itch, and then itch fiercely. The irresistible temptation is to scratch the bites more and more, often to bleeding.

Amateurs might wonder about the need to collect birds in the late Twentieth Century. Didn't collecting die out with the advent of field guides? Aren't there museums full of bird specimens that can be used for study?

Ask any ornithologist whose research involves the study of museum collections, and you will be told that although collections of some European and North American species are well represented, those for other parts of the world are nowhere near complete. Many species are represented in the museums of the world by only a handful of specimens, and often these specimens are old and poorly documented. Thus, there is uncertainty about where the specimens were collected, and little or nothing is known about weight, eye color, or color of the bill and legs or other parts that show perishable colors.

Aren't photographs as good as specimens for documentation? Never. A bird in a photograph cannot be measured and remeasured, nor do the colors in the photograph last for a century or more. A well-prepared and well-documented study skin can reside in a museum for more than a century with virtually no noticeable degradation. It serves as physical documentation that a particular type of bird (species, subspecies, color morph) inhabited a specific point on the earth at a specific time. The specimen label often indicates habitat, altitude, breeding status, molt status, and other valuable ancillary biological and ecological data. Taken together, the specimen and label form an invaluable biological record that can be checked and examined decade after decade. Also, for each species there may be several age- or sex-related plumages that require documentation. Anyone who has purchased a field guide should know that the artists who painted the birds had to refer, invariably, to museum specimens; also, field ornithologists, in solving identification riddles, require the use of these specimens for their work.

Those who collected the birds in past decades could never imagine the number of fascinating questions that have been answered using their specimens. A photograph or a notation in a notebook, such as "I saw this bird," would never be able to take the place of a museum specimen. Scientists today are learning about the evolutionary relationships of the Passenger Pigeon by using DNA that is extracted from minute quantities of skin from specimens in museum collections. The relationship between DDT and eggshell thinning in the Peregrine Falcon was studied by measuring eggs in museum collections that had been assembled over a long span of time. Even *new species* of birds have been discovered in museum collections. Enterprising and sharp-eyed ornithologists looking through trays of specimens have found novelties that had been originally misidentified and overlooked by earlier researchers.

The birds I collected for the U.S. National Museum of Natural History form a valuable reference series of birds from the Huon Peninsula. I have referred to them many times since, as have other scientists. They will remain in the museum, serving researchers, long after I am gone. I have no regrets about collecting them. Their value will grow as time passes, because they will become a historical record of a place and its fauna at a past point in time.

Paul had wonderful success collecting endemic rhododendrons, including a remarkable oddity with a greenish yellow tubular flower (*R. pachycarpon*). In addition, he found another species with a short, broad, two-toned flower, yellow and red (*R. cristi*). These plants thrive in the cool mists of the high slopes of these north coastal mountains, and occur nowhere else on earth. Birds were relatively few in diversity, but many that inhabited this stunted forest were novel to me. These, too, inhabit only this north coastal range. The noisiest in the area was Foerster's Melidectes, a close relative of Belford's Melidectes, so common on Mount Kaindi. Foerster's Melidectes, though, is bigger and shows a brighter pattern of facial wattles. Another, even larger honeyeater, was more unusual. Like Foerster's Melidectes, the Spangled Honeyeater is endemic to these north coastal mountains. It is a big black bird with a mess of white spots on its breast and belly. Like the Common Smoky Honeyeater from the central ranges, this bird has a striking orange facial wattle that blushes deep red when the bird is excited. More often than not, I initially mistook this bird for a bird of paradise. It superficially resembles the marvelous Huon Astrapia, one of this region's little-known birds of paradise. The astrapia, which in fact sports a much longer tail and no face patch, was common around

Salvadori's Teal

the camp—an exciting discovery for me because the species had not previously been recorded above 7,500 feet.

One evening after dark we were startled by the explosive report of the shotgun of one of our guides. This was followed by excited thrashing about in the thickets and splashing in the pond. Our guide had shot a pair of ducks that nightly came to roost on the water. After a few minutes the excited hunter brought the birds to the shelter, lit by the harsh light of the Coleman kerosene pressure lantern. Using my copy of the *Handbook*, I identified the birds as Salvadori's Teal, New Guinea's only endemic duck. I explained to the man that the shooting of this species is proscribed by Papua New Guinea law. That did not prevent us from deciding to dine on the contraband fare. After hanging them for a day, Paul marinated the breasts in red wine and cooked a delicious duck meal. I still don't know what inspired Paul to bring a bottle of wine all the way up this mountain, but he saved it for the right occasion.

On the appointed day, the "superwomen" arrived and spent the night; early the next morning we were off down the mountain. I had made it through my first expedition without a mishap. Neither Paul nor I had made any earthshaking discoveries, but Paul had assembled a splendid collection of live cuttings of rhododendrons that had never before been cultivated. These would be distributed as horticultural breeding stock to botanical gardens around the world. I made a valuable collection of birds for the Smithsonian and also obtained novel observations on the distribution, ecology, and diet of a number of the little-known forest species. Most importantly, I had witnessed, first-hand, how a field expedition is organized, provisioned, and directed. This would be invaluable when I had to organize and lead trips on my own into the Papuan wilderness.

Opposite: Sunrise vista from Abid's Camp, Bulldog Road

3 *Bulldog Road*

*D*uring World War II, the Australian forces constructed a truck road linking Edie Creek and Wau with the lowlands of the southern watershed, ending at a barge depot named "Bulldog." The purpose of the road was to supply Allied units battling the Japanese in the hills of the northern watershed. The road followed a ridge of Mount Kaindi that ascends gradually to a pass on the central cordillera and then descends down through rough country into the gorge of the Eloa River and finally out into the flat alluvial country to Bulldog. This hastily constructed track was passable for trucks for only several months, but it continued to be used as a native walking path, and, in the early 1970s, as a research area for biologists studying the montane forest.

A group of ecologists based their studies at Abid's Camp, a rough shelter set about ten kilometers up the old roadbed from Edie Creek. The site was named for Abid beg Mirza, a field collector who established the site in order to collect marsupials, rats, and their ectoparasites. I first visited Abid's Camp in early 1975 and returned a number of times during the next four years. I developed a love-hate relationship with this isolated spot, for the weather was often abominable, but the natural wealth of the forest was alluring.

The trek to Abid's Camp began at Edie Creek, atop the Mount Kaindi road. In 1975 this tiny mining community probably looked not terribly different than it did in 1929 at the height of the gold rush. If anything, the settlement was now smaller. Edie Creek is an upland basin southwest of the Kaindi summit. All of the forest in the basin has been cleared by prospectors, and the area gives the appearance of an isolated wasteland, often shrouded in mist and rain. Gold continues to attract the attention of miners, whose efforts produce gaping wounds in the earth. Gravel, mud, rain, shanties, shovels, and silty creeks characterize the place.

On my first trip to Abid's Camp, five of us debarked at the road-head, amidst the Edie Creek mining settlement. I did not think to hire a porter, but it would be the last time I made this mistake. I soon found that there is rarely any advantage to be gained in conducting biological fieldwork with a heavy pack on my back.

I suffered for lack of appropriate camping and hiking gear. On my feet I wore the poorly made canvas-and-rubber "jungle boots" sold in trade stores throughout Papua New Guinea. They were fairly comfortable, but the canvas was not water-resistant; hence, excess water in the humid environment tended to concentrate in my socks. The boots provided little support or protection, and the canvas around the toes began to wear thin after only a fortnight of rough treatment. My backpack had been borrowed from the much-tattered general supplies of the institute. It was an old, army-issue, steel-frame pack, such as was used by hikers before the advent of the modern hiker's designs. My pack must have been created by a sadistic fiend or a total incompetent, for it held little, its straps dug into the flesh of my shoulders, and its steel frame jabbed ruthlessly into the lower parts of my back.

Into the pack I had stuffed an ancient, down-filled, army-issue sleeping bag. This was wonderfully warm, yet it gave up feathers each night by way of numerous small rents in its green cotton cover.

From the roadhead we began to wind our way towards the forest, following a track that zigged and zagged around pits where men labored in pursuit of gold. After about twenty-five minutes, we entered the forest. The track became relatively regular and well graded, for we had settled onto the old bed of the Bulldog Road.

As we walked, I pestered the leader of our group about the birds that we heard singing and about what we might expect to see up at Abid's Camp. Over and over again I asked him what a certain prominent call was, and he patiently replied each time: "Belford's Melidectes." This species, a ubiquitous dweller of these tracts of montane forest, has a song varied and complex enough to fool beginners time after time. I call it a "song," yet it is more a garbled series of caws, coughs, gurgles, and whines—oddly phrased in endless variety of fashions.

The track led upward at a steady grade. It was a fairly good walking track in 1975, but it would have been difficult to guess it had once been a truck road. Green tangles of vegetation had grown up everywhere. Only a narrow path between the thick shrubbery permitted passage. Small trees grew in profusion in any open spot, and larger ones crowded the spaces on each side of the old bed. Much original vegetation had been felled and used in road construction, then replaced by vigorous regrowth. Within a hundred feet of the track, great forest trees remained, with their branches reaching out to shade us.

We rested and lunched at a grassy site where there had been a large landslip across the original path of the road. Here we gloried in dropping our loads and hungrily devouring the hard Navy biscuits and the cool water that a field assistant drew from a little creek below the track.

The climb from less than 7,000 to 8,600 feet is gradual but wearing. I arrived exhilarated but bone tired. Abid's Camp lies at the junction of the Kaindi ridge and one of the main mountain masses of the Ekuti Divide, overlooking the deep gorge of a high tributary of the Bulolo River, which drains northward into the Wau valley. The camp was situated on a flat site formed when the wartime roadbed was cut from the flank of the mountain. Looking out from one of the several vistas near the camp, I was struck by the vast tracts of untouched mountain wilderness.

In April 1975, Abid's Camp itself was a small clearing bracketed by two tall pandanus trees. The shelter was a low, broad lean-to, fashioned from rough poles and several pieces of wartime corrugated metal. Our source of water was a zinc-lined fifty-five gallon drum filled with naturally chilled rain water. We made the camp livable by first stoking up a big fire, laying on a pot of water for tea, and throwing our smoke-darkened sheets of roofing plastic on the leaky roof and more on the rough sleeping area below.

After dinner, the three ornithologists collapsed into their sleeping bags, while the two Papuan assistants sat talking by the crackling fire. Their habits differ from ours. They are more sociable and more addicted to a hot fire. To sleep, they wrap themselves in a blanket and curl up as close to the fire as possible. Every hour or so they awaken, stir the fire, then catnap again until the fire dies down. We slept in our warm, cocoonlike down bags until our tea-filled bladders forced us to wander out into the miserable cold of predawn, in search of a bush.

━━━━

I was here to observe the high-altitude forest birds. There is a subset of the Papuan avifauna that inhabits only the highest mountains, and it usually remains above eight thousand feet. We had encountered a tight flock of Pink-faced Sittellas on the hike in. The next morning I was able to closely observe another party of these squeaking and nervous little beasts right beside our camp. Superficially, the birds have the look of a nuthatch, but their coloring is generally blackish, relieved by a pink mask, pink tips to the tail, and yellow legs and feet. The party moved through the twigs and limbs of roadside trees, then illuminated by the pale sunlight of early morning. Several birds even dropped down into the shrubbery in their quest for insects, but almost as soon as they arrived they nervously set off for another feeding site. In more than a decade since then, I've never again seen this species so well.

Another high-altitude treat was the Crested Berrypecker. It resembles a crested jay because of its handsome patterning in blue, black, white, and green. This is a confiding, sociable fruit-eater that moves through the upper montane shrubbery in search of ripe berries. We captured several of these birds in the three mist nets I had erected the evening before. I got a quick indication of the bird's morning diet when the individual I was holding snugly in my hand evacuated a jet of warm, wet, deep purple excreta onto my shirt and pants. Dark stains permanently marked this avian encounter, and I learned to beware of berrypeckers.

What, exactly, is a "berrypecker"? That is a question not easily answered today, because recent systematic studies indicate that the assemblage of small fruit-eating songbirds formerly placed in the family

Dicaeidae actually comprises unrelated lineages lumped together because of their similar diets and habits. Our nomenclature still lags behind this discovery, and what we today call the Crested Berrypecker may next year be called the Crested Paramythia, because it probably is not a member of the true berrypecker alliance! Suffice it to say, all of these "berrypecker" types are of obscure affinities and occur only in New Guinea.

We were most pleased to net a small, brown-plumaged night bird, the Mountain Owlet-nightjar. When I removed it from the net, I was handling a member of a little-known family of birds I had only read about, the Aegothelidae. This group is even more obscure than the berrypeckers! We were uncertain at the time as to its specific identification, so it was the focus of much scrutiny, measurements, notes, and photographs.

Hunting for birds in the high mountains did have its costs. After lunch, I decided to trek up to the pass south of Abid's Camp. This pass divides the northern and southern watersheds of the island and is the high point of the road. The track up to the pass continues to follow the old roadbed but is much overgrown. I slowly worked my way upward, stopping to observe the following: a large, soaring hawk that I could not identify; the creeperlike Blue-capped Ifrita, giving its buzzy call; a male and female Plum-faced Lorikeet carrying out a mating display on a low tree limb; and a Painted Tiger-Parrot foraging in a low conifer.

I took copious notes on the raptor, and upon return to Wau I pored through Rand and Gilliard's *Handbook* to try to pin down what it was. Trying to identify a large, brown-streaked hawk in New Guinea was a real test at that time. The descriptions in the book are accurate, but they were based on examination of dried museum study skins, not live birds in flight. I would later come to realize that the bird I saw was the very common and wide-ranging Long-tailed Buzzard. It is the only streaked species that soars over mountain forest at this altitude. Back in 1975, the many immature raptor plumages (mostly streaked brown) were a nightmare for field identification. Subsequent work has helped clarify this muddle.

The Blue-capped Ifrita, formerly called the Blue-capped Babbler, is another one of the high-altitude species that is common but poorly known. There are still disagreements about its systematic affinity. Its

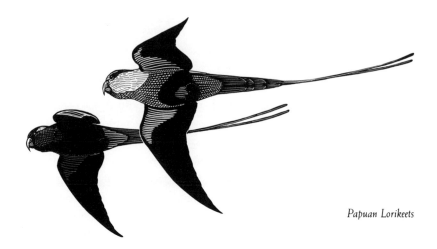

Papuan Lorikeets

size, shape, plumage, and behavior help little in answering this question once and for all. Is it related to the fairy-wrens, the scrubwrens, or some other Australo-Papuan group? At this time we don't have a clue—that's how little we know about many of these montane specialties.

The lorikeets on Bulldog Road are one of its most remarkable features. For a first-time visitor, these colorful and graceful parrot relatives seem to be everywhere. Pairs of the streamer-tailed Papuan Lorikeets whizzed through the trees. Most of the birds I saw wore the common red plumage, although in one instance I saw a black individual paired with a red one. The Papuan Lorikeet exhibits color morphs in the same manner that our Eastern Screech Owl comes in both gray and rufous "phases." I observed this mixed lorikeet pair feeding at pale yellow flowers in the low canopy of a trailside tree. Whether black or red, this species is always a favorite of naturalists visiting New Guinea. It is perhaps the most streamlined and graceful of the parrot family, with a sleek body that graduates into a slender and long, pointed tail. And what colors—red bill and eyes, orange feet, blue hindcrown, green wings and back, red vent, and yellow tail! The red of the red morph is a deep, lustrous red, whereas the black of the black morph is a shiny purplish black that almost gleams.

Flocks of the tiny, jewellike Plum-faced Lorikeets raced through the openings in the forest canopy, heading who-knows-where in search of plants with nectar-filled flowers. Orange-billed Lorikeets, colored in green and orangy red, foraged in the pale blossoms of a *Xanthomyrtus*.

How different are the sluggish tiger-parrots from the frenetic lorikeets! Quite difficult to observe, the stolid but beautifully patterned tiger-parrots creep amongst the thick shrubbery and low trees at the edge of the track, giving their mournful, catlike calls. The two larger members of this genus inhabit the forest of Abid's Camp. Both appear to specialize on seeds of montane conifers.

At one point, Paul Kores and I had two tiger-parrots and three lorikeets as free-ranging house pets, and the behavioral differences were vast. Because of their retiring habits and lack of personality, Paul called our two tiger-parrots "the coprolites," an unflattering nickname, considering it is the technical term for fossilized dung. A tiger-parrot is more like a feathered sloth than a parrot. The difference in behavior between the lorikeets and tiger-parrots almost certainly relates to diet. The lorikeets subsist on nectar and pollen, rich and quickly metabolized nutrients. The tiger-parrots survive by preying on seeds of forest trees, many of which are protected by chemical defenses, and which are made up of complex resins and essential oils, more difficult to digest.

My hike up the track was productive, but when I was nearing a level section of road that I thought was the top of the pass, a chill rain began to fall. At nine thousand feet, a rainstorm is a nasty affair, especially to one clothed in a thin gingham shirt and khaki pants. Before long I was soaked and shivering. Luckily, there was a tiny lean-to, made from a large sheet of metal, some war relic. I huddled under this for fifteen minutes, while the worst of the rain dumped into the stunted forest around me. Although safe from the rain, I was getting neither warmer nor drier, so I decided to begin my miserable descent to camp. The overgrown trail, thick with prickly raspberry and other tangles, was torture. Each time I brushed these plants I was doused with a new freshet of water. Since I had no change of clothes, I was forced to dry what I wore by perching beside the camp blaze.

In New Guinea, chiggers were my nemesis, or perhaps my invertebrate mascot! They seemed to follow me wherever I went. In Papua New Guinea, Abid's Camp seemed to be a center of abundance for these trombiculid mites. It seems I always managed to sit down in the place where hungry chiggers were waiting, in swarms, for a naive and tender, white-skinned field biologist. Even when I returned to sites (like Abid's Camp) where I knew chiggers to be abundant, my preventive measures were inadequate, and the little devils managed to feast on my midriff, ankles, and more tender regions.

The chigger population at Abid's Camp must have blossomed during the period when I visited. After a single day I could count dozens and dozens of swelling pink bumps on the skin of my midsection. They itched fiercely, and I usually could not resist scratching them until they bled. At some points it was difficult to sleep because of the irritation. To my great chagrin, not all of my fellow field-workers suffered as I did. It didn't seem fair.

Our last morning at Abid's Camp dawned misty and gray, a change from the spectacular orange-and-purple dawn that I had witnessed the previous day. We had to break camp and hike down and meet the institute's jeep, due to pick us up in the early afternoon. The trek down was more difficult than the ascent, mainly because of the heavy rain. The intrepid, heavily laden Papuan assistants moved out far ahead of the three ornithologists, who grew more weary with every turn in the track. As we emerged from the forest out into the scarred gold workings of Edie Creek, the rain pelted us unmercifully. This, certainly, was our lowest moment. The jeep, a green speck in the distance, was our goal—a dry, warm haven and a promise of transport home to hot showers. When we arrived at the jeep, we must have looked like something that might wash up on a beach in northern New Jersey. Nonetheless, once we were in the warm and dry vehicle, bouncing down the rutted road to Wau, we felt like a million bucks.

My trying experience there in April 1975 was ridiculously tame compared with the hardship and deprivation visited upon the Australians and Papuans who spent months in the forest, constructing that path over the mountains. Their efforts will always hold me in awe.

Building the Road

When the Japanese forces swept out of the northwest, moving over the broad expanse of the Pacific, they captured the entire northern coastline of New Guinea and shortly thereafter began to penetrate the interior at key points. The Australian military, on the defensive, was quite worried about the prospects that the Japanese might "turn the corner" at Milne Bay and follow up by taking Port Moresby as preparation for an assault on Australia. The Australian plan, then, was to complete a strategic road link from the south side to the northern watershed, in order to supply their forces engaged with the Japanese. Because of the presence of a road from Bulolo to Wau and thence up to the heights of Edie Creek, engineers believed this might be the simplest site for forging the desired transisland connection.

The construction began in January 1943, with Australian engineers and 450 Papuan laborers clearing sections of track from the southern roadhead at Bulldog. After a daring reconnaissance of the proposed route over the high mountains by C. Keith Johnson, C. W. Ecclestone, and party, the work began in earnest. Different sections of the planned road were assigned to discrete teams, with the idea that they would link up when completed.

The final route was to be sixty-eight miles from Wau to Bulldog. The highest point on the road reached 10,500 feet. Seventeen bridges were erected. All of the high-altitude work was carried out by hand. Men worked with relatively crude construction equipment; dressed in clothing that was always dirty and wet; slept in inadequate shelters on beds fashioned from whatever could be had; and consumed food that was scarce in quantity and poor in quality. In spite of cold, clouds, and frequent rain, the teams worked seven days a week. Lines of supply were long and difficult. Morale was often low, especially when the construction was raided by enemy aircraft in early June.

In spite of the hardships, the work teams suffered only four fatalities (by landslide, tree fall, and explosives). Malaria struck many of the Australians, however, with 70 percent of one unit suffering from the disease. Pneumonia was the chief sickness to afflict the Papuan laborers, all of whom were lowlanders unaccustomed to the cold.

The upshot of all of this was that the completed road served no important strategic purpose in the war, which had bypassed this area by the end of 1943. In addition, landslides small and large often broke the single-lane route, which demanded a high level of maintenance and repair that could not be supported. Within a few months of its completion, the road was abandoned. It has never been reopened nor replaced. There still is no link from the capital in the south over the mountains to the northern watershed—this, in spite of tremendous advances in engineering methods and equipment. This is testament to the remarkable feat performed on the Bulldog Road in 1943.

New Guinea and the War

One of the fascinating aspects of my first sojourn in Papua New Guinea was my personal discovery of "the War." Local memories there of the Pacific conflict remained strong, even after forty years. Evidence of the war was never far from view. The Bulldog Road is one of the icons of the war effort. Most of the people in the area knew of the road, even if they had not actually walked on it. A surprising number of adventurous souls (many of them young Australians) wished to walk a segment of it. The Kokoda Trail, site of some of the most brutal fighting between Australians and Japanese during the War, has been declared a national monument. It is the more famous track through the mountains, but it has lost some of its mystique because it is so well traveled and well maintained.

Anyone who spent part of the War in New Guinea has significant memories of that time. The names Milne Bay, Finschhafen, Nadzab, Port Moresby, Buna and Gona, Aitape, Wewak, and others elicit vivid recollections, even about natural history. An acquaintance, James Bruce, for example, was stationed for a time on Numfoor Island, off the coast of Irian Jaya. He still has his small field notebook listing his bird observations; his watercolor sketch of that island's endemic paradise-kingfisher is striking. Another man, the father of a high-school classmate, told me he remembered an annoying morning birdsong that woke him each dawn at Milne Bay. Men christened it the "F——k You" bird because the syllables of the monotonous refrain sounded so much like that expletive. The offending species was most likely the everpresent Helmeted Friarbird.

———

The war in New Guinea had a well-defined script. After the swift Japanese occupation of the northern coast and the numerous Bismarck islands, there was a period of consolidation, during which time there was little Allied activity. The Battle of the Coral Sea, off the eastern tip of the New Guinea mainland, is recognized as one of the slowing points in the Japanese expansion, and after this there was a gradual growth in Allied strength, until the Japanese strongpoints were entirely neutralized by MacArthur's bold leapfrogging maneuvers to the northwest, back toward the Philippines.

Some of the most significant fighting took place about a hundred miles southeast of Wau, between the north coastal beaches of Buna and Gona, inland along the tracks that led to the tiny settlement of Kokoda, and from there in the montane rainforest in the mountains south of Kokoda, on the walking track that led to Port Moresby. The centerpiece of this series of engagements was the infamous Battle of the Kokoda Trail. What began as a surprise invasion and rout of the meager Australian outposts, finished as a complete destruction of this Japanese invasion force and the end of their push towards Australia. Fighting on the heights of the trail, often in the cold mossy forest much like that along the upper portions of the Bulldog Road, combined all the hardships experienced by the road-building crew with the terror of jungle combat.

Things got pretty hot in the area around Wau, as well. The Japanese occupied the two coastal communities nearest Wau, Lae and Salamaua, with the intention of moving inland and capturing the valuable mining settlements of Bulolo, Wau, and Edie Creek. Since there was no motor road linking Wau to the coast, the invaders were forced to make their way through the forests of the Kuper Range, and thence down into the interior valleys. The invading troops were much hindered by the forest, and when they struggled down the slopes of Mount Missim and Mossy Knoll, they were met by fierce resistance of the small militia force that defended Wau.

The battle for Wau signaled the end of Japanese efforts to penetrate and control the rich Wau-Bulolo goldfields. The success of the Australian forces at Wau is often credited to the daring resupply flights made by the air force in the face of harassing Japanese fire.

In terms of Pacific strategy, after Japan's first major defeat, in the Battle of Milne Bay, the War turned to the advantage of the Allies. MacArthur devised his grand plan of overstepping the main concentrations of Japanese; this isolated the enemy forces and severed their lines of supply. In New Guinea, the Allies jumped from Milne Bay to Buna.

Then, from their big air bases in the Milne Bay area and Port Moresby, they made a grand airborne drop at Nadzab and took Lae. The next big step was to Hollandia (Jayapura) and then a series of points along the north coast of Netherlands New Guinea (now Irian Jaya).

Any Australian can recount how MacArthur's grand strategy left the worst of the fighting for the Australian forces, who had the unenviable task of "mopping up"—a euphemism for fierce jungle battling to capture entrenched and fanatical Japanese units bypassed by MacArthur's advance.

═══

Moldering relics of the War litter the forests and villages of New Guinea. Lost fighters or bombers rest in nearly every valley. A bomber that lies in the thick scrub outside of Kaisenik village is a well-known local monument in the Wau valley, visited by curious expatriates on weekend excursions. Readily visible from the road above the village and even more obvious from the air, it appears as a silver cross in the green vegetation.

One of the longest-lasting War relics is Marston matting, the perforated, modular steel sheets that were linked together to form a runway surface for wartime airstrips. The matting is nearly indestructible, and one finds it today being used as fencing, for small bridges across creeks, and even for its original purpose, on airfields. The other artifacts of war are now either rusting junk or undetonated ordnance, overgrown by vines and forgotten by all but the old-timers who, as youngsters, remember the days when the population of many villages headed for the hills to hide.

Thus, the War is much remembered by older New Guineans as a time of fear and a time of marvels. One of the lasting effects of the War was the growth of cargo cults—ritually complex, quasi religions that sprang up among village groups in many parts of Melanesia, but especially on New Guinea, where hundreds of the "cults" have been recorded. Each cult is usually inspired by the messianic teachings of a self-proclaimed local prophet, who promises to bring a time of spiritual and material prosperity. An important component of many of the cults is the desire to gain access to the material riches of the white man's world—the "cargo"—that was exhibited by the Allied forces in such prolific abundance during the War. Villagers throughout the Pacific theater were able to observe, first hand, the arrival of huge stores of food and supplies, delivered by plane and ship. Why were similar riches never delivered to the Papuan villages?

Superficially, the most remarkable aspect of these cults was their focus on material wealth and the means of obtaining it through some form of magic communication with those powerful gods who controlled it. This was manifested in bizarre ways. In some instances, villagers went to great efforts to construct and decorate airplane landing grounds or else great piers along the coast in order to encourage the arrival of the "cargo" that they believed they rightfully deserved. In other instances, cult leaders encouraged cult members to donate money in order to convince the "cargo" gods to deliver the goods.

Anthropologist Peter Lawrence studied the cargo-cult phenomenon on the north coast of Papua New Guinea. He has postulated that these remarkable cults develop because of the deep conflict between the white culture of material abundance and individual acquisitiveness, versus the traditional Melanesian culture of communal sharing of the relatively sparse material wealth in their societies.

This was Lawrence's reasoning: the typical Papuan villager worked hard either in his garden or else in a menial job and received relatively little material reward for his efforts. By contrast, his white counterpart was observed to labor physically almost not at all, yet was able to sign a small scrap of paper and subsequently receive a huge quantity of goods from some unknown source overseas. The Papuan logically deduced that material wealth did not come from physical labor but instead was won by some magic (as in signing the scrap of paper). Thus, since the white man was not sharing equally his vast wealth, it must be that the white man had cheated the Papuan of his fair share.

Cargo cults often promised the removal of whites and their system and the supernatural appearance of material wealth to be shared beneficently among the cult members in traditional Melanesian fashion. The peculiarly Melanesian phenomenon of the cargo cult did not begin with the War, but it seems to have reached its zenith in the decade immediately afterward. Lawrence believes that its fundamental roots are a rudimentary nationalist movement, a revolt from European rule.

Rhododendrons

Paul Kores, my botanist friend, spent more time on the Bulldog Road than any other person I know. He visited Abid's Camp nearly every month in 1975 and 1976, in order to study the sixteen species of rhododendrons inhabiting the roadside scrub near the camp. Many of the species that inhabit the moss forest of New Guinea live primarily as epiphytes, often high in the canopy, where they can compete successfully for light and moisture. However, under the rather unusual roadside conditions found along the Bulldog Road, many of these primarily epiphytic forms live on the ground because of the clearing created by the road cut. The situation, then, is man created, but Paul didn't complain, given the botanically splendid result.

I traipsed up the long track to Abid's Camp seven times with Paul, and he visited the camp at least another dozen times. Normally, we spent three nights, which gave us two full days of work—not a lot of time, but considering the difficulty of carrying food and supplies and the troublesome weather, it was a satisfactory compromise. The pilgrimage was one that I faced with some mixture of dread and anticipation. I dreaded the possibility of heavy rain and the long walk up and back, but it was a perfect site to set up my mist nets, trap and band more birds, and make new observations on the foraging behavior of honeyeaters.

I began to learn from Paul the process of data gathering and experimental design. Paul's project seemed to involve a nearly ideal system, a suite of rhododendron species, all easily accessible along the roadside and exhibiting a great range of morphologies and colors. Paul wanted to test Peter Stevens' hypothesis that the colors and corolla types in these rhododendrons were the product of coadaptation with a specific group of animal pollinators. Stevens had suggested that the typical nonfragrant, red-flowered species were visited by birds; that funnel-shaped, yellow-flowered species were used by butterflies; and that the tubular white flowers were specialized for pollination by hawk moths. In addition, Kores' initial studies indicated that the large, scented, white-flowered species were used by nectar-feeding bats, a fact not recognized by Stevens.

I was interested in Paul's project because a major subset of his presumed pollinators were species of nectar-feeding honeyeaters that I was studying. It was useful to work with someone who looked at ecological problems from the plant's viewpoint. We discussed honeyeaters and rhododendrons with a mutual interest that made doing the fieldwork a lot more satisfying.

My work on honeyeaters was following several lines. I had been studying the cryptic yellow-eared *Meliphaga* species at several middle-altitude sites in the Wau and Watut valleys. That group of birds did not inhabit the montane forest on the Bulldog Road, so at this site I had devised another honeyeater project related to foraging behavior by five montane species.

In early 1975, Paul was still in the midst of the preliminary stages of the work—finding, tagging, and identifying the species of rhodo-dendrons that inhabited the Bulldog Road. When his assistant, Taine Gumine, brought in a novel plant, the excitement would run high. Paul photographed and then carefully sketched the flower and leaves in his field notebook, noting every detail. Then came the arduous task of working through H. Sleumer's keys to the rhododendrons in *Flora Male-siana*. This latter task was, by far, the more difficult, as anyone who has used a botanical key for a species-rich genus will readily admit. It was especially troublesome if one believed that the specimen might be a hybrid between two well-defined forms. After sketching and a prelimi-nary attempt at identification, the specimen was preserved between newsprint in a plant press.

One of the great differences between Papuan botany and Papuan ornithology was the level of taxonomic clarity within each group. The plants, by comparison, were poorly known, and species limits were not well defined. Botanists working in different regions tended to give new names to anything that possessed distinct characters. This did not take into account the possibility of clinal variation between populations at distant collecting sites. At the opposite extreme, the birds were very well worked, and ornithologists in the 1930s and 1940s had sorted out most of the questions related to regional variation, uniting the region-ally variable forms into polytypic species, each with geographic repre-sentatives, known as subspecies or races.

Thus, there was virtually no chance for me to discover a new spe-cies (or even a new race!) among the birds at Abid's Camp. By contrast,

Paul often had to struggle with the question of species identification. Was this strange-looking plant a hybrid, a regional isolate of a described species, or an entirely new species? Plants, by the way, show a great deal more morphological "plasticity"—they can exhibit non-genetic variation brought about by environmental and developmental conditions.

Once Paul had generally sorted out the tangle of forms into a discrete set of defined species, he began the task of learning something of their pollination biology. This effort was very time consuming, requiring long hours of patient observation at actively flowering plants, in the hopes that the pollinators would visit. For those rhododendrons that were pollinated primarily by birds (mostly honeyeaters), the job was relatively simple, but for plants suspected of bat or moth pollination, it was necessary to make observations at night. Paul individually tagged many plants, much in the same manner that I banded my birds. In addition, he bagged inflorescences. Some flowers he enclosed in coarsely meshed cloth bags. This bagging would permit pollination by wind and tiny insects but prevented visits to the flowers by vertebrate or moth pollinators. Other samples he enclosed in finely meshed bags, which prevented any outside pollen from entering and would allow him to determine which species were autogamic—able to self-pollinate.

Paul's results typify fieldwork on a complex system in a difficult environment. They provide tantalizingly suggestive data but do not close all of our gaps of uncertainty. He was *unable* to observe bats and moths actually visiting the rhododendrons, yet he was able to collect specimens of both bats and moths carrying loads of rhododendron pollen, clear evidence that they had been visiting the plants. He found that the so-called bat-pollinated rhododendrons apparently were pollinated both by bats (at night) and also lorikeets (in the daytime). Those white-flowered species that were coarse-bagged failed to set seeds, indicating that a vertebrate pollinator was necessary for reproduction.

The relationship between the red rhododendrons and the honeyeaters was messier. Both Paul and I documented that several honeyeaters regularly visited these plants, but their importance as pollinators is unclear for several reasons. Paul found that the reds typically are autogamic; his bagging tests proved that many could pollinate themselves. In addition, the honeyeater species were notably unfaithful to any one species of rhododendron and would forage at any available plants. Allied with this, Paul found large numbers of hybrid plants of the red species. How, then, would the red rhododendrons benefit from the sloppy pollination by the honeyeaters? Paul supposed that the plants benefit from a low level of outcrossing, to reduce genetic load. The production of hybrids is simply "slop" in an imperfect biological system.

Most rhododendrons bloom in profusion at the end of the rainy season. At this time, large sprays of red, white, pink, or white-and-pink flowers burst from the dark green vegetation. Although there was a flowering peak, at least some species were in flower every month, so each trip provided new encounters with this diverse group.

I had become infatuated with Paul's rhododendrons and spent a good bit of my time photographing them in full flower. The most glamorous species, and most photogenic, were the big tubular whites and the crimson-flowered reds. Inflorescences of these often bore dozens of flowers, bunched together to give a wonderful splash of color in the roadside greenery. It seemed no two plants produced exactly the same size, shape, and color of flowers. Moving from plant to plant, I could see why Paul often had difficulty with species identification. I was able to enjoy the plants for what they were—beautiful additions to the natural landscape and generous providers of nectar for the birds I was studying. I have spoken at length of the hardships of Bulldog Road, but they were always repaid by the varied environmental wonders I witnessed there. The chiggers may be fierce, but they would never keep me from visiting Abid's Camp again, if the opportunity arose.

Honeyeaters and Honeycreepers

In my work at the Bulldog Road camp, I studied foraging behavior by the five species of honeyeaters common on the site: Sooty Melidectes, Belford's Melidectes, Black-throated Honeyeater, Rufous-backed Honeyeater, and Red-collared Myzomela. All five foraged at flowering plants, so my observations concentrated on nectar feeding.

At that time, one of the ecological questions that excited field-workers was: how do foragers of different species manage amicably to share a single food resource? My honeyeaters at Bulldog Road provided a model for examining this question, because in certain instances the large, medium-sized, and small species could be seen foraging at the same flowering plants. The smaller species were able to forage at several locations in the plant that the larger species could not reach because of their weight, so there was some ecological partitioning based on flower position. The second factor was the more interesting to me and seemed to contrast with that for many other systems being studied then. Often the honeyeaters *did not* share the flower resource amicably. Individuals of the same species jostled among each other, and different species also fought among each other for favored perches. A foraging hierarchy, based on size and aggressiveness, determined who foraged where in the tree. The two most aggressive species were Belford's Melidectes, the largest, and the Black-throated Honeyeater, the third largest. These birds were the bullies of the feeding tree and would spend a remarkable amount of time driving lesser foragers out. In addition, Belford's Melidectes often attacked the Black-throated Honeyeaters, even following them far out of the tree in noisy, aggressive chases. Finally, one Belford's would chase another Belford's, so no species was immune from the violence.

The interspecific aggression among nectar-feeding honeyeaters was in sharp contrast to the foraging system employed by several species of honeycreepers in Panama, birds I observed at a flowering *Luehea* tree in 1977. Three species of these small nectar eaters tended to arrive and depart the flowering tree as a group, and there was virtually no aggression among them. A fourth species, *Chlorophanes*, behaved in yet another manner. A pair of this species would stake out a small part of the tree and defend it from the other foragers, but without the aggressive chases so common among the larger honeyeaters. Time and time again I was to find that, when looking at the solution to a general ecological question, the local answer in New Guinea differed from the evolutionary "solution" achieved in the New World. Is one strategy "better" than the other? That is not the point in this sort of comparison. It is more important to understand that there can be more than one "correct" evolutionary answer to a general biological problem.

The honeyeaters are New Guinea's largest family of birds, and one of the most diverse, morphologically. The five species at the Bulldog Road camp were typical of honeyeater assemblages elsewhere in the country. Although all did feed on nectar, they also spent time foraging on other items, such as insects or fruit. This would be a fascinating group for further study.

Frog Heaven

In early 1976, Martin Simon, a new volunteer, joined the staff of the Ecology Institute and split his time between science education and ecological fieldwork on frogs. Martin was a burly, athletic, and irrepressible sort who was always intensely involved with some activity or another. His interest in frogs eventually led him to the field camp on Bulldog Road, and it was there that he did the major part of his herpetological field research.

I visited Abid's Camp on three occasions with Martin. Our work projects were, in many ways, very different, so there was very little overlap in effort or in timing. Martin studied his frogs at night, and I studied my birds during the daylight hours. Thus, he often was asleep when I was awake, and vice versa.

Martin Simon studied a group of tiny microhylid frogs. Bullfrogs these are not. The species of *Cophixalus* that Simon studied are more like miniature toads than they are like the common frogs we know in the United States. First, the frogs are often less than an inch long and not uncommonly less than a half-inch. Second, they do not live in water but instead inhabit the moist vegetation of montane forest interior. Third, they are fossorial—spending much of their lives burrowed under the ground litter and moss. Fourth, they lay their eggs in wet moss, not in water as do typical frogs.

For such tiny creatures, the voices of these frogs are remarkably loud and distinctive. Perhaps this should not be surprising, considering that the vocalization is their main means of communication and given that much of the time the frogs are hidden in vegetation. Male frogs call in order to attract females for mating. The loud call may help the male signal to more females. The clicking and pinging calls of the little *Cophixalus*, along with the repeated cawing of Belford's Melidectes and the quick rattled warble of Papuan Scrubwrens, will forever be a part of my memories of Bulldog Road. Even on a sunny day one might hear

Small Cophixalus *frog,
Bulldog Road*

the distinctive cry of a tiny frog holding forth from a damp and shady spot by a trail.

These frogs are quite demanding as study animals. Like the rhododendrons, they can offer some serious identification problems. They are often polymorphic, and the best means of identification are their voices and skeletal characters. Thus, it is not always possible to identify a frog by external looks alone.

Finding frogs during the day or on a dry night was nearly impossible. Each frog gives its high, ventriloquial call, *ping . . . ping . . . ping*, one note every twenty seconds or so, and the searcher first must try to locate the general area from which the sound emanates—no simple task—then must begin to home in on the point source, the burrowed frog. The searcher is on hands and knees, ear close to the ground litter, and still the quest can be futile. One does not actually wish to begin digging into the litter until one is certain of the location of the hiding frog; but pinning down the location, even on hands and knees, is very difficult because of the frog's ability to throw its voice, combined with its natural tendency to halt calling when it senses a potential predator approaching.

Luckily, on wet nights the little *Cophixalus* frogs emerge from their hiding places, ascend into shrubs, and sing lustily from atop leaves. These nights were sheer delight for Martin Simon. With the help of Timis Suri, an erstwhile ornithological assistant, Martin would scour the vegetation along the paths below the camp, often returning with bags full of frogs. Timis, invariably, brought back more than Martin, but, after all, Martin was a newcomer to Papua New Guinea. After learning the various species that inhabited the forest around the camp, Martin began ecological studies of them.

Martin found that one of his study animals, *Cophixalus parkeri*, displayed well-developed parental care. In this species, the female lays a mass of eggs on wet moss, and it is the male who broods after fertilizing them. He remains with the eggs for a period of eighty-five to one-hundred days, until hatching.

In these frogs there is no tadpole stage. At hatching, the "froglets" remain with their father for an additional thirty days and receive their nutrition by way of absorption of a large abdominal yolk mass, a by-product of the development process.

Martin performed several manipulations of this brooding system and found that parental care significantly increased the success of the broods. It seems that the parental care reduced mortality that can be caused by fungal infection, egg cannibalism, and predation by arthropods. The brooding behavior in *Cophixalus parkeri*, although ingenious, is not without its costs. Parents that brooded eggs lost weight and held significantly smaller fat reserves than free-ranging adults. This was primarily caused by the relative starvation of the brooding individuals, who were unable to search freely for their invertebrate prey.

Another of Martin's more interesting encounters was with the *Cophixalus* frog "apartment houses." He pointed out to me that an arboreal species, *Cophixalus riparius*, relied on the empty chambers of epiphytic ant plants as roosting and laying sites. An ant plant is the name for one of several genera in the coffee family that produce enlarged, bulbous stems that are often used as a nest by ants. The relationship between the ants and the plants appears to be symbiotic. The ants provide the plant with some nutrition (their waste) and physical protection from herbivorous pests. The plant provides the ants with a nest shelter. The frog connection is another twist to the story. The bulbous stem of the plant, which usually can be seen hanging up on the branch of a tree, has a number of openings that give entrance to sizable chambers inside the stem. It seems that females of *Cophixalus riparius* like to enter these stems to lay their eggs. There is no conflict with ants, which are absent at altitudes above seven thousand feet in New Guinea. The ant plant provides a thermally protective nesting place for the frog, one that is presumably safe from predators as well. Whether the frog provides any direct benefit to the plant is unknown.

Changes

I have not visited Bulldog Road for more than a decade, but colleagues from the Ecology Institute have, and they tell me that the splendid isolation we savored is gone, victim of a new gold rush. In the search for new "lodes," the local mining company has made test digs in many of the high mountain watersheds south of Edie Creek. Men hike into a site, make a big clearing by felling trees, and then build a helipad for delivery of supplies. A sizable clearing was made for this very purpose right beside Abid's Camp. If no gold is found, the very localized desecration of the wilderness will remain for all future hikers to see for decades. If gold is found, the hopes for having access to an undisturbed high mountain research site for the Ecology Institute may be doomed. It seems this is a story told over and over by researchers in the tropical world.

*Opposite: Mt. Oiamadawa'a,
from Ulatuya village*

4 *Goodenough Island*

J ust north of the eastern tip of New Guinea lies the D'Entrecasteaux Archipelago, comprising three main islands, Goodenough, Fergusson, and Normanby, and a scattering of tiny islets. Goodenough Island was the site of the huge Allied air base at Vivigani, not so many miles north of the battlefields of the Milne Bay region, across Ward Hunt Strait. This entire area was alive with military activity during 1943. The Battle of the Coral Sea, thought by many historians to be one of the turning points in the Pacific War, took place less than a hundred miles to the east. In recent decades these islands have more or less returned to sleepy anonymity.

I visited Milne Bay Province in 1976 in order to climb into the mountains of Goodenough Island. I was drawn to this area, rarely visited by naturalists, in search of the unknown. As the gold prospector is lured to a new region by rumors of a strike, I was drawn to Goodenough Island by tales of a black bird, an undescribed bird of paradise that inhabited this rugged island's mountain forests.

The Black Bird

I knew nothing of the black bird until I received my copy of the March 1976 newsletter of the New Guinea Bird Society, which noted a recent observation, by James Menzies, of an unidentified species of long-tailed black bird on Goodenough Island:

> On Mt. Oiamadawa'a, Goodenough Island 28 December 1975. Altitude about 1600 m, moss forest of *Castanopsis*, pandanus and tall bamboo. At dawn—a group of medium-sized black birds with long tails moving about in the forest canopy. Observed against the rising sun, without binoculars. Call a short explosive rattle.

The editor added: "Several of the Archbold Expeditions tried unsuccessfully to find a bird similar to this description."

I visited the institute's library and located the 1956 report of the Fourth Archbold Expedition, which visited Goodenough Island in 1953. On page 144 I was held by the author's words, as he spoke of a similar encounter:

> In the forest one morning I saw a black bird the size of a small crow which seemed to be a bird of paradise but not *Manucodia comrii* or *Manucodia keraudrenii*, the only members of the family reported from the island. Our native hunter confirmed the absence of *Paradisaea decora*, endemic on neighboring Fergusson Island, and on Normanby Island, as far as is known. He described, however, a small black bird with a long tail, which dances in the treetops in the mountain forests of Goodenough, a description that suggests an *Astrapia* or ribbon-tailed bird of paradise.

Reading these accounts, I began to speculate about what this mystery bird might be. The dark body and long tail did suggest a typical bird of paradise. The prominent vocalization suggested that it was not an astrapia, but more likely a sicklebill. Of course, with such a vague description, it could be just about anything at all, including some sort of undescribed drongo, or even a long-tailed starling. Whatever it might be, it would almost certainly be new to science.

I began to feel the fever that must perpetually heat the blood of the prospector, and which occasionally excites the imagination of the zoologist. I wanted to get down to Goodenough Island and find out the identity of that black bird.

Mount Oiamadawa'a

Within a week of reading James Menzies' brief account of his observation, I was on a plane south to Port Moresby. I spent two nights with Menzies, and I interviewed him about his observations, his field trip, and his guesses as to the mystery bird's identity. Menzies could provide nothing more on the mystery bird, but he gave me all the details of getting to his field camp, including the names of islanders who could assist me in my effort.

I flew to Alotau, capital of Milne Bay Province, in a DC-3, the two-engine, twenty-six passenger aircraft made famous during World War II. Air Niugini relied on a small fleet of reconditioned DC-3s for its domestic flights to Papua New Guinea outstations. The oddest thing

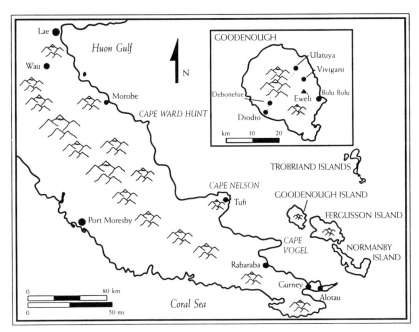

Milne Bay region with inset of Goodenough Island

about the plane is that when on the ground it rests on a tail wheel, and the fuselage is canted back, with the cockpit well above the passengers. It felt odd to race down the runway in this position, only to right upward just before taking off. One gets the feeling that the pilot has to be very careful not to bring the tail up too far, lest the craft end up on its nose!

We landed at the wartime strip at Gurney, a fifteen-minute drive from Alotau. I had hoped to connect on a Talair flight onward to Vivigani, my destination, but that flight had been canceled. I was fortunate to catch a ride into town, because there was absolutely nothing at Gurney in 1975. I had no contacts in Alotau, and I had no information on lodging. I learned that there was but a single guesthouse. I stayed there to await my flight out to Goodenough Island.

The geography of this part of Papua New Guinea features rugged forested mountains and deep salt-water embayments. The eastern extremity of New Guinea is actually a four-pronged affair, with three major capes on the north (Cape Nelson, Cape Vogel, East Cape) and one on the south (South Cape). The three main D'Entrecasteaux islands stand off the northern coast of East Cape and east and northeast of Cape Vogel. To the south of the East Cape is Milne Bay proper, a deep bay that lies between two mountainous peninsulas. On the northern side of the head of this bay lies Alotau.

Because I needed to economize, I had hoped to avoid spending any nights in Alotau. Also, I only had two weeks to do my fieldwork. The tariff for the guesthouse, which included three meals, was quite high. Planning to camp in the forest, I had not budgeted for this. Worst of all, the Talair pilot told me that the Vivigani airstrip was closed for an indefinite period. At this point I began to doubt that I would ever reach Mount Oiamadawa'a, and one of my worst traits came to the fore—impatience. I have all the impatience genes that an American can inherit, and here I was stuck in an environment where time has no meaning; where "tomorrow" might mean next week; where a brief afternoon siesta could last four hours. I didn't want to "take it easy"; I wanted to get up on that mountain!

Alotau was a hilly, quiet harbor town, with little to distinguish it from any of a hundred other coastal towns in the Pacific. "Downtown" was a cluster of Chinese trade stores and tiny offices for the two airlines. The port itself held a number of fishing boats. There were lots of tall shade trees, yet when the afternoon heat settled on the community, my brain began to fry. I was tortured by the uncertainty of it all. I did some bird-watching around the town and managed to see quite a few birds, but this did not quell my fierce frustration.

Tropical biologists have to get accustomed to being trapped by unforeseen circumstances. It is never easy, especially when one's hopes have been pinned on a certain field plan, only to discover that clouds have grounded the aircraft; or that a bridge has washed out; or that permission cannot be granted; or that the local people, in a protest, have blocked a road. It seems that one is forced to wait, with little relief from boredom or discomfort. The heat grows more oppressive. The waiting room grows claustrophobic. Three days can seem like a month. It all grows unbearable.

=====

After those three wasted days in Alotau, I was told by the pilot that we could fly. The gods smiled on me that day: restrictions on the landing ground had been lifted, and the sun shone. Leaving Gurney, we flew up and over the mountains of the East Cape, and then along the grassy coastal hills in the rain shadow created by Cape Vogel and the line of high islands. The small plane then crossed Ward Hunt Strait heading towards Goodenough Island, fifty miles to the north.

Goodenough Island is nearly circular in shape, except for a small protrusion of land in the southeast. Twenty miles by twenty-five miles in size, it is a small island with mountains higher than eight thousand feet. It is said to be the most mountainous island on earth, as measured by mountain height in relation to island diameter. Goodenough is no volcanic remnant, and thus lacks the spires and cliffs typical of the French Polynesian islands. It is an old granitic mass that will not be eroded anytime soon. It is solid and imposing, looming out of the rough sea. Most of the island is forested, and the population is confined to lowland areas, mostly near the coast, especially on the broad, northern alluvial plain.

As the plane circled the airfield, I could easily make out the vast extent of the wartime installations here. One of the two bomber strips had been converted to the present landing ground. It was huge. The sister strip, parallel to it and equally long, was overgrown with scrub. Scattered around were low, crescent-shaped antiaircraft revetments that once offered protection to the wartime gunners. Now there was nothing except for the strip, a small roofed shelter, and a gravel road that led south to Bolu Bolu, the administrative center. In 1975, the entire area around the landing ground was grassland and scrub, but fewer than two miles east was the rugged face of Mount Oiamadawa'a, the smallest and most accessible of the island's peaks, and my destination in the search for the black bird.

I had been given instructions to make my way to the Catholic Mission at Ulatuya, a few miles north of the landing ground. I was lucky that there were several young men loitering about the airstrip, for I needed help carrying my packs and boxes of food and someone to show me the way to the village mission. I had no map except for one sketched by James Menzies on a small scrap of paper.

The mission, headed by Father Anthony O'Brien, a quiet, ruddy-faced Australian, was my base of operations. Father O'Brien agreed to put me up for the night and to arrange for four porters to take me up the mountain. The mission had a small chapel, a school, a playground, and a corrugated metal dwelling for Father O'Brien. The complex was remarkably spartan, yet I could tell that it was an important cultural center for the people of the area. Here was a man who was giving his life to help a group of people in an isolated corner of the planet.

Before dusk, I walked through the scrub on the outskirts of the mission station. At that time I knew little of lowland birdlife, and this was my first visit to a small South Pacific island. One of the few bird species endemic to the islands off southeastern New Guinea is the oversized, ungainly, Curl-crested Manucode. I found one of these crowlike birds of paradise in a clearing, perched quietly out on a leafless canopy branch. How atypical of a bird of paradise! Many tropical island species are neither rare nor shy, yet I took it as a token of good fortune that I saw this unusual island endemic on my first evening on Goodenough Island.

———

Early the next morning I was met by my four porters. They had walked over from the two neighboring villages of Lakalakuya and Debatutu.

They sorted my supplies, added their things, bundled them all into four equal parcels, and led me toward the mountain. For the first hour, we picked our route through gardens, villages, and forest patches. The high conical form of the mountain seemed very far, and before we had reached the first foothill, the clouds billowed out from the summit and cast a drizzle upon us

There were lots of birds about, even in the rain. In the last village I watched a noisy group of Red-cheeked Parrots wheel about in the trees. High above, I could see the great dusky form of a Pinon Imperial Pigeon, heading to some foraging site afar. A pair of Channel-billed Cuckoos, oddly prehistoric looking, sailed overhead, giving their grotesque pretense for a call. We flushed a pair of Eclectus Parrots from a garden planted with corn. This is one of the species in which the female is more striking than the male. Both are handsome, but the female is bright red, with a blue breast and belly. The male is largely green, with red wing linings.

We left the alluvial plain and began to struggle up a steep ridge crest in tall forest. The ascent continued without a break until we came to the grassy opening of an old garden. As we rested, we gazed over the plain below to the South Pacific. Scanning with my binoculars, I could see the wakes made by a school of porpoises. A flowering hibiscus plant rose from the thick grass—evidence that this may have been a ridgetop village during the war. More interesting to me was the superbly elegant black-and-green male birdwing butterfly that clung to one of the flowers. The deep yellow of the abdomen added to the creature's splendor. I had seen these before, but never at such close range. More commonly I saw individuals flying across clearings—the huge pied female like some decorative kite, the smaller and more graceful-looking male moving with what seemed to be more purpose. It is remarkable to be able to refer to the male, with its five-inch wingspread, as "smaller."

One porter called me over to point out a small Death Adder that he had just dispatched with his bush knife. I knew that grasslands were the favored habitat of the region's poisonous snakes. This particular one seemed puny and harmless, but to a bare-footed islander, a nip from one of these could be painful and debilitating, if not deadly.

As we climbed higher, the topography grew increasingly steep and dissected. We began to follow a rocky stream bed, which we crossed and recrossed. The rain continued. By midafternoon we had reached the site of James Menzies' low camp, although I could not see sufficient flat ground to accommodate five sleeping bodies. Somehow the men built a small lean-to, and as the rain poured down, we huddled under it, drinking tea and chatting about our ultimate destination—the rock cave 2,500 vertical feet above, where Menzies had spied the black bird. Before dark, the rain abated, and we were able to see clear skies out over the ocean. I went in search of birds, while the men collected firewood and made a dinner.

——

Goodenough Island is a mere seventeen miles, as the crow flies, from the tip of Cape Vogel, and yet for rainforest birds, it is a world away from mainland New Guinea. Here at my first camp, at slightly over 2,500 feet above sea level, I encountered fewer than ten species of birds. Except for the big manucode, all were species quite familiar back in Wau, approximately 250 miles to the northwest. At a similar altitude on mainland New Guinea I could have counted thirty or forty species during the same period. It was not a matter of great geographical distances, but it was, instead, a matter of salt water. Tropical forest birds are exceedingly sedentary, and most rarely venture across salt water.

Goodenough Island is a true oceanic island and has probably never had a land-bridge connection to New Guinea. It supports an impoverished bird fauna. I was to be reminded of this day after day in my stay on the mountain. The impoverishment was double—fewer species, and fewer absolute numbers of birds in the mountain forest, because the few species that occurred did not "fill up" the empty space that was left by the absent species. The forest on Mount Oiamadawa'a was remarkable for having few birds. This is in contrast to the open and scrub habitats of the lowlands that support an abundance of wide-ranging "tramp" species, for whom salt water is less of a barrier to dispersal.

A second lesson in island ornithology was taught by two of the most common species in the forest, the Little Shrike-thrush and the Tawny-breasted Honeyeater. I heard both of these species calling in the forest as we hiked up the mountain. Their vocalizations were much

Birdwing butterfly at hibiscus

like those I had heard back in Wau, but looking at these two, I might have mistaken them for new species. Both were strikingly different in appearance from their mainland counterparts. The honeyeater showed a prominent pale eye patch absent in the mainland race I knew, and the shrike-thrush was green and gray rather than rufous and tan. These were distinct island races.

The sedentary habits of these forest birds, which prevent significant movement between island and mainland, also permit development of genetic differences between related populations separated by even small salt-water barriers. The plumage differences exhibited by the honeyeater and shrike-thrush are evidence of minimal movement of these species between Goodenough Island and New Guinea. This simply means that the two discrete populations have had an opportunity to reproduce in relative isolation from each other. The combined effect of random genetic mutation and natural selection, because of the differing demands of the two discrete environments, has been the evolution of geographic races.

The next morning we awoke to a wonderful orange sun rising above the Pacific horizon, yet we were still under a blanket of wet clouds, which sat atop the island's mountains like a cap. Thus, we could see the sun shining on the sea as drizzle beaded on our plastic tarp—typical weather on Mount Oiamadawa'a in March. The only time we saw the sun was at dawn and sunset, when it was able to peek under our mountain's cloud bank.

We broke camp in the rain and continued our ascent. There was no trail, only a path formed by the rocky stream. Before long the stream became little more than a collection of moss-covered boulders, under which water flowed. There was no stream bed, per se. We had to rock-hop to make our way upward. The moss and dampness made every step treacherous. Luckily, it lasted only until noon, when we reached the site where Menzies had glimpsed the black bird. That was the only good news. The clouds were so thick that it was like dusk. The rain continued to fall as we struggled to construct a rainproof shelter on the tiny rock platform available for sleeping space.

The location certainly was not a place I would have chosen to camp. There was no flat ground here, just lots and lots of large boulders covered with wet, green vegetation. To move about, one literally had to hop from boulder to boulder. Somehow these managed to stay put on the steep mountain slope. The "cave" Menzies mentioned as a campsite was a small overhang of a gigantic boulder, barely big enough to accommodate five men.

Knowing I had only a few days to find and collect the mystery bird, I did not wait for good weather (it never *did* come). After setting up, three of us went out to look around. Two of the men had been up here once before, and they mentioned a cave full of bats that they were eager to visit, in order to secure a dinner more fortifying than what we had packed.

Clouds hung in the trees, and we were soaked to the skin within minutes of launching the reconnaissance, while the boulder-strewn habitat continued to provide a challenge to exploration. The forest itself was draped in the heaviest moss I have ever seen anywhere. The trees were low, gnarled, and hidden in coats of green epiphytes. Where a tree trunk had not managed to shoot out from a crevice between boulders, clumps of bamboo or a spiny *Pandanus* took its place.

We heard the whistling wings of a flock of Papuan Mountain Pigeons and could see their dark shapes as they passed overhead in the mist. The low *hoo* notes of the White-breasted Fruit-Dove attracted our attention. We also glimpsed several small forest songbirds: a white-eye, a leaf warbler, a small honeyeater, and a small myzomela. That was all, aside from the periodic serenade of weird, almost ghostly, low tremulous notes of the Curl-crested Manucode.

The men took me to the bat "cave," which turned out to be a crevice leading to a dark space between two huge boulders. Two of the men armed themselves with stout sticks and launched into the den with shouts, swinging their clubs wildly back and forth. This stirred the sleeping bats, and the swings brought a few down. Most escaped through several vents, but the men were happy to have four fruit-bats to cook over the fire that night. This small species of *Dobsonia* was much like the species I had first heard at night outside the hostel at the Ecology Institute.

I had hoped to set up a long line of mist nets in the forest. The reconnaissance indicated that this would be impossible. With the greatest difficulty, the men set up three nets above our camp. First they had to find suitable straight poles for the nets, and then they had to locate forty feet clear of boulders and bamboo for each length of net.

We spent four days searching for the black bird in the rain and clouds at Menzies' campsite. We hiked upward into the grasslands that flank the eastern side of the summit area. We neither saw nor heard a bird that might have been something new. The weather was so debilitating, and the conditions were so poor, that my guides insisted that we retreat down to the comfort of the village. They did not have to argue long to convince me.

Back at Ulatuya, I was depressed about our failure to encounter the bird, but my men had described it to me while we were on the mountain, saying that it was mostly black, with a short bill, white throat, and long tail. After returning from this trek, I had spoken to Laurance Iaubihi, one of the island's big men, and he told me that the bird was named Huutua and was difficult to observe. So I still had hope. I planned to go back up into the hills in another, less-difficult part of the island.

Eweli Camp

After a night at the mission school at Ulatuya, I packed my things and headed southeastward to Vivigani. I wanted to make contact with the resident officer-in-charge to plan a strategy for the second leg of my stay on Goodenough. I found him at the airstrip, awaiting the flight from Alotau. He took me to Bolu Bolu and put me up in his home for a night, before driving me out to the village of Eweli, about half the way between Bolu Bolu and the landing ground. He arranged for three villagers, including one of the headmen, to take me into the mountains behind their village. They led me up a track, through garden after garden, onto the side of the broad height of land that runs southeastward from the high peaks.

We established a camp about eighteen hundred feet above sea level. Here we found a thatched hut. I wanted to get higher, but my guides assured me that this was impossible. We had a rather heated discussion about it but they prevailed. The English spoken by these men from Eweli was much less intelligible to me than that spoken by the men I had worked with from Ulatuya and Debatutu. They understood little that I said, and I understood practically nothing that they said. They were amazed that I had difficulty with their English. I tended to lapse into Pidgin, a language equally obscure to them.

The Eweli camp was quite different from that on the mountain. Although much of the terrain was steep, there were patches of flat ground to establish a net line and to walk around in search of birds. Also, we had a superb, unobstructed view of the coast, the sea, and neighboring Fergusson Island.

Here I observed a remarkable phenomenon exhibited by two species of parrots, the Eastern Black-capped Lory and the Eclectus Parrot. Numbers of these birds roosted at night in the montane forest above our camp and spent the day foraging in the lowlands two thousand feet below. In the early morning I watched the birds sail down the mountain, wings folded, at high speeds, their bodies making remarkable rushing sounds when they passed over the camp. Near dusk, the birds made their way up, slowly, gaining altitude by flying in a lazy circling pattern, flapping higher and higher, like soaring hawks gaining altitude under a thermal. Why these birds choose to roost in the mountains and

Marbled Frogmouth

forage all day in the lowlands remains a mystery.

One evening, puzzled by a strange moaning call near the hut, two of us went out to investigate. We found a Marbled Frogmouth perched on the branch of a tree at the edge of the forest. In the beam of the flashlight, the bird's eyes reflected like ghostly red beacons, and only with binoculars could I just make out the bark-and-lichen pattern of its cryptic feathering. Its broad, blunt bill seemed oversized for its body. Without calling, the bird disappeared silently into the surrounding darkness.

Larger night creatures in New Guinea are fairly common but often elusive. In 1976 I rarely ventured out in search of them. Now I have learned that the forest at night is a fascinating realm with a totally different "feel" than the forest in daylight. Distances are longer, rustling leaves sound louder, and every voice or glow in the night can be a mystery for solving.

The birdlife at this lower altitude was quite distinct from that on Mount Oiamadawa'a. Here, the birds were primarily lowland species, most of which do not range up into the rain-soaked, mossy forest. The common fruit-dove on Mount Oiamadawa'a was the White-breasted, whereas here it was the Claret-breasted. The common myzomela honeyeater on the mountain was the Red-collared. Here, it was a lovely red-capped race of the Papuan Black Myzomela. Whereas I counted no more than fifteen species at our first mountain camp, the second camp produced almost forty.

However, there was still no sign of the "lost" black bird of paradise. This absence, and the precipitation, were the two points of similarity between the first and second camps.

At times, the rain came in buckets. This explained why the ground in the forest interior was entirely devoid of loamy soil, dead leaves, or other detritus. Our feet skidded on the bright orange claylike soil, washed of any litter or nutrients. Late one afternoon, clouds darkened the sky and all of our group returned to the hut to have a cup of tea and wait out the rain. What started as a tropical shower grew, until it seemed that the heavens were falling. The myriad heavy raindrops fell for about an hour, and even the Eweli men were surprised by its intensity. After the rain, we began to prepare for dinner, and I noticed that the soup pot, which had been left out in the open, was filled to the brim with fresh rain water. It had rained more than six inches in that hour period.

A few days later I saw the power of this sort of rainfall. The road between Bolu Bolu and Vivigani crosses a broad floodway. A concrete ford had been paved to permit jeeps to cross. The first two times I crossed the floodway it was bone dry, yet this natural floodway was a broad avenue of water-worn boulders and smaller stones, entirely without growing vegetation. It led up into the forested hills like a rock-strewn highway, and at first glance could have been mistaken for a road under construction. On the day of my departure there was a brief morning shower. As we came up to the floodway, we saw that the ford was blocked by a raging brown river. I could hear the rocks and boulders popping and cracking against each other as they tumbled ocean-ward. We had to wait twenty minutes for the flood to subside before the Land Cruiser could be eased across the turbid flow.

Just before the plane arrived, I saw Laurance Iaubihi coming up to the little rain shed where I waited. When I had spoken with him a week before he had seemed very knowledgeable about the mystery bird, Huutua. After greeting me, he said he had secured a specimen! He carefully drew a roll of newspaper from his *bilum*. He unfolded this to reveal the skin of not a black bird but a brown bird—a Black-billed Cuckoo-Dove. This is a species widespread through this part of the Pacific, certainly not the bird James Menzies observed.

Island Birdlife

Anyone who works in New Guinea tends to forget that it is an island. This is because it is so big, and it is surrounded by so many smaller satellites. The birds seem to recognize the distinction as well. There are clear differences between bird communities inhabiting small islands and those of New Guinea proper. This is a fact that was probably first recognized by ornithologists who had surveyed many of the Melanesian islands before World War II, but it was Jared Diamond, ecologist at the University of California at Los Angeles, who made a detailed study of the phenomenon and highlighted the remarkable dichotomies presented by island-versus-mainland faunas. This work, in turn, was sparked by the imaginative theoretical analysis of the evolution of island animal communities carried out by Robert MacArthur of Princeton University and Edward O. Wilson of Harvard.

Diamond classed Goodenough Island as an oceanic "high" island—one that has never been connected to New Guinea by a land bridge and that has mountains big enough to support a distinct montane avifauna. My observations on Goodenough accord well with Diamond's predictions. I found the open lowland habitats to be relatively rich in species and numbers of birds that are good island colonists, species that favor nonforest habitats. Diamond has termed these "tramp" species for their ability to cross saltwater barriers. The forests of Goodenough Island, by contrast, held relatively few of the mainland forest bird species, which are known to be poor at over-water colonization. Finally, the mountain forests were poorest of all and held only a very small subset of forest species known from mainland New Guinea. That these birds have lived on the island for a long period is evident by the fact that all or nearly all have evolved into distinct island subspecies.

Islands, then, are wonderful natural laboratories for biogeographers and ecologists. The complexity of the rainforest environment can be dissected and examined in miniature on an island, where the number of species is smaller and the conditions often change in predictable ways. Jared Diamond has used this natural laboratory to its fullest to help us understand the details of island biogeography and also to help us understand that tropical forest communities are not made up of species that are all alike—different species perform different roles, thus inhabiting differing types of habitats.

Still, questions remain. To me, one of the greatest mysteries is why any but the most mobile parrots and pigeons ever would deign to leave the comfort of their forest home and attempt to cross the sea in search of an island. The oft-cited argument that founding populations of forest birds have been "blown" onto islands by storms simply is not convincing. First of all, these birds inhabit the forest interior and never fly above the canopy for any purpose, nor are they migratory. No matter how strong the storm, one cannot imagine the bird being plucked from the interior of the forest and blown across a ten-or twenty-mile strait in a strong wind. Here is a question that would benefit from further study.

Return to Goodenough Island

Four years after my first trip to Goodenough Island, I returned to continue the search for the black bird. This time, I decided to work on the western slope of the highest mountains, which appeared to be more promising because of its topography and better access to the high terrain. I asked Harry Sakulas, ornithologist and acting director of the Wau Ecology Institute, to accompany me on this field trip. Harry had no difficulty securing our needed permits before departure.

The plan was to take a small coastal vessel from Lae to Goodenough Island and to be dropped off at the village closest to what we had determined to be the best route up into the mountains. In 1980, we had obtained a wonderfully detailed topographic map that had been produced after my 1976 venture. We were able to pore over the map and devise a detailed plan of action. I was confident that we could mount a successful ornithological expedition to Goodenough.

Harry and I loaded an aging institute jeep at Wau with all of our equipment and drove down to the coastal port of Lae. After purchasing food and supplies, we visited the docks in order to find our vessel, the Koonwarra, owned by the United Church on Fergusson Island, Goodenough's easterly neighbor in the D'Entrecasteaux Archipelago. We had timed our trip to coincide with the boat's departure for the islands. I climbed aboard the Koonwarra and was greeted by a scruffy but cheerful crew of Milne Bay seamen.

By joining the crew of one of the small coastal vessels that ply the seas around the great island, it is possible to learn something of what it might have been like for earlier seafarers to explore New Guinea by ship. We traveled the Solomon Sea in a small craft, spending nights on the water, mooring at dusk in uninhabited coastal anchorages, or else rocking to sleep out on the open water as the boat beat its way towards its destination.

We traveled the coast, never more than three or four miles from land, but because this part of New Guinea has no coastal plain or shelf, the water here is deep and rough. For most of the trip the view to shore was of forested hills. The water was choppy and showed various tints of murky green, depending on the sky and weather. Heading southeastward, the craft fought for headway against the blowing trade winds. Prominent features of land moved by ever so slowly from our marine perspective.

Looking shoreward, I was mesmerized by the dark hills that rose in ridges upward into the clouds. This was a repeated visual refrain for much of the journey. From our position off the coast, the scattered beachside villages were usually out of easy sight.

The coastline along the northern portion of our route to Goodenough Island is dotted with headlands, rocky stacks, points, and harbors. A strip of beach, brilliant white in the sun, would stand out against the somber colors of sea and forest. Straining the eye, from time to time one could make out a regular row of columnar trunks, each topped with radiating fronds. The coconut palms and beach indicated a village. With my binoculars, I could make out houses. These were constructed of Sago Palm, their roofs thatched with woven fronds of coconut. A row of outrigger canoes in the shade above the high-tide line proved the settlement was still occupied. From this distance I could imagine I was seeing the New Guinea coast of two hundred years ago.

The trade winds grew in power as we approached the island. The boat bucked the chop without relief. Harry and I shared a small cabin with two wooden bunks. After a dinner of rice and stew, we would chat until dark closed in and then attempt to sleep on the narrow pallets provided us. Although I had a sleeping bag, this was no padding from the hard planks. The only convenience was a folding wooden side-board that prevented me from rolling onto the floor in my sleep. This was important, because the boat thrashed terribly. I was eventually lulled into a shallow sleep by the constant rocking back and forth and side to side.

During the daylight hours I kept to the back of the deck, away from the heavy bow spray, and I searched for sea birds. Aside from the relatively abundant groups of terns (of various species), there was relatively little to watch—a few frigatebirds, a lone storm petrel, some Brown Boobies, and some shearwaters. More novel to me was a strikingly patterned black-and-yellow sea snake that I watched swimming just under the waterline. Porpoises visited the boat on several occasions, once playfully leaping out just beside the bow. Nearly every day I saw groups of flying fish skitter out over the surface of the sea, briefly become airborne, then splash back into the water. Most of the time, I had little to watch besides the slowly changing coastline.

Late on the third day, we pulled into the deep "fjord" that leads to the tiny port of Tufi, in July a dry, forlorn place. Tufi lies in a rain shadow, and the vegetation was brown from drought. Up on the headland above the harbor the wind was blowing fiercely, and I was happier down in the shelter of the boat. We rested and dined and waited until midnight to set out again, with the hope that the wind would have abated.

Goodenough Island lay across Collingwood Bay, sixty miles to the east-southeast. The crossing took twelve hours, in which the captain had to take the puny Koonwarra across the face of the strengthening winds and rising sea. We spent a lot of time wallowing in deep troughs, then bobbing up and over the next wave. Everything on the boat was soaked with salt water. As we fought this battle, the sun rose over the high spine of the island, and Harry and I began to prepare for our landfall.

The crew dropped a small dinghy as the Koonwarra stood off the sandy but unprotected beach at Diodio village. In three trips we had all of our things on land, and the boat departed. We had to get up into the mountains, do our work, and return in a brief nine days because at that point the boat would be returning to Lae.

We rounded up five men to carry our supplies to the head of the valley, to Debonefue village, from which we would launch our ascent. When we entered this interior village, I looked up, and to my surprise I saw the high peaks glistening in the sun. They seemed incredibly close.

The next morning, as we packed our supplies for the climb, the village was alive with birdlife. The big black manucode gave its mournful call; a pair of hornbills flapped by, their wings giving their distinctive puffing sound; starlings, friarbirds, and lories sang out from the forest's edge. The day dawned bright and clear.

On the first day's climb we followed a forest track to its end and then clambered up a ridge tangled with vegetation. Cutting a track through this proved slow, and when we stopped at dusk, we were about 3,500 feet above sea level. We dined in the dark, with moonlight streaming through mist that settled on the mountain. At dawn the next day, two of the men set out in advance with bush knives to blaze a route. The forest gradually opened and permitted steady progress. At about 5,500 feet, we found an ideal site for our mountain camp, with accessible water, good areas for mist netting, and beautiful montane forest with great, moss-covered trees much like what I had known at Abid's Camp on Bulldog Road. We now had six days to learn as much as we could about the birds of this western slope.

We were camped on a well-defined ridge that led upward toward the high peaks. Each day Harry and I took turns making the trek up as far as we could go, often to a big expanse of fern-choked grasslands, rather like alpine grasslands, at about seven thousand feet above sea level. From there we could gaze up at the rugged main peaks, which, from this vantage point, looked forbidding and inaccessible. We could see that the highest peak had a metal beacon atop it, so someone had been up there—perhaps by helicopter—in the not-too-distant past.

Harry returned from an exploratory walk with the news that he had seen a big sooty-gray honeyeater that looked like Belford's Melidectes. That would be new for the island! I was busy setting up all of our mist nets in the wet forest. It was not raining, yet the forest held a great deal of moisture, presumably from clouds that strike the mountainside each afternoon and evening.

My first few mornings at the mountain camp were full of surprises. First, I encountered a Zoe Imperial Pigeon, a lowland species that I did not expect to see in moss forest. Then, when climbing up a moss-covered, sloping tree trunk to get a vista through an opening in the forest, I came upon a snake coiled on a pad of moss atop the same trunk. I was a bit put off, since both of us were twenty feet above the ground with no place to go. Using a piece of branch I was able to push the snake off the trunk. I was surprised to see a snake in this dark, wet forest at this altitude. Finally, I was struck by the silence. There was very little in the way of morning chorus of birdsong. I heard the big imperial pigeon, and the manucode, and the shrike-thrush so common on Mount Oiamadawa'a; but I heard little else. Where were the birds? It was early morning; the weather was good. This seemed unnatural.

The presence of the pigeon and the silence might have had something in common. I earlier spoke of the impoverishment of island avifaunas. This silence exemplified that phenomenon. The forest was not "properly filled" with the birds I had come to expect in a forest that looked like this. My expectations, of course, were based on my experiences in forests on mainland New Guinea. The pigeon, a lowland species in New Guinea, occurs at higher altitudes on Goodenough Island, as do many other species that are typical of lowland habitats on New Guinea. The shrike-thrush, the Tawny-breasted Honeyeater, and other common birds on Goodenough are species best known at lower altitudes in New Guinea. It seems that under conditions where the montane forest avifauna is much impoverished, this ecological void is filled, at least in part, by lowland species whose populations expand into the mountain forests.

This niche expansion is also expressed in another phenomenon— the segments of vegetation that the birds use for feeding. The Island Leaf-Warbler that dwells only in the forest canopy in the mountains around Wau was observed to forage in all levels of the vegetation at this camp. I have never netted it in the forests around Wau, and yet I netted dozens on Goodenough. The leaf warblers are chasing insects that in richer habitats would have been snapped up by flycatching birds that populated the understory vegetation.

In the mountains of Goodenough Island the common birds were indeed very common, and the rare birds were very rare. On my first trip to the island I repeatedly encountered the common species: the Little Shrike-thrush, White-breasted Fruit-Dove, Dwarf Honeyeater, Red-collared Myzomela, Sclater's Whistler, Curl-crested Manucode, and the Island Leaf-Warbler. These birds were abundant, often filling our nets on the second trip; but what of the Trumpet Manucode that I knew so well back in Wau? It has been collected on Goodenough Island but was never heard nor seen by me on either trip. The same could be said for the Black Monarch and the Black-capped White-eye, both known from a single collection in earlier decades. One of the mysterious birds of the island was the gray-headed race of the Island Thrush, originally collected by William Armit at the turn of the century. No subsequent collectors found it. Some ornithologists doubted that it had come from Goodenough. I never saw it, but Harry Sakulas managed to collect a single individual high up on the mountain.

And what of the black bird, or Harry's mysterious sooty honeyeater? We have no conclusive proof of either, in spite of our long hours spent each day in search of forest birds. They will remain ghosts in our ornithological memories until someone proves their existence by securing a specimen or an identifiable photograph.

Is the long-tailed black bird anything more than a misidentification of a more familiar species by a botanist and a mammalogist? That is impossible to say. Goodenough's endemic race of the Island Thrush was not seen for nearly a century until Harry Sakulas encountered it in 1980. The mountains are high and imposing and support large tracts of untrammeled forest. Ornithologists have had too little time to do a proper survey of the forests. As I shall detail in chapter six, the existence of the Ribbon-tailed Astrapia was noted in an adventure book four years before it was formally described for science. Certainly, undescribed forest birds could be living in the mountain forests of the D'Entrecasteaux islands. As with the Loch Ness monster, it is impossible to prove that a creature *does not* exist, only that it *does* exist.

Salt-Water Culture

Until I paid my first visit to Goodenough Island, I had been dwelling in an interior valley having little in common with the coastal lowlands. I was to find that life on the islands and coastal areas around Papua New Guinea differed greatly from that in the mountainous interior. The differences extended to race, diet, activity, custom, education, and language. How could two populations be so divergent, while inhabiting the same country?

Coastal life is easier than life in the mountains. The main reason for this is the natural abundance of the seas, readily harvestable by coastal people. Reef fish, migratory sea fish like tuna and mackerel, spiny lobsters, conchs and giant clams, shrimp, and crabs are part of their diet. Everyone spends time in or on the water in search of these resources.

To accomplish this, nearly everyone has a dugout canoe. These are constructed from a straight trunk of any of several easily worked and durable tree species. The log is trimmed to size, and the outside is slowly fashioned into the shape of the canoe's hull, while the dugout's interior is hollowed out with fire and a gouging tool. Most are adorned with a single outrigger, which makes the craft less tippy.

Fishing is a varied sport here. Small boys usually employ an "iron"—a long metal rod that is sharpened at the tip. This can be used by hand to spear fish, or it can be propelled under water with a *gumi* (a large rubber band) wrapped around the hand. Women do a lot of fishing with a baited hook and line. They either wade in and toss the hook by hand, or else they drop the line from a canoe. Men often cast large, handmade nets from a canoe, or search for schools of tuna or mackerel, "pulling" them with a large, unbaited hook on a strong line.

The coastal lowlands are almost as productive as the sea. It seems that every coastal village has abundant plantings of coconut palms. These produce a staple crop of coconuts, whose meat is dried and then consumed, or shredded and soaked for use in cooking, or else sold as copra, from which coconut oil is made. Other edible fruiting plants common in coastal villages are mangoes, bananas of various sizes and colors, papayas, and various citrus fruits, as well as the *okari* and *galip* nuts that are harvested from the forest.

Although life is easier along the coast, to my eyes it is not idyllic. The coastal villages I have visited tend to be rather drab places, with an abundance of unfenced pigs and dogs and the attendant noise and disturbance. Sleeping at night can be next-to-impossible if pigs have access to the sheltered spot below the house. It seems that some pigs wake and squeal every hour, while others prefer not to sleep at all but instead to rub their big backsides against the pilings on which the house stands. A large pig can rock a house—I know from personal experience.

The Papuan villagers' propensity for tossing all refuse, including beer bottles and tin cans, into the water in front of the village, seems to be a habit that dies hard. The rationale is that the tide will carry off the waste, and no one is inconvenienced, but this rarely works efficiently.

The reefs that fringe the islands are a source of rich sea life for villagers and also a source of wonder to the naturalist. Papua New Guinea sits atop the northern arm of Australia's Great Barrier Reef, and the wealth of New Guinea's reefs equals those to the south. To explore these, all one needs is a diving mask, snorkel, and perhaps a pair of diving fins. The best diving is away from villages, because of the deleterious effects of over-harvesting of reef life and long-term waste disposal. Reefs are highly sensitive environments, and the coral dies off with remarkably little provocation. The difference between a reef that has died and one that is alive is too great to describe.

The living reef in Papua New Guinea is probably the nation's most beautiful natural resource. Unlike the flowers and birds of the rainforest, the life of the reef is not elusive and hidden from view. Scores of colorful fish species dart and shimmer in schools around the snorkeler: parrotfish, angelfish, wrasse, poneyfish, emperors, and many others. Little clownfish, bright orange with white and black patterning, dance about in protected cavities in the coral. Blue starfish move ever so slowly over the sandy bottom. Dull sea slugs race with the starfish. Deep black, long-spined sea urchins hide in crevices. A foot-long *Tridacna* giant clam peers out of its wavy shell, the indigo blue-and-black mantle and yellow eyes unbelievably rich in color. Amazing forms and colors of corals constitute the physical structure of this environment. Any naturalist who visits New Guinea should be required to snorkel on a reef.

Lure of the Black Bird

In 1976, the black bird of Goodenough Island was, for me, a sort of Holy Grail. I was captivated by the mystery and excitement of uncovering something new, untouched by science. It was the sort of adventure that used to be given prominent play in articles featured in *The National Geographic*—staple reading of my youth.

In 1959, I can well remember reading with wonder and excitement a newspaper article about anthropologist Louis S. B. Leakey, who announced to the world his discovery of a new lineage of extinct man, a missing link that he gave the name *Zinjanthropus*. Reading the article in the afternoon paper at my grandfather's house, I was terribly excited about the discovery, although I knew little about what it actually meant. I did know it was very important and that I wanted to accomplish something like that some day.

In college I read of the discoveries of new species of birds in the montane cloud forests of Peru and Colombia. This sort of discovery usually was announced in a lead article, heralded by a color plate of the bird, appearing in one of the professional ornithological journals. These discoveries, too, excited my imagination, and I continued to think that such a discovery was the pinnacle of scientific achievement.

Once I started my work in Papua New Guinea, I learned two lessons. First, I found that a new species, even one like Goodenough's black bird, can create troublesome currents of suspicion and jealousy. Subsequent to my 1976 field trip, I learned that several Australian residents who were interested in birds complained loudly to the Wildlife Department about the fact that a young American was out searching for a bird that "belonged" to Australia and Papua New Guinea. These people did not want me to be involved with this new bird's discovery. Other, scurrilous rumors were circulated about my work. I was shocked to see this reaction to my endeavors.

The second lesson came with the realization that there are many lines of valuable field research that have nothing to do with expeditions and fantastic discoveries. Scientific advances do not usually come in a flash or as easily as taking a new species of bird from a net. Instead, meaningful discovery is typically a slow process: one of attempt, trial, and error, new insight, and repeated attempt.

By the time I visited Goodenough Island in 1980, I had no illusions about the discovery of a new species. I knew that it would have been great fun if we had found the black bird, but I hope I would not have exaggerated its importance. My trip with Harry Sakulas to Goodenough Island was more of a lark, a chance to break the routine of my ongoing doctoral work at Wau, than a real end in itself. I knew that the research I was doing back in Wau, if done well, would have an impact that would last longer than any discovery on Goodenough Island.

After dredging up all these memories of past adventures in search of the black bird, I know that I would love to return to the Milne Bay Province and continue work on Goodenough, for getting out into the field, especially onto one of those wonderful islands, is worth all the effort: sights of little-known birds in rarely visited forests; the morning sun burning in rays through the mist of the moss-laden forest; the deep maroon sunsets over the mountains of nearby Fergusson Island. In the final accounting, perhaps these are the deepest and longest-lasting benefits of doing tropical field work.

Following page: Mount Missim, as seen from the Wau Ecology Institute

5 Mount Missim

*I*n the early 1930s, the field naturalist Herbert Stevens visited eastern New Guinea in order to observe and collect birds. In October 1932, he trekked up onto the flank of Mount Missim, on the northeastern edge of the Wau valley, where he spent several months camping and working. Here he discovered new races of the Blue Bird of Paradise and the six-wired bird of paradise now known as Lawes' Parotia. It is evident from Stevens' field notes that he considered Mount Missim to be a splendid place to observe birds, especially birds of paradise.

Herbert Stevens was the first ornithologist to visit the grand forests on Mount Missim, and it was more than forty years before another ornithologist, Thane Pratt, returned to camp and study there. In 1974, when Pratt established his four field camps on Mount Missim, the forest and the birdlife were probably little changed since Stevens' time. The lowest slopes of the mountain had been logged over, but the upper slopes remain, to this day, untouched.

Pratt explored the eastern slopes of the 9,600-foot Mount Missim and learned a great deal about the birdlife of this rich tract of midmontane forest. His research centered on population dynamics of rainforest bird communities, with special focus on the avian fruit-eaters. This initial research not only set the stage for his subsequent doctoral research in this same forest, but it also opened Mount Missim to a number of field-workers who followed in Pratt's footsteps. During my first year in Wau, I visited Pratt's four Missim camps and discovered that here was an ideal research area for future investigations.

Birds of Paradise

After two years of graduate study at Princeton University, I returned to Papua New Guinea to initiate my doctoral field research. I was here in pursuit of answers to a complex question about the ecology and mating behavior of birds of paradise. This was the beginning of a twenty-nine-month sojourn in New Guinea, from July 1978 through November 1980.

The forty-two species of birds of paradise comprise the avian family Paradisaeidae. This group inhabits New Guinea and its satellite islands, eastern Australia, and the northern Moluccan Islands. Still, the best place, by far, to study birds of paradise is in the mountainous uplands of New Guinea. This is where most of the species live, vocal but elusive inhabitants of the upper stories of the rainforest.

Ranging in size from a starling to a crow, the birds of paradise are quite diverse in color and form, yet all are robust in build, with strong legs and grasping feet. Their diets vary from primarily fruit to primarily insects, but most take a combination of the two. Birds of paradise forage for fruit in canopy and subcanopy trees and vines and obtain most of their insects from searching crevices in bark, dead wood, and gleaning from branches and vegetation. In many ways they are reminiscent of the New World jays. The most recent systematic analyses indicate that the birds of paradise are most closely related to the crow alliance.

Why were the birds of paradise of interest to me in 1978? I was focusing on the evolution of reproductive behavior and its relationship to ecology. The birds of paradise were known to exhibit a wide range of mating systems—some species monogamous and others showing a range of polygamous strategies. The group was ideal for study of interspecific differences in mating behavior. It was already known that most birds of paradise are polygynous—one male mating promiscuously with many females. The details of these polygynous mating systems, however, were poorly understood, and virtually nothing was known about how a species' ecology influenced these behaviors. Were there ecological explanations for why some species were monogamous and others polygynous? Could ecology explain the range of differences among the polygynous species? I wanted to explore these questions that were, at the time, very popular ones in the relatively new field of behavioral ecology.

The Study

My plan was to make an interspecific comparison of behavior and ecology in four species of birds of paradise. To do this I needed first to select a good patch of forest that was home to the desired focal species of birds. It was difficult to find a flat patch of forest within easy distance of Wau. The valley had been inhabited for centuries by Biangai people who cleared land for gardening. European mining and plantation and timber operations had exploited the remaining uncleared areas of flat forest during the previous five decades. I was left with the remnants. Not a single hectare of undisturbed forest remained in any of the valley bottoms, which are always the first to go.

I decided to return to Thane Pratt's "Camp One" on Mount Missim, just down the ridge from where Thane was then working (at Camp Two), and less than a half-hour's walk from the roadhead. The site included a superb patch of giant, old-growth forest, protected from natural disturbance in a deep, damp hollow. While being quite hilly throughout, it was less steep than the other sites I had visited. Most importantly, it was rich in resident birds of paradise.

══════

With my two recently hired field technicians, a Biangai named Ninga Kawa and a Kaintiba named Michael Lucas, I returned to Camp One in early August 1978. We made our way up the steep path to the main trail leading to the mountain's summit. After thirty minutes of hiking, we were deep in the oak forest and atop a flat spot on the ridge. This would be the heart of my study area. Thane's original campsite lay in the little hollow below the ridge, but the trail he had cut in 1974—the one I had used sporadically in 1976—was gone. I retraced the general course of the trail, with Ninga and Michael following, and in a few minutes we were among the great trees that marked Thane's campsite.

Miraculously, the camp shelter that I had constructed in 1976 still stood, but the main uprights were now completely dry-rotted, and the entire frame collapsed when we gave it a slight push. Rain, dry rot, and boring insects had taken their toll. Ninga and Michael worked rapidly, and in ninety minutes we had a new "house." The open face of the lean-to structure was oriented downhill, towards a deep gully that drained into the ravine of Poverty Creek. From this spot we had a lovely view of masses of green vegetation in this lush patch of old forest. I never grew tired of this site. It was a rich green oasis in a hilly and relatively dry area, whose ridgetops were dominated by the oak, *Castanopsis acuminatissima*, the most abundant tree species on the flanks of Mount Missim.

Although this oak was fairly common in the forest around the camp's house, there it was physically overshadowed by the great trees that populated the hollow: laurels, incense, elaeocarps, mahoganies, and members of other, more obscure, rainforest families. This site was richer than the other parts of the study area. I could feel this when first surveying the plot, and it would prove true by various measures.

These first few days on the site were eye-opening. In two years I had forgotten many of the bird calls. Most of the work I did in 1975 and 1976 focused on higher altitude bird communities. Now, each morning brought a remarkable swell of songs, many unknown.

One of the loudest and most persistent singers was the male Buff-tailed Sicklebill, a bird of paradise. He perched in the dead branches atop a huge Wau Redwood in front of the house. On our first morning we watched the male sing over and over from this high perch. This was only the second time I had glimpsed this elusive species, and I was happy to learn its vocalization. If this little-known species proved easy to observe, then I would include it in my study.

I searched for birds of paradise on my morning rambles around the vicinity of the camp. The habitat near the house was so rich that it was not necessary to go far in order to see interesting things. I observed another bird of paradise, a male Lawes' Parotia, foraging on the large red fruit of a canopy vine. Then I found a small, fruiting *Schefflera* vine, where a wary female Blue Bird of Paradise was testing the ripeness of individual fruitlets. I looked at the bewildering variety of plants around me and realized that I needed to learn a lot about the flora.

Four Birds

After several weeks of observing and deliberating, I chose four species for study: Trumpet Manucode, Buff-tailed Sicklebill, Magnificent Bird of Paradise, and Raggiana Bird of Paradise. Although in the same family, the Paradisaeidae, the species are remarkably different in morphology as well as mating behavior. This latter parameter was all-important, since I wanted to compare birds with contrasting social lives.

As most birds go, the Trumpet Manucode is very attractive, but the species is much outshone by many of the male plumages of the other birds of paradise that inhabit Mount Missim. In the Trumpet Manucode, both sexes share a metallic blackish plumage with blue-and-green highlights, further enhanced by a shaggy thatch of long, pointed feathers that hang off the crown and neck, forming a rough crest. The most remarkable physical characteristic of this manucode is the male's elongated trachea, hidden under the feathers of the breast. It leaves the neck cavity and curls down in several double loops that lie under the skin of the breast. Only with the bird in the hand is this looped trachea readily evident under the skin, once the breast feathers are blown up and away from the sternum.

This elongated trachea allows the male to produce its low, tremulous vocalizations that carry far through the forest. The male gives a series of haunting calls that are never heard from the opposite sex. Presumably the length of the trachea permits the particularly low frequency of the notes emitted. The adaptive function of the low calls is almost certainly related to sexual selection—the competition for females. Although this species is one of the few monogamous birds of paradise, there is still competition among males for mates, and presumably this anatomical adornment is an end product of that competition.

The other three focal species were polygamous birds of paradise, but each exhibited characteristics that readily distinguished it from the

Magnificent Bird of Paradise

others. The Buff-tailed Sicklebill is unusual in two respects: its very long, sickle-shaped bill (present in both sexes) and its solitary, territorial nature (most male birds of paradise defend no ranging territory).

At the time of my study, the Buff-tailed Sicklebill was one of the least-known birds of paradise. This sicklebill, and to a slightly lesser extent, the manucode, were the "mystery birds" of the foursome I was to study. The Buff-tailed Sicklebill differed from the Trumpet Manucode in exhibiting obvious sexual dimorphism—the male has several nuptial adornments absent in the female. In polygamous birds of paradise (and many monogamous bird species, as well), the males are more colorful than the females. The females tend to be cryptic and retiring, the males gaudy and active.

Both Buff-tailed Sicklebill sexes have a buffy tail and dull brown upperparts. The female's underparts are finely barred buff and blackish brown. In contrast, the male lacks the barring and sports two sets of erectile display plumes that course down each side of the breast. These plumes are sets of elongated, purple-tipped, gray-brown feathers. In addition, the male has a blackish face and two tiny feather "horns" that protrude up from above each eye. Although the male is vocal, both sexes are unobtrusive, and the female, because of her total silence, is very difficult to observe.

The diminutive Magnificent Bird of Paradise was the third species I studied. Less than seven inches long, quite compact and short billed, it was the most common species on the study site, and I thought (incorrectly), that it would be the easiest to study. Polygamous, the beautifully plumed male was known to set up a ground-level display area, like a very primitive bower, where he displayed to and mated with visiting females. Sexual dimorphism in the species is great. The female is dull brown above and finely barred buff and blackish below, in the very same pattern as in the female Buff-tailed Sicklebill. The male is wildly different, with no brown and no barring. Like the male Buff-tailed Sicklebill, the male Magnificent has sets of erectile plumes, but those of the Magnificent are on the back. The bird is a patchwork of color: entirely velvety green below, from chin to belly; golden brown on the head; orange on the wings and lower back; yellow on the midback; and deep red on the upper back. The legs are deep cobalt blue. Most remarkable of all are the two central tail feathers, which are modified into narrow, wirelike appendages that extend out from the brief tail and recurve in opposite directions to form two near-perfect circular loops. These wires are colored a dark metallic green.

The final focal species of the study was the Raggiana Bird of Paradise, one of the prototypical members of the family, of the type that most people know as a bird of paradise. The Raggiana is more than a foot long, robust, and heavy billed. The female is plumaged in muted browns, maroon-buff, and with a dull yellow crown and nape. The male, brown bodied, green throated, yellow hooded, with gorgeous orange pectoral plumes, is one of the most beautiful and unusual of birds. The true marvel of this species defies proper description, and the bird displays its plumage with vigorous motions and amazing postures.

━━━

In my study of these four birds of paradise, I concentrated on foraging ecology and mating behavior. Studying behavior was simple; I focused on interactions between males and females and among males, and I located territories or display perches and made repeated observations of the birds doing their behaviors. By contrast, in order to learn about ecology of the birds I not only had to learn what the birds ate and how they foraged for it, but also I had to learn as much as possible about the

Opposite page: Male Raggiana Bird of Paradise displaying to a female at his lek perch in the canopy of a Castanopsis *oak tree.*

Orange-billed Lorikeet, a common nectar-feeder in the forest along the Bulldog Road.

Kaindi Camp, 1975. Banding a bird at my small rain shelter on the study plot near the summit of Mount Kaindi.

Field assistant Timis Suri with a friendly Rufous-backed Honeyeater. Below: Treeferns in the sodden alpine grasslands of Mount Bangeta.

This Mountain Kingfisher, mist-netted at Camp One on Mount Missim, is a vocal canopy dweller.

Sooty Owl. A widespread nocturnal species whose whistled and screeched nighttime vocalizations can be as bizarre and bone-chilling as those of any bird. Opposite: Paul Kores looking down on a small village and church near Derim, in the Saruwaged Mountains.

Lawes' Parotia male, a common fruit-eating inhabitant of the lower montane forests of Mount Missim.

Raggiana Bird of Paradise. The close-up of the head shows the remarkable feathering of throat and crown. Opposite: Moss-encrusted subalpine forest on Mount Bangeta.

A ground orchid (Phaius tankervilliae) *from Mount Missim.*

Grass-skirted schoolchildren on Goodenough Island.

A lowland forest giant, probably an Octomeles sumatrana, *dwarfs a young field assistant (with white cockatoo feather in hair).*

A cryptic phasmid insect, relative of the walking-stick, has evolved to mimic a dried yellow leaf.

A Eupholus weevil, common in gardens in the lowlands near Kakoro.

Buff-faced Pygmy-Parrot, mist-netted in the forest at Ninga's Camp, Kakoro.

The author holding a Macgregor's Bird of Paradise, ready for release after color-banding, in the mists of the Lake Omha camp.

Green Tree Python, common in the lowlands and hills. The immature is a striking yellow.

Painted or Forbes' Ringtail, a small possum of the lower montane forests. This individual was captured by hand at Camp One on Mount Missim.

124   A Naturalist in New Guinea

Green tree frog (Litoria *sp.*) *photographed at Krisa Camp, West Sepik Province.*

Rhododendron alticolum, *one of the many colorful members of this genus inhabiting the Bulldog Road.*

Carol Beehler sharing one of Papua New Guinea's "public motor vehicles" (called PMVs) with a piglet, a small dog, and a crowd of highlanders, near Mount Hagen. Below: Small children carrying firewood at a village near Holuwon, Irian Jaya.

Highlander men place hot stones atop meat to be cooked in mumu fashion in preparation for a feast celebrating opening of a new church in the Baiyer River valley. Following page: Huli wig man, sporting a spray of orange flank plumes of the Raggiana Bird of Paradise, upper mandible of Blyth's Hornbill, and pig tusks.

food resources themselves, which was the most difficult hurdle for this field project.

How does one measure resources in a way relevant to the animals using those resources? In the birds of paradise, the resources come in two forms: arthropods (mostly insects) and fruit. Both required concerted effort to sample in a meaningful way. There are standard procedures for sampling winged arthropod populations, using the netlike Malaise traps, which can be hung at various heights above the ground. Although standard, this will not measure the availability of the type of arthropods that are taken by the birds of paradise—the invertebrate fauna of bark and rotten wood, creatures that spend most of their lives hidden in crevices. The standard method for measuring fruit availability is to deploy screen-net fruit traps, which collect fallen whole fruit as well as seeds that are regurgitated or defecated. The problem with this method is that in order to obtain a meaningful sample in a forest with more than a hundred fruit-producing species of trees and vines, it is necessary to deploy an impossibly large number of fruit traps.

During the study I would spend at least as much of my time monitoring the birds' food resources as I did observing the birds. I modified my arthropod sampling to include a series of bark traps. For the fruit sampling, I found that most of the species of fruiting plants in the forest were not consumed by the birds of paradise, so to avoid wasting large blocks of time with irrelevant fruit, I identified key plant species for each bird of paradise, and then I made detailed mapping surveys of these favored food plants, monitoring them once a month.

=====

By October 1978 I had selected the four focal species, and I also had a superficial knowledge of the mating behavior of each. The Trumpet Manucode established a monogamous pair-bond between male and female. Males of the other three species were polygamous. The latter three associated with the females only to mate and shared none of the responsibilities related to nesting and raising offspring. Instead of helping at the nest, the males, veritable avian playboys, established display "courts"—dance sites of varying complexity and placement—where they displayed for and mated with any females that visited and consented. Among the polygamous threesome, however, there were significant differences in male deployment. In the Buff-tailed Sicklebill, each male defended an exclusive territory of more than twenty acres, on which no other males were permitted. In the center of the territory, the owner-male had a song perch high in the canopy and a display perch in a sapling below this.

The Magnificent male cleared a small area under a thicket of saplings for his display court. He spent lots of time trimming leaves and sweeping the fallen vegetation from the ground below. The effect was striking—this little bird created neatness and order out of the chaos of a forest thicket. Perched on a single vertical stem in the center of this small cleared area, the male Magnificent would make his elaborate displays to visiting females.

The mating system of the Raggiana was a canopy-level, communal version of that of the Magnificent. A small group of adult males established a cluster of display perches in the canopy limbs of a single tree. The males shared the tree quite amicably, although they did fight from time to time, presumably in battles for dominance. At this cluster of perches (called a "lek"), the males would assemble and dance and display for visiting females.

During subsequent months I invested effort in piecing together more details of the mating behavior of the birds, but all the while I spent much of my time and energies learning as much as possible about their diet and foraging ecology.

Doing Fieldwork and Why

Today, nearly all field research is conducted only after a research program is developed on paper and money to pay the expenses has been obtained from a grant-giving agency. Camping and bird-watching in an exotic locale are not adequate reasons either to receive funding support or to justify the expense. More is demanded of the field-worker. Available grant support is limited, so it is necessary for those who receive funds to be able to produce some definite contribution to knowledge. In spite of a focus on an esoteric subject, there should always be a striving for scientific utility and generality. In other words, in a study of species x, the researcher should design his work to shed light on a question that transcends that particular species being studied. The discipline of biology is the search for order in the seemingly disorganized—even random—world of nature. Certainly, nature contains elements of both randomness and order, but in most instances the randomness is self-evident, whereas the order is subtly insinuated in the morass of environmental noise.

My project had the goal of attempting to discern some order at several levels. First, are there any clear dietary trends among the birds of paradise? I kept detailed observations on foraging by the eight species of birds of paradise that inhabited the forest of Camp One; in addition, I made several field trips away from Mount Missim to do the same for additional species in other parts of New Guinea. Second, at a more general level, I asked two questions: Are the behavioral and ecological oddities of the birds of paradise relevant to other bird groups, such as the fruit-crows and manakins of the Neotropics, the two families of birds that had long been compared to the Paradisaeidae? And, has the independent evolution of the complex, polygamous "court" mating systems, exhibited by many avian and mammalian groups, been produced by equivalent forces? Is there a unitary explanation for this remarkable behavior?

———

Science is a collaborative pursuit. My work on birds of paradise was nothing more than a recent increment in the gradual accumulation of knowledge and theory over a hundred-year period. Whatever the field, each new worker builds on the knowledge of his or her predecessors, so the research is never conducted in isolation. While working in the forest on Mount Missim, I often spent spare moments reading the publications of others who had worked successfully in similar forests, solving related riddles. Biologists Ernst Mayr, Austin L. Rand, E. Thomas Gilliard, Jared Diamond, and others had preceded me in New Guinea, and their writings were sources of insight and knowledge that I relied on regularly.

Still, scientific collaboration is not simply a linear sequence of discoveries. I was continually referring to the results emanating from ongoing field projects in other parts of the world that might shed light on the way my system was operating. Work done on the mating systems of bats, for instance, strongly influenced my way of looking at the birds of paradise. I was, in effect, one member of an informal world-wide team, researchers seeking solutions to a shared problem in behavioral ecology.

On the Mountain with Thane Pratt

The collaborative nature of my work was not just a matter of developing pen pals. Thane Pratt, then a doctoral candidate at Rutgers University, was working on a research project that broadly complemented mine. Pratt was attempting to determine the pattern and process of vertebrate seed dispersal on a patch of forest at Camp Two, a forty-minute walk up the ridge from my camp. Whereas I was interested in how dietary choice influenced the behavior of the birds of paradise, Pratt studied how plants achieved efficient distribution of their offspring (seeds) with the aid of birds and bats. We were looking at two sides of a system that is critical to the tropical forest.

Dispersal of seeds is complex, especially in humid tropical forests. There is intense competition for sunlight and space, and because of the presence of many animals that consume and destroy seeds, it is all the more important for plants to scatter their "offspring" far and wide. For this, many plants have evolved specialized fruit that is attractive to animals who can consume it and carry the seed away, unharmed, subsequently to regurgitate or defecate it elsewhere in the forest. By contrast, the typical dispersal systems in the temperate zone of eastern North America depend on physical factors, like wind, or else on animals that often consume more seeds than they disperse, such as squirrels and jays. In the tropics, there seems to be an obvious dichotomy between the seed *predators* (the plants' mortal enemies) and seed *dispersers* (the plants' important allies). This distinction is not nearly so obvious in the relatively impoverished temperate habitats.

In the tropical forest, entire assemblages of birds and mammals have evolved that consume fruit without harming the seeds. The intricacies of this plant-animal interaction attracted Pratt's attention.

Pratt made several important discoveries. Perhaps the most important finding concerned the widely believed notion that the best dispersers of seeds of rainforest trees are the pure frugivores, as exemplified by New Guinea's fruit-doves and fruit-pigeons. It would be natural to expect that an animal whose whole life revolved around eating fruit might also be particularly good at disseminating seeds. This assumption was not supported for his Papuan system. On Mount Missim, the most efficient dispersers were partial frugivores, primarily the birds of paradise. These birds take both arthropods and fruit.

Pratt came to realize that some insect-foraging adaptations that some birds of paradise exhibited, such as the ability to creep about on near-vertical surfaces, and the strength and prying ability of the beak, permit these birds to harvest difficult-to-reach and structurally protected fruits that pure frugivores (such as the fruit-doves) usually cannot take. In addition, Pratt documented that the plants that depend on birds of paradise for dispersal of seeds benefit from a more even "seed rain" through the forest. In other words, more of the seeds are scattered through the forest rather than being dropped in a heap under the parent tree or clumped under other food-plants, where the likelihood of successful seedling growth is much reduced. This, too, related to the different habits of pure frugivores vs. partial frugivores.

Pratt found that the pure frugivores (like the fruit-doves) spent long periods in fruit trees and often roosted or loafed for extended periods when not foraging for fruit. As a result, these birds dropped more seeds under the parent tree and also tended to drop their seeds in clumps. By contrast, birds of paradise spent short periods in feeding trees, took fewer fruits per bout, and moved about more, with minimal loafing. They thus scattered their seeds more effectively.

Finally, Pratt and I found that in New Guinea, fruit-eaters and food-plants are quite specific. Certain types of fruits were taken by certain types of avian foragers, with little variation. Conversely, each fruit-eater tended to take fruit of a certain size or type. Thus, small cherrylike drupes were taken by bowerbirds but not birds of paradise. Capsular fruit—those in which the edible portion is hidden in a tough husk that opens when the fruit is ripe—were taken almost exclusively by birds of paradise, and never by bowerbirds. Pratt was able to show that the bird-plant interactions were in no way random or haphazard. These were important discoveries that helped me better understand my birds of paradise.

Working at Camp One

I visited my study site nearly every week for twenty-nine months. It remains the most pleasant environment I have ever worked or lived in. The climate was perfect—never too warm nor too cool. During the day I wore shorts and a short-sleeved shirt. At night, never more than a light sweater was needed. The insects were few, and we were able to sleep without netting. At most, one to two mosquitoes arrived at dawn to wake us up. Noxious pests were scarce. I could range through the forest without worrying about poisonous plants. The only nuisance was a small species of paper wasp that built its nests in the undergrowth. Once or twice a year one of our party would bump into a nest and receive a few stings. The greatest danger here was that in our mad dash to escape the little wasps, we would thrash through the underbrush at top speed, risking a twisted ankle or a twig in the eye.

Our days at camp followed a fairly familiar regimen. We divided our time between monitoring avian visits to specific fruit trees, checking fruit and insect traps, observing display behavior by male birds of paradise, mist netting, and other tasks. Through most of the study we operated mist nets in order to continue capturing birds of paradise. I wanted to color-mark as many individuals of my four focal species as possible. These birds were difficult to capture, so patience and time were the only means of success. Since the birds spent most of their time in the upper part of the forest, it was necessary to place nets as high above the ground as we could. In many instances we rigged nets to ropes and pulleyed them up, strung between two tall poles. This was hard work, but it was effective.

Once we captured a bird of paradise, we took several measurements. If it was in female plumage, we had to determine whether it was really a female or perhaps an immature male, which can look nearly identical. In the polygamous birds of paradise, immature males may keep this female-type plumage for three or more years.

We also banded the bird with a numbered aluminum band, and we attached a brightly colored strip of plasticized cloth tagging to each leg for ease of reidentification in the field.

Not surprisingly, for each bird of paradise that we caught, we netted many more other birds. These, too, we banded and measured.

Sugar Glider

We also found other surprising things in our nets from time to time. One evening I looked up into our tallest canopy net (actually four individual nets strung one above the other) and saw a large, dark object hanging in the middle of it. Upon lowering this rig, I found the dismembered and mangled torso of a Common Scrubfowl! Apparently a New Guinea Harpy-Eagle had struck the net while carrying its dinner. The eagle was too large to be held by the net, but its meal was left for us.

We occasionally captured unlikely mammals in our nets. A lovely little Sugar Glider, a docile marsupial that looks just like our flying squirrel, was captured at dusk one night. We handled this demure little creature for a few minutes (it did not bite), and then released it. Sugar gliders were common in the forest here, and we heard their sweet squeaking notes nearly every night.

On another occasion we captured a Three-striped Marsupial Mouse. This looks like a graceful and attractive forest rodent, except for the three prominent black stripes on the back. It apparently had been tightrope walking across the top line of the net when it lost its balance and tumbled into the netting and became entangled.

Some of the birds of paradise that I netted were given special treatment. They were fitted with a tiny radio transmitter. This was fixed to the base of the tail feathers with thread and glue. After release, the movements of the radio-tagged bird could be tracked through the forest by using a special receiver and portable antenna. Radio-tracking was especially useful for learning how the birds of paradise use the forest and the size of their home ranges.

Although the technique sounds straightforward, in the forest it is a difficult and time-consuming task. While the bird glides through the forest, the tracker must huff and puff up and down steep grades to keep up. Mornings and late afternoons are devilish. By contrast, much of the middle of the day is incredibly boring since the birds tend to rest for long periods.

I was lucky, because I was able to solicit the help of five volunteer field assistants from two Australian universities to help with the radio-tracking. These assistants had lots of energy and perseverance, and they raced up and down the hills of our study area to map the movements of our birds of paradise. They worked in pairs, one to carry the receiver and antenna, the other to enter the data on the detailed map of the site. From all of this effort, we were able to show that each of the species occupied a relatively compact patch of forest, with little wandering. This is quite unlike a number of other species of fruit-eaters, exemplified by the fruit-doves, which wander far and wide in search of ripe fruit. The birds of paradise I was studying tended to stay right on this site the year-round. The only exception seemed to be the fig-eating Trumpet Manucode. One individual was found at a fruit tree in Thane Pratt's camp, some two miles distant.

We learned a lot about this little patch of forest, but some forest phenomena remain mysteries. I spent a considerable amount of time observing the behavior of the male Buff-tailed Sicklebill, yet we still have only a sketchy idea of its mating system. One thing in particular is unresolved. Where does the male mate? We know the male does his spectacular inverted display from a small sapling below his regular canopy song-perch, but I never did see him mate there. On several occasions, I found the male giving weird display calls from the protection of a low thicket. Here, the male was perched within inches of the ground. I built a blind to see what he was doing in this thicket, but the visibility was poor, and he came to the thicket only irregularly. Might this be where the male mated with visiting females?

Another, more vexing, mystery, was the bizarre "leaf-mulcher" sound that I heard dozens of times but never identified. It was definitely given by some sort of animal when near to the ground. It was either from a bird or a mammal. The sound was quite unpleasant and unlike anything I have heard in nature. The only thing it could be likened to was the sound of one of those big machines that tree-trimming companies use to grind up limbs and leaves. It would be given three or four times in a row and then end, only to be heard again a week or so later. What was it? I may never know. Luckily, this was not a mystery that was crucial to my studies of birds of paradise.

Discoveries

My fieldwork produced several interesting take-home points about the behavior and ecology of the birds of paradise. At the most general level, I learned that the relationship between the birds, their environment, and their strategies of reproduction is exceedingly complex. Complexity grew from two sources—the ecological relationship between the birds and their food-plants, and, in the three polygynous species, the behavioral relationship between males competing for females. I was able to penetrate important aspects of the bird-plant relationship but failed to do more than scratch the surface of the long-term behavioral strategies that males employ to obtain mates.

The bird-plant relationship is one of apparent mutual interaction between efficient seed disperser and valued producer of needed nutrients. The plant trades valued fruit pulp (often rich in hard-to-obtain lipid and protein) in return for safe distribution of seeds. The bird and plant form an alliance that is mutually beneficial. Contrast this to the relationship between the insect-eater and insect. The insect seeks to avoid consumption, whereas the bird attempts to benefit from the capture and destruction of the insect, with no mutually beneficial interaction.

In New Guinea, different species of birds of paradise probably consume fruit from hundreds of species of food-plants. Their relationship with different plant species varies, and this may be critical to the bird's life history. Those birds that eat large quantities of what I call "bird of paradise fruits" appear to be the most important dispersers of seeds in the family. Most remarkable among the specialized food-plants are those, like certain mahoganies and umbrella plants, whose seeds are known to be eaten and dispersed *only* by the birds of paradise. This is powerful evidence of a very close bird-plant relationship.

In contrast, some birds of paradise, like the Trumpet Manucode, feed primarily on figs. The manucode benefits in two respects. First, figs are available in the forest all year long. Second, most fig plants produce fruit in prodigious quantities. The manucode, being dependent upon figs for nearly all of its food, suffers from being tied to a nutritionally restricted diet. Figs are poor in lipid and protein, which is essential for growth of nestlings. In addition, figs produce their fruit on an unpredictable, asynchronous and nonannual cycle, making it difficult for these birds to develop an efficient foraging routine. Manucodes have to hunt for ripe fig trees each season. It seems safe to say that the manucodes are monogamous because both parents are required at the nest to provision the offspring.

In my study on Mount Missim, the three polygamous species of bird of paradise took fruit and insects and thus escaped from the manucode's nutritional dilemma. Moreover, it appears that certain anatomical features permit their specialization on the protected capsular fruit: the birds need strong prying bills and powerful legs and feet to clamber about in search of the hidden insects. These same skills can be used to gain access to specialized, nutritious fruit that is inaccessible to most other fruit-eating vertebrates in the forest.

The key to the evolution of polygamous behavior in the birds of paradise seems to relate to the development of a special foraging relationship between bird and plant. Thus, my results show that fruit-eating is influential in the evolution of polygamous behavior in the birds of paradise.

The details of this relationship are exceedingly complex—it is not only a matter of eating fruit, but also relates to nutrition, foraging ability, plant specialization, and other factors. The Trumpet Manucode eats fruit and is monogamous. The Raggiana Bird of Paradise eats fruit and is polygamous. Thus, for the birds of paradise, we need to know what kinds of fruit and how they are consumed in order to understand the behavioral ecology of this remarkable bird family.

One of the key discoveries of my study was that the evolution of the birds of paradise has been the product of very complex interactions between bird, plant, and even arthropod. My initial notion that some simple ecological "rules" could explain why one bird was monogamous and another polygamous was disproven. I learned, instead, that the tropical forest is made up of complicated, intricate relationships that are not immediately obvious to the observer. I also learned that the birds of paradise are more than just a group of beautiful birds adorning New Guinea's rainforest. With Pratt's help, I found that they are critical for the dissemination of seeds of rainforest plants and thus are an important force in the regeneration of the Papuan environment.

Return to Mount Missim

I returned to the Wau valley very briefly in July 1987, just to see what was happening in the town, at the institute, and on Mount Missim. I was, in particular, very curious about getting back to Camp One. How had it changed in the seven years since I had worked there? Were any of the color-marked birds still on the plot? Was the forest still intact? This last question is not an unusual one in tropical habitats, where the push for development often means that any accessible forest gets cleared for timber, mining, or gardens.

I rose before dawn and drove a borrowed jeep up the forestry roads to the Missim trailhead. The roads were in fairly good shape after all these years. The monoculture of pines that had been planted on the clear-felled lower slopes was now a maturing stand of sizable trees. This made hiking up through it a bit less of a chore. Once in the forest proper, the trail was much as it always was, and the forest appeared unchanged. I felt a pinch of anxiety as I approached the boundaries of Camp One. What would be there? Would I be able to find the camp site? Were the net lanes and walking trails still traceable?

I mounted the flat ridge that ran down the middle of the study site and saw that the forest looked unchanged, but any trace of the paths Ninga, Michael, and I had constructed in 1978 had vanished. Even the most heavily used camp path was obliterated by accumulations of detritus and tree falls. I made my way down to the camp area simply by my knowledge of the topography and of the great trees I had marked and identified. Without too much difficulty, I found what was left of the camp clearing—a scrubby, flat area, filled with ten-foot-high saplings, most of which had still been seeds when I worked there. The actual camp house was long-gone, and where we had once laid our sleeping bags on the ground now was rank grass and the typical debris of an undisturbed forest. The forest had swallowed up most indications of human disturbance. The only proof that I had indeed worked here was evident from the numbered aluminum tree tags that still marked the larger trees in the clearing.

After seven years, I supposed there would be little chance of seeing birds that I had marked, with one exception. I had hopes that the male Buff-tailed Sicklebill might still be singing here a decade after I marked him. The other birds of paradise move over such a large range that it would be mere chance to see one in a few hours of looking about in trailless forest. So I stood by the site of the house and began listening for the Buff-tailed Sicklebill's lovely, mournful, whistled song. Within a few minutes I heard it, and I then answered with my own whistled version. Five minutes passed; then I glimpsed a flash of buff as he wheeled overhead onto a large branch in the canopy. I did not see any sign of the bright green tag I had affixed to the right leg of the adult male I had marked in 1978. It took a minute to get the bird into view with my binoculars, but once I got him, I instantly saw what I was looking for, an aluminum band on his left leg, the one I had placed the day I put on the tag. I had always put multiple markers on all of the birds of paradise because I knew that the difficult-to-see bands would last much longer than the more obvious (but temporary) tags. This was he—Sicklebill No. 957—a bird that was a territorial adult on 1 November 1978 when Michael Yamapao took him out of a ridgetop net. The bird was at least twelve years old (it takes several years for these birds to develop adult plumage). One reason it is so difficult to come to grips with the biology of birds of paradise is because they live so long. If there was one thing my doctoral research taught me, it was that I had only begun to get answers to the complicated biological story of this remarkable family of birds.

Opposite: Mount Erimbari, Chimbu Province

6   *The Highlands*

The Highlands informally denotes that upland segment of Papua New Guinea west of Morobe Province, southwest of the Ramu River, and centering on several mountain ranges that surround the Wahgi River valley. Although the area is extensive—more than two hundred miles from east to west—the heart of the highlands district ranges from Goroka, in the east, to Mount Hagen in the west. Here lies a series of interior highland valleys that support large populations of robust, aggressive mountain people. It is a region often visited by tourists, and it is ornithologically rich. In 1979 I planned a trip to the Baiyer River Sanctuary in Papua New Guinea's Western Highlands Province. Based out of Baiyer, I planned to spend a month studying bird-of-paradise species not found in the Wau area.

Baiyer Valley

For more than two decades, Papua New Guinea's finest collection of captive wildlife has been displayed at the Baiyer River Sanctuary, an hour's drive north of the town of Mount Hagen. Nearly every visiting naturalist has felt compelled to visit Baiyer, not only because of the wonderful zoo collection, but also because it is an excellent base for observing highlands wildlife, both in the tracts of forest on its own extensive grounds and also in the surrounding countryside.

In June 1979, I drove from Wau to Baiyer, taking with me my chief field assistant, Ninga Kawa. I left Michael Yamapao in Wau to look after my Missim camp and the weekly ecological sampling program there.

Baiyer is some 250 miles northwest of Wau. The first day, we drove my small Suzuki jeep down the rough dirt road to Lae, and then up the Highlands Highway to Goroka. Ninga was a good companion and could spell me in the drive. The road was much improved since I had driven it in 1975, with long stretches of the Markham valley, the passes, and several other flat parts, paved in asphalt. This also made for a speedier, though not necessarily a safer, trip. Huge transport trucks, laden with goods, lumbered up and down this highway and paid little heed to lesser vehicles such as ours.

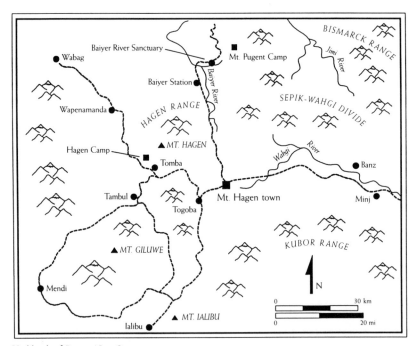

Highlands of Papua New Guinea

After overnighting, we departed Goroka early. We wound through rugged Chimbu District, passing picturesque Mount Erimbari, Daulo Pass, and the Chimbu Gorge, on our way to the Western Highlands Province. A smooth ride down the broad and lush Wahgi valley brought us to Papua New Guinea's rowdy frontier town—Mount Hagen. Though it is not physically on a frontier, the town in 1979 had the atmosphere of the rough-and-tumble wild West. This is not so much a matter of looks as of feel. It was a mix of hard-working and hard-drinking Australian planters and cattlemen, New Guinean highlanders of varying degrees of sophistication, missionaries, and government employees. This commercial center, the main western depot for material goods trucked inland from the coastal port of Lae, attracts villagers from the hills for many miles around. Here, these tribal people, who in many instances have walked several days from their village, find a sort of material nirvana. Their small caches of money, hoarded for so long, are quickly spent to purchase valuable goods: a woolen blanket, a second-hand tweed coat, a plastic water bucket, perhaps a battery-powered radio.

Arriving in downtown Mount Hagen, I was struck by the variety of people. An aged, bare-chested warrior caught my eye, dressed in nothing but his traditional costume of bark belt, loin cloth, and *ass gras* (leaves of *Cordyline* tucked into the belt to cover the posterior). The old man was standing on the concrete pavement, inspecting a brand new, brick red, flatbed Toyota Land Cruiser. The automobile was obviously fresh off the sales lot. Since several persons lounged in the rear bed of the car, I concluded that it was a purchase made by a village cooperative, a group of highlanders who were prospering by their coffee plantations. The driver appeared, wearing sunglasses, a rumpled white cotton shirt, shorts, heavy Aussie-style socks, and a pair of work boots. He epitomized Papua New Guinea's modern man.

In 1980, Hagen itself was a relatively small town, with only two streets of shops. Several stores catered primarily to the white residents (a pharmacy, two grocery stores, a news agency), and a few trade stores served the populace (selling fried foods, pressure lanterns, Chinese-made pots and pans, axes, bush knives, flashlights, and blankets). The town itself is not particularly pretty, but I always felt invigorated by visiting it because of the brisk weather, the mix of people, and the view of the rugged hills and mountains that ring the valley.

Ninga and I made a shopping list and purchased ten days' worth of food and supplies. We hefted this into the little Suzuki and headed north along the Baiyer Road. This leads by the town dump, home to some of New Guinea's largest pigs, and thence upward over a gradual, deforested rise that forms the watershed between the north-flowing Baiyer and south-flowing Wahgi. From here we dropped into a picturesque gorge, with fine vistas of the looming slopes of the ancient Mount Hagen volcano and the river below, a small white thread in a deep ravine. The banks on the uphill sides of the road were dotted with clusters of the diminutive, pale yellow blossoms of *Rhododendron macgregoriae*, one of the species that prospers in open midmontane grasslands.

Leaving the gorge, we crossed the clear, rocky river and proceeded out into the broad Baiyer valley, a miniature of the Wahgi valley, but less developed and with a smaller human population. Here the road is broad, stony, and straight. Remarkably, it passes right through the middle of several villages, and it seems that something is always going on in one of them. That day, we passed a group of twenty or so young men, carrying their bows and arrows, their faces colored with a yellowish clay. It looked like a war party. I stopped, and when Ninga inquired, he was told the men were preparing for the formal mourning of the death of a village elder.

The valley bottom is open range—grasslands of various types, much of it grazed by cattle. There is even a local group of cowboys who tend to the cattle on horseback. This interest in cows can be credited to the government-run livestock research station located in the heart of the valley. We passed that on our right as we sped toward the tiny Baiyer River Patrol Post. We recrossed the river and followed the branch of the road that led up the watershed of the Trauna River, a tributary of the Baiyer. Here we came up to the steep ridge that delimits the northern edge of the valley. The Baiyer River Sanctuary was situated in a sizable tract of remnant humid forest at the base of this ridge.

Entering the sanctuary, we left the sunny grasslands and entered the relative gloom of the forest. The gravel road wound through forest to the main residential compound: a cluster of buildings that includes a large hostel/office/laboratory, and two staff houses. Ninga and I would share one of the small bunk rooms in the two-story cinder-block hostel that was shaded by tall forest trees growing right up to the edge of the compound. I was pleased to see a hostel built in the forest. As we unloaded our things, I could hear several calling birds, most prominent of which was the loud mix of cawing and whistling that I knew belonged to a group of male Lesser Birds of Paradise. I had been told that this species occupied a lek tree on the sanctuary grounds, and I was eager to study them. My ear also caught the musical howling and yodeling of the captive group of New Guinea wild dogs, dingolike relatives of *Canis familiaris* that have colonized several high mountain areas of Papua New Guinea. The music they made put the birds of paradise to shame!

The finest thing about the Sanctuary is the skillful combination of exhibit and jungle. All of the captive wildlife was displayed in cages scattered through clearings in the forest. Ninga and I toured the displays that afternoon, taking time to have a look at the action at the lek tree of the Lesser Birds of Paradise. The plumed males of this species shivered their yellow flank feathers from perches in the upper branches of a tall tree at the forest's edge, permitting us a splendid view from the path beside the wild-dog pen.

Studying the lek behavior of the Lesser Bird of Paradise became the focus of my research at Baiyer. Although during this month I made two side trips to isolated field sites, I kept returning to that display tree to watch what was happening in the lek. Doing this, I learned one of the secrets of lek behavior in birds of paradise.

The Lesser Bird of Paradise is a yellow-plumed version of the Raggiana. The two are sister-species—recently differentiated and geographically isolated forms that share many traits because of common descent. The Raggiana inhabits the forests of southeastern New Guinea, whereas the Lesser ranges through the forests of the north and far west. Where the edges of their ranges meet, they hybridize. Like the Raggiana, the Lesser exhibits a classical lek mating system, with a series of courtship displays that are nearly identical to those of the Raggiana. In 1979 I had little success obtaining good observations on lek behavior of the Raggiana in the Wau valley. I now had hopes that I could gather data of a similar type for the Raggiana's closest relative, and this substitute data could help me to understand the Raggiana's breeding behavior.

On my first morning at the sanctuary, I walked down to the Lesser's display tree and watched what took place. It was barely light; plumed males were already active in the treetop. Three birds perched together on some dead branches in the open. They preened their golden pectoral plumes, and at intervals one would give a loud and raucous *kwau kwau kwau kwa kwa kwa*—an advertisement song. Often this incited one or both of the other males to respond with the same song or a variant of that. After preening, the males hopped lightly on their perches and occasionally flew short distances between other perches in the open branches.

All of a sudden the lek erupted. The three plumed males were joined by several more, as well as several unplumed birds. Each plumed male took a perch, spaced two or three feet from his nearest neighbor, and began posturing, flapping wings, and erecting the cascade of yellow flank plumes over his back, all the while giving a high-pitched series of agitated notes that announces that a female is present in the lek. This was a lek "convergence," when all attention was focused on the lek and the displaying males. It is one of the breath-taking events in the animal world—and I was seeing it on my first morning on the sanctuary.

The birds are so exaggerated in their behaviors that interpretation of their signals is usually straightforward. The convergence is a veritable call to arms. In this case the battlers are the individual males in the lek and the displaying males. It is one of the breath-taking events in the animal world—and I was seeing it on my first morning in the sanctuary.

My attention was drawn to a nonplumed bird that was moving warily through the branches. Any time a plumed male left his perch to approach this bird, it withdrew, avoiding contact. A female, she was here to examine the males. As she moved about, the males no longer gave their agitated calling and flapping display but instead assumed a fixed, motionless posture, in which the body is bent low over the branch, the head lowest, and the great thatch of yellow plumes are erected into a radiant array over the back.

I watched the female perch close to one of the males, a bird near the center of the aggregation. She looked him over and even pecked at him a few times, and then she crouched beside him. By crouching, she had signaled her desire to mate. The male took over as the active participant. He sidled up to her and began a vigorous precopulatory display in which, while rocking from side to side, he gave powerful downstrokes with his wings, pummeling her with his nearest wing; holding his head over her back, he pecked at her nape in rhythm. After nearly a minute of this, the male mounted, and it was all over in a few seconds. The female flew off, and the male resumed his position on the branch.

The lek is a male bordello. Females can visit, examine the lek males, and mate. The males faithfully attend the lek tree every day for nearly the entire year, calling to, and waiting for, females. This, apparently, is the extent of the relations between the sexes.

What is the secret of lek display of the Lesser Bird of Paradise? During my observations at the sanctuary lek, I was able to keep track of mating activities of seven different males who regularly attended the tree. I counted twenty-six copulations. Twenty-five of these were made by a single male. Five of the seven lek males failed to mate even once. The various other males who only visited the lek on occasion I never saw mate in the lek either. Thus, the successful male is able to dominate mating in the lek and control reproduction in the population. This highly selective mating regime serves to explain how the remarkably exaggerated nuptial plumes can evolve in the birds of paradise. In this very directed breeding program, natural selection can operate with considerable effect and speed.

Why would all of the females mate with a single male, when there are a large number to choose from? Some researchers believe that it is the product of acute female discrimination and that the females are choosing the "prettiest" or "sexiest" male. I tend to believe that it is caused, in part, by a despotic control of the lek mating hierarchy by the dominant bird. The alpha male, by periodic physical aggression and continual psychological intimidation, is able to keep control over the subordinate males in the lek. The females are able to perceive this hierarchy in the lek, just as humans can make the same perception about dominance and subordination in a social situation. Females will naturally tend to mate with the alpha male, because his genetic material will most likely give the female the best chance of producing offspring with his qualities—the qualities that may help her male offspring dominate a lek of the next generation.

Does evidence for psychological control exist? In the Baiyer lek, I once observed a female crouch beside a male whose subordinate perch was in the lek periphery. He displayed to her repeatedly but never copulated, even though she remained next to him for several minutes. She had made a choice but apparently was denied access to this male because of his refusal to mate in the presence of the alpha male.

Subsequently, my observations of other lek-breeding birds of paradise have corroborated this finding, with some emendations. In some leks, the domination by a single bird is incomplete, and two or more males share "the spoils." Typically, in these mating groups, the mating hierarchy is less well established and more physical aggression between rival males is observed. One sees lek males fight, sometimes quite fiercely. It is not rare to see two birds, claws locked in combat, tumble out of the lek and fall all the way to the ground. In other instances, one male will interfere with another male who is in the process of courting a female. All of these interactions reinforce the view that lek behavior is very competitive and that these clusters of beautiful males are not assemblages of comrades but are instead arenas populated by fierce rivals.

Mount Pugent

Mount Pugent, sometimes called the Trauna Ridge, rises up behind the Baiyer River Sanctuary and forms a watershed between the Jimi River to the north and the Baiyer. A saddle in this ridge offers a low point for passage between the two drainages, and it presumably has been the crossing point of a traditional walking track for generations. In the late 1970s, the government began construction of a road through this pass. The high point of the road is about five thousand feet above sea level. I was particularly interested in spending some time observing birds in the forest above this pass.

After being dropped off at the point where the jeep road crosses the height of land, Ninga and I, laden with heavy packs, followed the small ridge-crest trail upward for an hour, to about 5,600 feet. With our loads, the climb was fairly grim, and we were glad to find a spot with some level ground. Ninga hacked his way down into a likely ravine and found good water. Here we set our camp for a week.

There are two advantages to placing a camp on a ridge crest. In the mountains, this is usually the most productive place to set mist nets, and we could thus string ours right along the trail, on either side of the camp. In rainy areas (and this was one), drainage is best on the ridgetop. I had learned the importance of a well-drained camp area from mishaps on earlier field trips.

I was most curious to see what birds of paradise inhabited this forest. A colleague had told me to expect Carola's Parotia, one of the remarkable six-wired birds of paradise. As we set up our camp, a group of these birds appeared in the nearby forest canopy, announcing their presence by a lovely, loud, quavering whistle, quite distinct from that of its eastern relative, Lawes' Parotia. Finding a display site of this species would be one of our priorities, but first it was necessary for us to set some mist nets. This is a time-consuming chore best done on the first day so that they can be operating throughout the stay. After we had set two lines of nets, about twelve in all, I went off in search of good localities for observing, while Ninga went in search of a display ground of Carola's Parotia.

I observed little that afternoon, but on the way back to camp, I was bowled over to find a male Yellow-breasted Bird of Paradise entangled in one of our nets. This species, one of New Guinea's most reclusive birds of paradise, is a small, unobtrusive, fruit eater that inhabits the forest canopy. The male has golden brown upperparts, silky yellow underparts, and a bulbous, pale green wattle sitting atop the base of the bill. Here was a bird I had not expected to find. Thus, one day's work had produced two birds of paradise new to me. The other good news was that Ninga had found an active dance ground of Carola's Parotia.

By dusk, our camp was enveloped in clouds. This ridge was a cloud catcher. Although in the highlands it was the middle of the dry season, to the north, on the coast, the rainy season prevailed, because of the effect of differing wind patterns. This ridge overlooked the flat Jimi plain, which led northward into the Sepik. The wet weather of the coastal East Sepik rolled up this valley system, and our little ridge was the first barrier it struck. Because of this, we would be draped in clouds and rain much of the time we camped there. Thus, the heavy mossing on the vegetation was a natural result of the high rainfall.

The Yellow-breasted Bird of Paradise was an exciting discovery. I thought it was a remarkable stroke of luck that the bird hit my net until I trapped another five individuals, all of them adult males. On subsequent days, I observed individuals foraging quietly in the mossy canopy on several occasions. Jared Diamond wrote that this species "exemplifies to an extreme the patchiness of distribution characteristic of numerous New Guinea birds." This was one of the "patches" where the Yellow-breasted Bird of Paradise is common, even abundant. In most parts of New Guinea it is rare or absent altogether. I had looked for this bird for months on Mount Missim, without success. A single individual had been collected there in 1932 by Herbert Stevens. The species has not been observed there since. No wonder it was a surprise to find it so common on Mount Pugent.

Why are some bird species so patchily distributed? Why is a particular species common on one mountain and absent on another? That is one of the unanswered questions in Papuan ornithology. It is a question that Diamond first raised in 1972, yet I am not certain anyone has produced a completely satisfactory answer. In the case of the Yellow-breasted Bird of Paradise, it may relate to the localized distribution of some types of fruiting plants, since the bird is almost exclusively frugivorous. However, this is only speculation. Perhaps the species only prospers in a habitat with high rainfall. I suspect it will be decades before we understand this mystery of the Yellow-breast's spotty distribution.

There are other mysteries surrounding the Yellow-breasted Bird of Paradise. Most prominent is the question of mating behavior. As I have pointed out earlier, the sexually dimorphic species (wherein male and female differ in looks) are all known to be polygamous, with specialized mating display by males (though not all so extravagant as that of the Lesser Bird of Paradise). The Yellow-breast is sexually dimorphic, yet no one has reported any elaborate courtship display. While on Mount Pugent, I had hoped to get some evidence on this question, but this was not to be. Each time I encountered a bird it was solitary, silent, and sluggish. This species has been grouped in a section of the family that is little known and rather cryptic. Might they all be monogamous species with no elaborate courtship display? It is a question that nags a number of ornithologists working in the region.

I had better success observing Carola's Parotia. In contrast to the reticent Yellow-breast, Carola's Parotia is both gregarious and active. Carola's is the most beautiful of the six-wired birds of paradise, also known as flagbirds because of their six, spatulate-tipped head wires, used so remarkably in display. Most of the species are nearly all black, but Carola's has marvelous white flank plumes, a golden eyebrow, and prominent golden "whiskers" that give it an oddly human look. It is also adorned with a maroon, metallic breast shield, a white crown stripe, and a golden iris.

The male dances on a cleared terrestrial court not unlike that of a Magnificent Bird of Paradise. The court that Ninga found was about three hundred feet off the ridgetop, on slightly sloping ground in undisturbed forest. The male had cleared a display ground of about three feet in diameter next to the site of a fallen tree. The light brought in by the tree fall had permitted a small thicket to grow, and it was in here that the clearing was made. Several viny tangles sheltered the small cleared area, and this constituted the female's observation deck.

Ninga had constructed a blind about thirty feet from the dance site. Into this I crept in the predawn, in order to be ready when the bird arrived. I was surprised to hear a party of males arrive above the dance ground just as it was becoming light. They darted among the midstory branches and called excitedly. They moved off after a few minutes, and after some quiet, I noticed that a single male had dropped down into the thicket. He made light scolding sounds and pleasing interrogative notes, as if under his breath. He was the owner.

The male began hopping about on the tidy dance ground, which was so free of leaves and other debris that it stood out, an unexpected sight to see in the forest. The male preened his long flank plumes, picked up a small twig in his bill, and then moved up into the branches. A juvenile male with just a hint of adult plumage visited the thicket and was driven out by the owner. Then a group that included adult males and others in female plumage arrived and clambered about in the vegetation, vocalizing, while the owner returned to his clearing on the ground. Several times the birds seemed to call to each other, and the level of excitement rose, but no female entered the dance ground.

Several days passed before I saw a male and female interact, but it was worth the wait. Late one afternoon, a male was in attendance at the dance ground when a female arrived, followed by a juvenile male. The adult male first picked up a leaf in his mouth and slowly chased the female around the small arena. She kept just out of reach. He then dropped to the clearing and began his marvelous courtship dance. In an upright posture, the male erected his flank plumes and head wires and suddenly transformed, before my eyes, from a rather peculiar-looking bird into a creature of bizarre beauty. In this bird of paradise, the transition is extreme, and it is startling to see. What looks like a single flank plume is expanded into three segments, a white cape that covers the wings, a golden segment that highlights the flanks, and a black skirt that is arrayed in front of the bird. All the while, the six head wires are thrown forward and bob like jewel-tipped antennae. The movements of the bird highlighted this transformation. He made dainty hops, moving jerkily side-to-side, in order to display his finery. He danced back and forth in his clearing for about a minute. During this time the female perched about a foot above, on one of the vines. The male then flew up to the female, but she retreated. He then repeated his dance, and she returned and watched intently. Another female appeared, and the first quickly drove her off. A young male moved into the thicket, and the male permitted his presence until the young bird closely approached the female; then the dancing male attacked him, before returning to the dance. I was held spellbound while this sequence was repeated, with varying levels of interruption, for more than thirty minutes. The male repeatedly approached the female but she did not allow him to copulate that afternoon. Thus, his displays were for naught. This, actually, is a common end to display efforts of a male bird of paradise. The competition is stiff, and copulations go only to a few.

The display behavior of Carola's Parotia seems to be one step from that of a true lek system, like that of the Lesser Bird of Paradise. In the Lesser, a group of males share a display tree, although only one or two dominant birds control the action. In Carola's Parotia, the males, although very sociable, do not assemble into fixed groups for display. Instead, apparently only the top males hold personal dance grounds, and these are visited by a large and mobile group of subordinates.

Carola's Parotia

I repeatedly watched interloping males visit the site, often in small groups. If they had ruled their own courts, they would most likely have spent time there. Steve Pruett-Jones' studies of Lawes' Parotia show that the males have a variable dispersion in the forest, with some clustered into leks and others scattered about solitarily. More fieldwork is required to obtain a complete picture of the mating system of Carola's Parotia. Nonetheless, my brief stay on Mount Pugent allowed me to get to know two rarely seen birds of paradise, invaluable for coming to grips with the biology of the family as a whole.

Mount Hagen

One of the goals in my visit to the highlands in 1979 was to gain field experience with species of birds of paradise that did not occur around Wau and Mount Missim. Baiyer Sanctuary offered a lowland species (the Lesser); Mount Pugent was home to two midmontane varieties (Carola's Parotia and the Yellow-breasted Bird of Paradise). In order to round out my experience I decided to camp high up on the south-western slopes of Mount Hagen, where I could observe the species inhabiting the highest altitudes. A good, all-weather road led up through the pass between Mount Hagen and Mount Giluwe and gave access to high mountain forests north and west of the tiny community of Tomba.

Ninga and I drove up past the Tomba sawmill and through heavily logged forest. After several more miles we branched off on a small logging track and found a place to hide the jeep in a gravel pit. On foot, we followed the logging track up the slope, hoping to come upon a trail that led into the forest. I was glad to have Ninga choose the route, because he could pick out the best among a myriad of possible choices, and he led me up a track into superb, untouched forest quite unlike any I had ever seen. This was open pandanus forest, visited annually by the local people for its crop of nutritious pandanus nuts.

I call this pandanus forest, although really it was dominated by several large species of gymnospermous trees in the family Podocarpaceae (relatives of the familiar yew bush). The forest is very open, with a much-broken canopy, and where the canopy is absent, it is filled either with pandanus or else with mounds of impenetrable scrambling bamboo. We were lucky to have a well-marked track. After about an hour's walk we came to a small clearing and a low, thatched hut, where the nut pickers stay during harvest time. Since we were there during a nonharvest month, there was little chance that we would be disturbed. We used the hut as our camp. From here, several subsidiary trails led to groves of pandanus, and these were perfect to use as netting and observation trails.

I had camped at equivalent altitudes in other parts of New Guinea, but I had not seen forest like this. It was unusual for two reasons. First, the soils are of volcanic origin and very rich. The topographical relief is quite low; we were on a very gently sloping ancient volcanic shield. Second, periodic heavy frosts had apparently killed many trees, producing the openings in the canopy that permit the abundance of pandanus and other lower vegetation. Thus, at 9,400 feet on Mount Bangeta, the forest was altogether different—stunted subalpine forest, heavily encrusted with thick mats of moss, and very low statured, with a nearly complete canopy. Here on Mount Hagen, the mossing was not as apparent because of the open aspect and the abundance of scrambling bamboo, and the canopy trees were big-trunked, sizable trees.

———

Three species of birds of paradise inhabited this forest on the upper slopes of Mount Hagen: the Crested Bird of Paradise, Brown Sicklebill, and Ribbon-tailed Astrapia. A fourth species, the King-of-Saxony Bird of Paradise, is abundant in the roadside forests at the head of the Wapenamanda Gorge, a few miles west, but absent here in the forest proper. I spent most of my time observing the Sicklebill and the Astrapia.

The Ribbon-tailed Astrapia is remarkable for several reasons. Weighing only 160 grams, the species has the typical, compact body of the members of this genus. The sexes differ, and it is the male's beauty that takes one's breath away. His head is, all-round, a deep iridescent blue-green, with a velvety pom-pom of the same color perched atop the base of the bill. The body is generally blackish, but the splendor of the bird is its central pair of tail feathers—narrow, three feet long, and streamerlike—entirely white but for the black, pointed tips. These wonderful adornments are light and flexible, and they switch and bend every which way. In flight, the two streamers ripple and loosely trail the bird, producing a marvelous effect. The female is a blackish bird with a foot-long tail, lacking much of the male's beauty.

Besides having one of the most beautiful male plumages, the Ribbon-tail is notable for its geographic range, its interaction with Stephanie's Astrapia, and the history of its discovery. The Ribbon-tail was the last described of the birds of paradise. It was first mentioned in print by patrol officer J. G. Hides, in his 1936 book, *Papuan Wonderland*. Hides described an expedition west and south of Mount Hagen that he took in the company of fellow officer L. J. O'Malley. This was the trek in which they discovered the Tari Basin, in 1935. When he saw the white-tailed birds, Hides realized he was observing something of scientific interest. A local ornithologist, Fred Shaw Mayer, read this description and queried O'Malley about the birds. In 1938, Shaw Mayer was able to ask the Fox brothers, wide-ranging gold prospectors, if they had seen the species west of Mount Hagen, and they were able to describe the species well, confirming that it was apparently a new type of astrapia.

At that point, Shaw Mayer put out the word that he wanted a pair of those tail feathers from any source. He eventually received the feathers from a missionary who had taken them from a Mount Hagen native's headdress. At virtually the same time, Jim Taylor and John

Black had collected several complete specimens of the species on their remarkable patrol west to Telefolmin and back to Mount Hagen.

Taylor and Black sent their specimens to Roy Kinghorn, at the Australian Museum. Shaw Mayer sent his feathers to C. R. Stonor, at the British Museum. Stonor lost no time in describing the new bird after Shaw Mayer (*Astrapia mayeri*). A few months later appeared Roy Kinghorn's description of the complete specimens received from Taylor and Black. Stonor had beaten Kinghorn to the honors, and in that manner the last species of bird of paradise came to be formally presented to science.

Why did this species elude ornithologists for so long? The bird occupies a tiny range, high in mountains that were traversed by explorers only at the end of the 1930s, more than 160 years after Linnaeus formally named the first species of the family *Paradisaea apoda*, the Greater Bird of Paradise. Even today we only have a vague idea of the distribution of the Ribbon-tailed Astrapia. We know it has not been recorded east of the Hagen Range and occurs westward for at least eighty miles, only in forests above eight thousand feet. This is the most restricted range of any bird species inhabiting New Guinea's central cordillera.

The ranges of the Ribbon-tail and the more widespread Stephanie's Astrapia (common around Wau) overlap, although the latter species tends to live at a slightly lower altitude. Where the two species co-occur they are known to hybridize, forming offspring that share a mixture of traits of the two parental types. This mixing of genes probably should not be surprising for two reasons. First, the two species appear to be very closely related. Second, the mating systems of the two are polygynous, with no bonding between the sexes. The males on the display ground will mate with any willing female. In the 1970s some biologists worried that the Ribbon-tail might get genetically swamped by the more widespread Stephanie's Astrapia. It now appears that hybridization occurs only in the lower segment of the Ribbon-tail's population. The birds I observed in the undisturbed forest on Mount Hagen showed no evidence of Stephanie's genes. By contrast, many of the males that I observed along the roadside between Tomba and the Wapenamanda Gorge were of hybrid origin. These hybrids sported remarkable tail feathers, broad and long, mostly white, with irregular patterning of black.

Male Ribbon-tails, confiding and seemingly imperturbable, were common around my Mount Hagen camp. On the first afternoon in the forest, I repeatedly observed males in the trailside vegetation. Birds visited the little *Schefflera* vine, grappling with the tough green globular fruit. Each "globe," some three-quarters of an inch in diameter, is a complex fruit, made up of dozens of fruitlets that must be pulled from their attachments. The *Schefflera* fruit looks a bit like a small sycamore fruit, but each seed is set in a coating of woody pulp that presumably has some nutritional value. They certainly did not look very edible.

Often I encountered the Ribbon-tails foraging in the upper limbs of the canopy trees, in search of arthropods and, presumably, small arboreal frogs and lizards. This was done by methodically poking into the moss, often peering down around the side and underside of the branch as well. A single bird might spend many minutes in the upper branches of a single tree, then move to the next, to repeat the process.

My daily observations of the Ribbon-tail taught me several things about this species. It was clearly nonterritorial. Males were not aggressive to other males in shared patches of forest. Territorial species are commonly very vocal, the voices conveying ownership of land. The Ribbon-tail was notable for its limited vocal ability. The birds gave no far-carrying call of any type. The only individual I heard to give any vocalization was a subadult male, who repeatedly gave weak, growling notes while foraging for arthropods. The species is remarkably unwary, and I assume this relates to the lack of natural enemies. Highlanders rarely use the bird's plumes for headdresses, and at nine thousand feet there is only one species of bird-eating raptor, the Black-mantled Goshawk.

The habits of the Ribbon-tailed Astrapia contrast with those of its neighbor in the forests of Mount Hagen, the Brown Sicklebill. This is the high-altitude relative of the Buff-tailed Sicklebill that I studied on Mount Missim. Whereas the Ribbon-tail has a short bill, that of the Brown Sicklebill is long and strongly decurved. The Ribbon-tail's central tail feathers are narrow and white, while those of the Brown Sicklebill are equally long, but broad, black, and sword shaped. The Ribbon-tail is virtually mute, whereas the Brown Sicklebill produces a penetrating, machinegunlike *TAT-AT-AT-AT, TAT-AT-AT-AT-AT*. The

Ribbon-tail shows a strong predilection for fruit; the Brown Sicklebill is largely insectivorous. For all of these reasons, it is not surprising that the two are able to share the forest amicably, with no apparent competition. They are birds of different genera, performing different ecological functions in the habitat.

From my campsite on Mount Hagen, I could hear the staccato calls of four male Brown Sicklebills. These males vocalized repeatedly through the morning, usually several times a minute. In contrast to the sociable Ribbon-tails, the male Brown Sicklebills were never seen together. It was evident that males were stationed on nonoverlapping foraging territories. To document this, I made morning censuses along the main ridge trail, mapping the distribution of calling male Brown Sicklebills. By estimating distance and taking compass directions of the calling birds from different points along the trail, I could generate data for triangulating their positions. This technique, useless for the silent and wide-ranging Ribbon-tail, was ideal for the Brown Sicklebill. I refined the method in subsequent field trips to gain an understanding of how males of different species of birds of paradise spaced themselves through the forest.

The Brown Sicklebill exhibited the behavior typical of a territorial bird of paradise: oft-repeated, far-carrying vocalizations, and sedentary habits. There are vocal birds of paradise that are nonterritorial, but these latter species tend to give their vocalizations in a much less-regular fashion, based on the presence or absence of females at or near a display area. In contrast, the territorial species tend to repeat their calls over and over, usually with a fairly regular periodicity.

The adult male Brown Sicklebill is a more majestic bird than the Ribbon-tail. Whereas the Ribbon-tail is compact and quiet, the Brown Sicklebill gives the impression of being much larger than it really is. In coloration it is nothing remarkable—largely dull brown and black—but its pale blue iris stands out from the dark face. The iris highlights the small round head and the deep sickle shape of the bill. The upper pectoral plumes that typify the family (but which are strangely absent in the astrapias) are rather small and generally hidden under the wing. In display, however, they form a splendid ruff that arches up over each cheek, forming a sort of fan, through which the bird peers. The tips of all of these shimmer an iridescent purple, forming a metallic rainbow from shoulder to shoulder, up and over the bird's crown. The lower pectoral plumes form a fluffy skirt much like that of Carola's Parotia.

The tail feathers are the Brown Sicklebill's most obvious asset. The two heavy, lanceolate central rectrices can grow to more than thirty inches, and they are glossed with iridescent greenish blue. They are flanked by a graduated series of smaller tail feathers, arrayed longest to shortest. Because of this, the tail has a look of great substance. To see this bird high up on a mossy bough, jerking its neck as it belts out its jackhammer call, is to understand the beauty that is inherent in the highest expression of avian behavior.

People, Plumes, Bride-price, and Warfare

One of the intangibles of our trip up to Mount Hagen, as well as our stay at Baiyer Sanctuary, was the uncertainty of tribal relations. This upland region is peopled by volatile tribes who, on a moment's notice, will express a grievance by means of violent action. Their sense of territoriality is strong, which may relate, in part, to the high demand for arable land. On Mount Hagen, Ninga and I worried about encountering local landowners in the forest. Such a worry would never have crossed our minds back in the Wau valley. Around Wau, an encounter in the forest would begin and end with polite conversation. On Mount Hagen, meeting local landowners in the forest could have sparked an interrogation as to our intrusion into a tribal domain, followed by a request for compensatory payment. Fortunately, we were left undisturbed during our stay.

One of the unexpected pleasures of driving the Highlands Highway is encountering a truckload of singing revelers on the way to some sort of traditional celebration. Dozens of headdresses adorned with plumes of birds of paradise wave in the wind; bodies glisten with charcoal and pig fat; tribal voices carry a haunting chant. The highlanders have a real sense of ceremony and pageantry, and they love traditional decoration. The women often dress nearly identically to the men— often, both are equally striking to behold. Nothing is more valuable to them than the feathers that they wear in their headdresses: a gift from their bountiful forests.

Every tribe has its own style of ritual dress, but all use plumes of birds of paradise in some capacity. Some Melpa tribesmen from the Baiyer River area prominently feature plumes of these birds. The typical headdress rests on a woven net cap. A carved piece of bailer shell covers the forehead, attached to the woven "hair net." Above this rises a series of wonderful plumes: first, the glittering blue breast shield of a Superb Bird of Paradise, topped by the velvety black head plume of that same bird. These two form a horizontal forelock, above which projects a huge array of plumes: on each side in the foreground stand the black-and-red flight feathers of Pesquet's Parrot. These parrot feathers bracket as many as six pairs of the fifteen-inch head wires of the King-of-Saxony Bird of Paradise that rise vertically, with their dozens of little pearly enameled "teeth," like small square leaflets of some primitive fern. As a background to all of this stands a row of six Raggiana Birds of Paradise, the remains of their shrunken and dismembered skins inserted into the foundation of the headdress, their deep orange pectoral plumes like rising flames forming a halo above the warrior.

Other tribesmen feature the tail feathers of Stephanie's Astrapia. These rise in groups of six or more from the headdress, swaying gracefully, blunt tipped, like standards in the wind. The men of Tambul, southwest of Mount Hagen, favor a more geometric arrangement of plumes, with two tall bunches of the deep cobalt plumes of the Blue Bird of Paradise, a centered block of cut feathers attached to a backing of the white tail feathers of cockatoo, and four pairs of rigidly vertical King-of-Saxony plumes, all of which is topped with a high row of Raggiana plumes.

Feathers only provide part of the decoration of the bodies of highlanders. Pierced nasal septa are variously adorned with tusks of wild boar, carved shell, cassowary wing quill, or bamboo plug. Faces are painted black or brightened with patterns of red, ochre, or white. A strip of skin of Boelen's Python, or else a woven cloth band encrusted with the emerald green elytra of cetoniine flower beetles, crosses the upper forehead. Around the neck go strings of red or black beads, a choker of pearl shell, or a long breastplate of *pitpit* (called an *omak*), forming what looks like a narrow venetian blind for the chest. Arm bands of woven cane, into which are inserted colorful flowers, are very common. The lower body is adorned with a large loin cloth, either of

Highlander in headddress

woven string or cloth, held up by a broad belt. The hind quarters are cloaked with a fresh bunch of *tangket* leaves, tucked through the belt.

To see a line of these men, dressed for show, holding bows and arrows or else *kundu* drums, is awe inspiring. This is the sight one encounters at a tribal *sing sing*—a traditional festival to celebrate a pig feast, a marriage, an adolescent initiation, or today, even the sanctification of a new church. The rhythmic movement, the sounds of drums and low chants, the colors in bright, repeated patterns, and the surrounding environment of rugged hills, dark peaks, and deep blue sky filled with billowing cumulus clouds, is a true highlands phenomenon.

Although the special nature of the *sing sing* has been commercialized in the annual "Highlands Show," the color and beauty remain little changed; and it is still possible to observe these tribal rites in their original village setting if one is willing to spend some time in the market, asking about the schedule of planned events. Certainly, the advent of evangelical Christianity has affected the way the people look on these *sing sings*, but the strong cultural ties to these traditions have prevented the ceremonies from being swept away or even changed in content.

In the highlands, the most important ritual relating clans and tribes is the exchange of wealth. It occurs in at least three forms: ritual exchange that binds alliances, purchase of brides, and compensation for acts of violence or destruction. In all three there are complex and detailed ceremonies. Exchange of wealth includes the wearing of traditional dress, dancing, and the actual exchange. The big man who is able to give away a great deal is considered to achieve high status. This act of generosity is conducted with the idea of eventual reciprocation. Thus, sharing of wealth is a remarkable evolution that ensures that a region's resources are distributed to the less well-off. It remains an important tenet of modern highlands culture.

Today, this system of communal sharing survives as the *wantok* system, a form of communal social security difficult to reconcile for the western mind long inured to worship of personal property. *Wantok* is Pidgin for "brother" or "cousin"—literally, it means "one talk"—someone who shares your language. Given the diversity of tongues in New Guinea, and the often tiny populations of unique language groups, New Guineans tend to keep tight bonds with those who share a native tongue.

In the *wantok* system, when a working man is paid on Friday, he may be visited by several of his unemployed *wantoks* on Saturday, with the unspoken understanding that part of the working man's salary will be broken up and distributed to those without jobs. This occurs with all material goods, food, clothing, money, beer. It is an ancient system of redistribution of the wealth, and it is one of the reasons that Papua New Guinea so easily grasped the nature of the parliamentary democracy based on social welfare that was adopted from the Australian system.

These days, wealth includes cash in the local currency (Kina), pigs, and cassowaries. The exchange with which I am most familiar is that related to bride-price. In the highlands, as in most other parts of Papua New Guinea, a wife is purchased from her family, usually at great expense. Price will vary according to local tradition, available wealth, and prestige of the woman in question. Several thousand dollars is not an uncommon price to pay for a wife in the highlands. This price is worked out through long sessions of bargaining between the heads of the two families, often over a period of several months. The bargaining is tough, and the father of the wife-to-be attempts to extract as much as possible, because this reflects well on himself and his family's status.

The purchase price is a mix of currency and traditional items. In the highlands, a large pig is an exceedingly valuable piece of livestock. It is worth far more than the retail price of its pork and bacon. This is because large pigs are required for the periodic feasts, as well as for exchanges and bride-price. The same can be said for cassowaries, always numerically rare and difficult to propagate. Cassowaries must be captured wild or raised from chicks found in the forest. Cassowaries are prized for their meat, their value in exchanges, and their feathers, which are important in the headdresses of many tribes.

Thus, a wife might be purchased with a payment of one thousand Kina cash, plus six pigs, and a cassowary. This wealth is presented to the wife's family. Some or all of the pigs may be butchered and cooked in a *mumu* as part of the marriage celebration.

A *mumu* is the traditional method of cooking large quantities of meat and vegetables for a feast. A large fire is built, and onto it are laid many stones. Next to the fire is dug a *mumu* pit, broad and shallow. It is lined with fresh green leaves of banana or whatever is available. Onto this lining are laid the pieces of meat. Often, there are several layers of meat and vegetables, interlayered with green leaves. Atop this are laid all of the hot stones, which themselves are covered in a final thick layer of green leaves, to hold in the heat. The hot stones steam cook the fare below in an hour or two.

Almost invariably the centerpiece of these feasts is the pork. This is the delicacy favored above all others. The big men are given the cherished portions—cubes of fat—whereas the women and children must make do with the tough skin and the firm white meat. A pig feast in the highlands is a bit of a binge. Rarely does it occur more than once or twice a year, and the habit is to overeat.

In spite of official bans and threats of legal retribution, intertribal warfare remains a part of the highlander's way of life. Traditional violence appears to evolve from the McCoy-Hatfield type of disagreement. In other words, a member of one clan is killed or injured by one of another clan, and this foments clan vengeance. These days, the initial act might be the result of an automobile accident, rugby injury, or bar brawl, but the result is, usually, a traditional response. On several occasions I have observed the product of tribal conflict. While Ninga and I were camped on Mount Pugent, we discovered that we were on the main path between two feuding Melpa-speaking clans. On more than one occasion, passing war parties stopped to chat with us and rest around our fire. Armed with their axes and bows, these were fearsome-looking men.

On a later visit to Baiyer Sanctuary, my wife and I were told in Mount Hagen that the Baiyer road recently had been closed for a week because of warfare. We hitched a ride with a local bread-delivery truck, and the New Guinean driver gleefully pointed out the roadside destruction that had been done by the warring factions. One village beside the road had been ravaged: houses burned, gardens wasted, coffee and banana plants uprooted or cut off at their bases. The road was closed during the fighting because it is not uncommon for one side or the other to place barricades across the road to halt traffic. All vehicles would be checked for members of the enemy tribe, and it was not unusual for the inconvenienced drivers to be robbed of their valuables as well.

In 1975, when I was camped outside of Kundiawa with an Australian tour group, we witnessed a traditional "payback" that sought to end warfare that had gone on between two neighboring clans for many months of that year. A school teacher from one clan had been killed, and the payback (money and pigs) provided suitable retribution that could end the blood feud amicably. The payback ceremony involved the ritual turning over of the agreed indemnity to the aggrieved village. The money was arrayed festively on tall poles, which accentuated the amount being given. These were marched, along with the pigs, to the recipient village. From our distant vantage point by the road, we could see the noisy procession of villagers, their tall money poles rising up from the crowd. Such public displays are a common phenomenon in highlands' culture. These sorts of colorful ceremonies, like the ritual displays of the birds of paradise, make the highlands a fascinating place for visiting naturalists and tourists alike.

Opposite: Mount Trikora, from Lake Habbema, Irian Jaya

7 Irian Jaya

*I*rian Jaya, the western half of the great island of New Guinea, was
the portion first contacted by the Europeans, first explored, and
first colonized. Nevertheless, since 1963, when control of this region
passed into the hands of Indonesia, it has become a land shrouded in
mystery. It has been shielded from the outside world by a host of official restrictions on travel and research, in part because of a politically
troublesome Irianese insurgency movement, Organizasi Papua Mer-
deka. To the ornithologist and tropical ecologist, Irian Jaya beckons,
with its great snow-capped ranges, vast tracts of untouched forest, and
its little-studied rainforests.

History

Western New Guinea was visited by Malay traders and seamen as early
as the fifteenth century. It was from these adventurers that the first
natural products of this island realm began to appear in western societies—skins of birds of paradise, spices such as nutmeg, and tamed
cassowaries and cockatoos. The pioneering Malay traders were fol-

lowed by the Portuguese, then the Italians and French, and finally, and most notably, by the Dutch, who claimed all of the island east of 141° east longitude.

Dutch New Guinea, the easternmost segment of the Dutch East Indies, remained less developed than its more westerly island provinces, probably because of the many hostile tribes inhabiting the island and the physical barriers to effective large-scale colonization. There simply wasn't much the Dutch could do to develop this region economically, so it remained an untouched resource, awaiting a time when technology and demand would foster development.

As the Japanese forces were being driven from the Dutch East Indies in the final days of World War II, the strong Indonesian nationalist movement sought full independence. These nationalist elements had hoped that Japan would help them to become a sovereign republic, but such did not come about, partly because of the unanticipated speed with which the Allied forces regained control over the western Pacific. After the cessation of hostilities, the Dutch struggled for several years to regain full control over their colonial possessions but failed and, in 1949, granted Indonesia its independence. This agreement, however, did not include Dutch New Guinea. Nonetheless, the young Indonesian state claimed western New Guinea as its own and finally was able to take possession of this region in 1963, by dint of diplomatic and military confrontation.

Many of the inhabitants of western New Guinea had little desire to become a part of the vast and populous Indonesian nation. The Dutch had promised a free and independent West Papua. The disappointment turned to anger, and an insurgency movement developed among those in "West Irian" who felt independence was denied them by trickery.

During the mid-1970s a secret war developed in Irian Jaya. It was a war fought by a small band of ill-equipped West Papuan freedom fighters against the mighty Indonesian military. This little-known war was fought in the jungles and villages far from the eyes of the western press, which were focused on Watergate and the final stages of the war in Indochina. In Indonesia's little war, jets bombed villages in attempts to suppress the insurgency. One Australian paper reported that in the period from 1977 to 1978 as many as several thousand people were killed in the conflict. Although this figure is probably inflated, there is no doubt that the military did conduct intensive, though fairly ineffectual, war against the Irianese who were deemed to be anti-Indonesian. One can, therefore, understand the Indonesian reluctance to allow Westerners into Irian Jaya during recent decades. Publicity about this conflict would not endear them to their more powerful allies in the West, allies who supported Indonesia as the Pacific bastion against Asian communism.

First Look

In March 1980 I decided to take a break from my work in Wau and visit Irian Jaya. I had little difficulty obtaining a tourist visa, although I understood that I would need additional special permissions, obtained from the police, to travel anywhere outside of Irian's capital area. Most fortunately, I had made contact with a Protestant missionary stationed

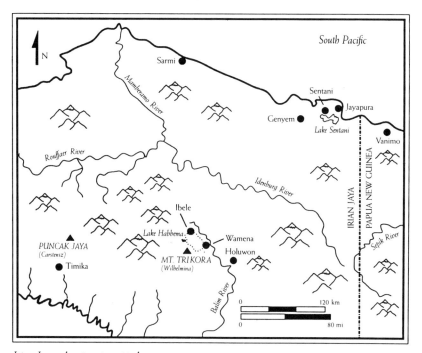

Irian Jaya, showing sites visited

deep in the back country and had received permission to visit his mission station in the hills south of the central cordillera. I built my travel plans around this special opportunity.

When my Air Niugini flight from Papua New Guinea touched down on the huge, wartime-vintage runway at Sentani, I was entering a world foreign to me. I was leaving the influence of Australian custom and outlook and taking my first steps in southeast Asia. I was surprised by the magnitude of the differences.

The airport is beautifully sited, tucked between Lake Sentani and the southern scarp of the rugged Cyclops Mountains, a small but steep coastal range that rises up from the outskirts of Jayapura, the capital of Irian Jaya. The lake is a peculiarity, a now landlocked, former arm of the sea. It is home to a species of freshwater sawfish and a sizable population of local people who make their life off the natural products of the lake. As I departed the international arrival lounge I was besieged by solicitations from a throng of self-appointed guides, taxi and jitney drivers. Each implored me to hire him. They shouted at me in Indonesian, of which I knew but a few words.

One of the throng, an Irianese national named Henke Ibo, spoke some English and fell into step with me as I tried to make my way through the confusion. Being lost and bewildered, I took up his offer of assistance. He convinced me to check the Mission Aviation Fellowship (MAF) Guest House for a room. This was the first of several splendid suggestions he had for me. The guest house was only a short walk from the airport, and it was quiet and inexpensive. However, my tenure there depended on luck. Missionaries were given priority, and if the hostel filled, I would have to move out. Mission Aviation Fellowship is an organization that transports and supplies the myriad of Protestant missionaries in the isolated communities scattered throughout Irian Jaya.

After I settled into my room, I met Henke again and he showed me around Sentani, a nice little community about an hour's drive from downtown Jayapura. Sentani is, by far, the more desirable location to get one's initial bearings. It is quiet, rural, and near the lake and the spectacular mountains. Henke's brief tour taught me about the various important components of Sentani: the main marketplace; the strip along the main street where, in the evening, food stalls are opened for the evening diners; the post office; the MAF headquarters. We agreed to meet early the next morning so that I could register with the police and obtain a *surat jalan* (travel authorization) for permission to visit the interior. Without this crucial document, I could not legally travel in Irian Jaya.

The next day I visited the crowded station of the Jayapura police, where, with Henke's help, I learned the Asian system of bureaucracy. First one tiny office, a few minutes with an official, then on to another tiny office, another brief conversation, periods of waiting, followed by more offices and officials, as we worked our way up to the only office that counts—that of the boss, where the wait is longer, but the reward is the travel permit that would allow me two weeks in the Grand Valley of the Balim.

Jayapura itself was a rather small town, wedged into a flat patch of ground that is backed by the steep coastal hills on three sides and a beautiful natural harbor on the fourth. The city center is unprepossessing, but the market is a memorable sight for the first-time visitor to Asia: shop after shop (*toko* in Indonesian) crammed together along a series of narrow lanes. The town's main street looks much like a main street in one of the lesser towns in Papua New Guinea. While we were there, a furious rain squall hit, and the street flooded with a brown swirl of water more than a foot deep. We took shelter in a food shop, and there I learned that restaurant food in Irian is tastier and less expensive than in Papua New Guinea.

The third morning I rose very early to catch the flight inland. Getting to the terminal early was critical because, in spite of an official passenger manifest and reserved seats, boarding was a free-for-all that began several hours before the departure of the flight. This was apparently caused by overbooking and frequent cancellations due to bad weather. The pilots use a single gap through the mountain ranges, and it often fills with clouds, forcing the plane back to Sentani.

For two reasons I was fortunate in this struggle for a seat. I was much taller than the others, and I was the only American in the mass of would-be passengers. Very politely, I was given priority because I was a "tourist." The flight boarded on time and the aging Fokker F-27 noisily lumbered off the long concrete airstrip, bound for the interior.

After clearing the notch in the high northern spur of the Jayawijaya cordillera, we began to descend slowly into the valley of the Balim

River. The Balim is to Irian Jaya what the Wahgi is to Papua New Guinea. Both montane rivers have cut wonderful midmontane valleys that serve as home to hundreds of thousands of New Guineans. In the same manner that the mountain peaks are higher in the west, the valley of the Balim is a slightly more spectacular setting than its eastern counterpart. The valley floor is broad and grassy, with tiny hamlets scattered here and there among the geometric patterns of walled sweet potato plots. Gazing down from the plane, I thought the remarkable quiltwork of potato gardens gave much of the valley an extraordinarily ordered look. Clearly, the local populace has been long-established here. I was seeing agriculture quite different from the slash-and-burn system practiced in many areas of the island.

My arrival at Wamena was uneventful. No hassles, no pressing crowds of guides offering their services. This is because Wamena is a small government station that supports little besides bureaucratic offices and missionary headquarters. I was the sole westerner to debark the plane, but I was surprised to see a sleek Gulfstream jet parked on the runway. People gazed at me with evidence of mild curiosity, but otherwise I was on my own. The airport superintendent directed me to the Hotel Balim as the only suitable lodging. I engaged two young Irianese men to carry my boxes of food and, with my pack on my back, set off with them along the grid of roads to my destination, a modular and modern-looking hotel. Since I spoke little Indonesian and the reservations clerk spoke little English, we communicated through gesture and phrase. He insisted on taking my passport, which I gave up with some reluctance. I was given a room—a nonattached unit modeled after a highlander's thatched hut. The interior had been planned with great care and would have been elegant except that someone had apparently vandalized it thoroughly since its completion. Screens over the windows had been ripped up, fixtures in the bathroom broken, and so forth. Still, I was just happy to have a room.

I was not the only westerner at the hotel. When luncheon was announced, I was seated at the table with a large, red-faced, white-haired man. I introduced myself and found that I was speaking to the Australian ambassador to Indonesia, who was making his initial tour of the nation. The Gulfstream was his.

====

The purpose of my trip inland was to get into the mountain forest. That afternoon I visited the Wamena police station in order to obtain permission to do this. I worked my way slowly upward through the levels of power until I was shown into the office of *Bapak* Franz, the police superintendent. I was in great luck, for Franz (*Bapak* means "father" and is an address of respect) was a friendly and intelligent man who was interested in what I had to say. I told him I was here to camp in the forest and study the birds. He said that as long as I kept out of trouble I could move about freely but that I could stay in the area only two weeks, the absolute limit for tourists.

Now it remained for me to get some guides. I visited the local MAF office. Because of the number of missionaries in the highlands around Wamena, this was a very large operation. The manager of operations hired for me two Irianese guides for the next morning's departure to the forest.

Sight-seeing through Wamena was a lesson in cultural incongruity. The streets were gridded in much the way they would be in small-town America, yet there were virtually no motor vehicles. Many of the government offices and dwellings were of a modern design and construction but were within spitting distance of the Balim River, home of the warlike Dani people, made famous by Robert Gardner's classic movie *Dead Birds*.

Walking down the dirt paths, one encountered clusters of Indonesian youths who giggled and boldly shouted "Hello Mister! Where are you going? Where do you come from?" so as to exercise the English learned in school. With my camera around my neck, I encountered a Dani man in his traditional state of undress—a colorful headband, and ornamental penis sheath made from a dried gourd, a string bag, and nothing else. I was amazed to see such sartorial "purity" amidst the modern streets of Wamena. I signaled to my camera and asked him *"poto?"* to which he replied: *"dua ratus rupiah."* He wanted two hundred rupiah for the privilege of photographing him! So much for cultural purity.

I was in for an unpleasant surprise that night. Preparing to sleep, I turned off the lights and climbed into the modular bed, set in the curved wall. Within a minute I heard the high whine of a mosquito. It landed on my cheek and I brushed it off. I then heard the whine grow as more mosquitoes came to hover over my bed. The little beasts attacked by the hundreds, having free access through the ripped-out screens of the bathroom windows. They must have been breeding in profusion in the network of tiny drainage ditches that serve as the local plumbing. Closing the bathroom door did no good because the mosquitoes could enter through the space between it and the floor. I was beginning to despair when I remembered that I had a mountain tent. I flipped on the light and set up the tent on the wall-to-wall carpeting, right in the middle of the room. I guyed the ropes to shoes, bags, and boxes. Once inside this little safe haven I slept peacefully.

The next morning I greeted the Australian ambassador at breakfast, only to find that he suffered a miserable, sleepless night, the victim of the voracious mosquitoes. In spite of being ambassador, his room was no better than mine. He, however, had no mountain tent for refuge.

Sawmill Forest

That same morning I was met by my guides and took them to the MAF office so that one of the missionaries fluent in Indonesian could tell them, in detail, what I wished to do. I had made a list of the critical phrases I needed to communicate: *bikin api*, "make a fire"; *makan*, "food"; *burung*, "bird"; *Saya mau pergi ke hutan*, "I want to go to the forest." I figured things would work themselves out, simply because I had done this same sort of thing in Papua New Guinea in 1975, at a time when I knew few Pidgin words.

The three of us took off, each of us carrying a load. We ascended the course of the swift Wamena Creek, a broad torrent that emptied out of the main ranges to the south. There would be no wading across this one. We crossed it on a small bridge under construction by the government, and then we took a tributary that led us southeastward toward the forest and the mountain wall. We passed gardens and small Dani settlements. Everyone was quite cheerful, and, of course, much surprised to see a white face passing through their neighborhood.

The typical Dani village is small and well laid out. It is usually a compact cluster of low thatched huts, surrounded by a stout protective

Dani men in traditional dress, Balim valley

fence. Casuarinas and bananas are planted around this fence, which is ringed by gardens. Thus, when looking across the valley, one could make out dull green patches of the casuarina groves, each marking the site of a small settlement. The gardens are very tidy and well tended. All of this gives the impression of industry. The Dani are hard-working people.

This impression was fortified by my next encounter. As we toiled up a small path that led into the forest, we noticed that lengths of cut timber had been left leaning against trees beside the trail. I gave this little thought until we came up to an elderly Dani, clad only in his penis gourd, carrying one of these lengths of timber. It must have been very heavy, since all of this timber was hardwood. He rested the timber and spoke with my guides. I could make out that he was earning cash by portering timbers from a sawmill in the forest down to town, where they were sold for construction. He was paid a small fee for each timber brought to market.

I soon found that I was being led directly to the sawmill. Before long, we had entered the very lush forest on the first slopes of the great mountains. Birds were calling all around, and I heard familiar notes from a Friendly Fantail and Black-breasted Boatbill—forest birds common back in the hills above Wau.

We made our camp in the small clearing where there were two tiny huts and lots of stacked timber. A small brook tumbled over a rocky course where several Torrentlarks squawked and dabbled. This was the "sawmill." In fact, the timber operation was nothing more than two young Indonesians and a long timber saw. Everything was accomplished by hand. I did not meet the men until after dark, when they returned to camp in a steady rain, soaking wet, but cheerful and friendly. They did not in the least resent my intrusion.

I was lucky to be camped here, because the forest had been opened slightly and made more accessible by the web of trails that had been cleared for the timber extraction. Before the rain, I quietly walked about in search of birds. The bird of the day was the all-black Short-tailed Paradigalla, one of the atypical birds of paradise. Little is known of its habits, mainly, it seems, because the bird is relatively unobtrusive. It is still unknown whether the male exhibits the flamboyant polygamous behavior typical of its more colorful cousins. The bird is not entirely without adornment. Both sexes possess the brightly colored blue-and-yellow wattles that mark its forehead and mouth, although the male's are brighter. I watched an individual hopping through midstory vegetation, probing moss and bark in search of arthropods with its long, slender bill. The only calls I heard it give were froglike croaks and scolds—not the loud cries that typify most of the polygamous species.

I learned something of the sawyers' methods the following day when I visited their current work site. The two would select a forest tree, fell it, then cut the trunk into segments. This, in itself, must take several days. They would then construct a scaffolding and work one of the sections of trunk onto this. They would proceed to mark, dress,

and cut the log in such a way as to produce lengths of needed timber—
$6'' \times 6''$, $4'' \times 4''$, $2'' \times 8''$, etc. I marveled at the patience and effort
required to produce the finished product. Each day, the men rose be-
fore dawn, cooked a large pot of white rice, consumed heaps of this
with some chilies and salt, packed what was left into small lunch pails,
and made off for the entire day, to return only after dark. They would
bathe vigorously in the icy brook, consume a dinner of more rice,
smoke and chat around the fire, then sleep. This was a very wet area,
and rain fell much of the time I was present. These men had to do
much of their backbreaking labor in the rain.

The second day, accompanied by one of the Irianese guides, I
hiked up the ridge in search of birds. The moss-laden forest was bathed
in heavy mists. As we struggled up the mountain trace, our clothing
was quickly soaked, but for some reason there were no leeches. This
was a pleasant surprise. I was excited to see, perched up on some of the
epiphyte-laden limbs, the huge white blossoms of a rhododendron. I
estimated the corolla to span five inches from lip to lip. This species,
Rhododendron leucogigas, has the largest flower known for any member of
the genus.

Next my eye was caught by the candelabralike fruiting head of an
epiphytic *Schefflera*. It was much like a species I knew from my study
area on Mount Missim, where it was popular with the birds of paradise.
I waited to see who might sample its ripe fruit, and before long I heard
a swishing of wings and an adult Splendid Astrapia, with its lovely
emerald green throat and its curious club-shaped tail, sailed into the
vine to feed. It made not a sound as it moved about, searching for the
best fruits. After half a minute it was gone, its wings giving the rustling
sound typical of this genus. Astrapias are characteristic birds of paradise of the Papuan mountain forests. Three species inhabit segments of
the main cordillera, and two others are found only in the isolated
mountains of the Huon Peninsula and the Vogelkop Peninsula, respectively. The species I found here, the Splendid Astrapia, ranges through
western Papua New Guinea and central Irian Jaya.

We moved yet higher up the ridge, far from any disturbance by
the encroaching civilization. We must have been following a Dani
hunting track. Gunandi, my guide, touched my sleeve and pointed in
the direction of a bird sound. I do not say "song" because the sound was

so unlike a song. It was a long, discordant, spitting and gurgling that continued for several seconds. What a bizarre concoction of notes! Although I had not heard this previously, I knew right away that it must be the infamous vocalization of the King of Saxony Bird of Paradise. Jared Diamond has written that the song "has such a weird quality that one is unlikely to suspect a bird as the author. It is a very dry rattling, a spitted jumble of insect-like notes poured out at a machinegun pace and suggestive of bad static on the radio, which briefly turns into a twittering at the climax of the crescendo." We tried, in vain, to see the author of this remarkable song, but it remained hidden in the misty canopy of the forest. This was one that got away. The next day I had to return to Wamena to prepare for the next leg of my trip.

Holuwon

Before visiting Irian Jaya I had corresponded with John and Gloria Wilson, Protestant missionaries who ran an isolated station on the south slopes of the central cordillera, where the tumbling Balim River cuts a deep gorge through the great wall of the Snow Mountains. The Wilsons' station was situated on one of the few relatively level spots in this terribly rugged gorge country. Level is a relative term, and to the pilot flying me into the airstrip, the term would probably not apply. My pilot, wearing a crash helmet, told me that the Holuwon strip was one of the more treacherous landing grounds in the area. It sloped steeply, was short, and very rough. I was the single passenger in the plane when the pilot skidded the single-engine Cessna up the grass-and-gravel landing strip.

I was now in Yali territory, one of the last parts of Irian Jaya pacified by mission and government influences. Much of the area was truly uncontrolled until the 1960s. This had been dangerous territory: one pioneering missionary had been butchered in a bloody raid by hostile Yali warriors. This was, to use a Pidgin expression, *bush tru*—"wild country." I would have to learn about it on my own, because the plane that brought me in was to carry the Wilson family out on their annual leave. They were very graciously allowing me to stay in their wonderful house, at the top of the airstrip, looking out over the foothills and low alluvial expanse of the Vriendschaps floodplain. Aside from a Dutch missionary at Ninia, a dozen miles to the north, I would be the only white-skinned person for many miles around, in a land starkly wild and with a people as "unwestern" as I had yet seen

———

The Yali territory is forbidding, steeply mountainous, rain-soaked country. This is an area that seems downright inhospitable and terribly demanding of the meager population that survives there. From the mission station I could see the nearest settlement on a knoll a few hundred meters away. It was a cluster of dwellings. The huts were very low and small. The people were small and wore very little clothing, in spite of the cool, damp, cloudy weather.

I spent two nights in the Wilsons' cozy house, being looked after by several of the Wilsons' Irianese assistants. One in particular, a youth named Sahaliek, was assigned by the Wilsons to be my guide, interpreter, and general factotum. He was one of the "city slickers." By this, I mean that he wore shorts and a T-shirt and spoke Indonesian. Most others spoke only Yali and wore only the traditional attire. Also assigned to me was a young hunter named Filile, who wore nothing but a penis gourd. Filile was the true Irianese "mountain man." He could walk interminably without appearing to tire; he carried my heavy backpack balanced on his head (the straps were too confining for him); and all the while he carried his bow with an arrow at the ready, in case some feathered morsel should appear within shooting range. I wanted to camp in the mountains above Holuwon, and Sahaliek and Filile would help me do this.

The third morning, we locked up the Wilsons' house and headed up the mountain. We first stopped at Filile's village of Yali Sili, no more than a dozen low circular huts, clustered on a flat bare ridgetop. The soil was sparse, and white limestone sand formed a barren playground for the naked children, who timidly fled to the protection of their parents as I approached. In Yali Sili I was seeing, for the first time, a New Guinean culture physically untouched by the influences of the West. As mountain people had traditionally done for centuries, they built their village on a ridge crest, where it was relatively safe from sudden enemy attack. Their huts were low, the walls formed by overlapping wooden planks driven into the ground, the roof made of thick layers of pandanus leaves. Each door, not more than a meter high, was barely two feet wide. The women about the huts were naked but for a small square of thatch, which hung strategically over the pubic area, fastened by two strings. The children, naked, bellies distended, clung to their mothers' legs in fear.

Looking about me, I had to wonder how these people managed to survive in this hostile land. Level terrain for gardens was nonexistent. The soil on the cleared, sloping patches of cultivation was poor. Rain fell in violent downpours. I was told that there is virtually no dry season. Crop failures are common. What a contrast to the sunny, lush, fertile Grand Valley a few minutes' flight to the northwest.

Filile picked up a few items at his hut, and we proceeded up the trail into the mountains. Dark gray clouds rested atop the higher ridges. I had a sense of foreboding. We labored upward, the trail a typical moss forest trace. The forest interior was dank and depressing. I saw no birds.

For much of the length of New Guinea, the southern scarp of the central cordillera presents a harsh environment for settlement. The slopes are much steeper than those on the north. The rain is heavier, and the conditions are more demanding for the inhabitant and naturalist alike. The northern slopes are a joy by comparison. This point was brought home in Yali territory. In the four nights I camped atop the ridge above Yali Sili, rain pestered us on and off for most of the day and night.

Birds were few in this patch of forest. Thanks to generations of skillful and dedicated hunters, the wildlife was scant, and skittish. I had to be content with hearing birds call from inaccessible spots. That was tantalizing, at best. A song I attributed to Loria's Bird of Paradise, a musical note (*kerrrng!*), was delivered dozens of times an hour from the canopy foliage not far from our camp lean-to. I never saw the bird, in spite of repeated efforts to locate it. Even more frustrating, daily I had to listen to the far-carrying, liquid *kwiik kwiik* notes of the mighty Black Sicklebill ringing from a neighboring ridge. This is the largest bird of paradise and one of the more elusive species. We tried to make our way over to the bird, but without success. It seemed that no large birds lived within arrowshot of the hunting trail on which we had camped.

The afternoons were deathly silent, punctuated only by the occasional flock of Papuan Mountain Pigeons racing overhead with the whistling of wings, or the screeching calls of a small flock of Josephine's Lorikeets.

How could hunting by a small Yali population, equipped with nothing besides bows and arrows, have such a noticeable impact on vertebrate populations? For the Yali people, wildlife was their main source of protein. I saw no livestock of any sort in the two villages I visited, though I am told domestic pigs are present in small numbers. The men spent many days a year hunting for the necessities of life— game for the table. I saw no evidence of cassowaries or wild pigs. This means that the people had to obtain their meat from birds, cuscuses, wallabies, tree kangaroos, and forest rats. The mammals would be hunted using dogs, while the birds would be hunted by stealth and with blinds. On our hike up, I came to understand the prowess of the true hunter when Filile shot down a small tiger-parrot that had been perched thirty feet up in the vegetation. He did this as we were hiking and as he was carrying a head load of gear. He dropped the pack and released the multipronged arrow before I knew anything was up. I heard the sound of the arrow and bird dropping out of the tree. This bird weighed no more than a few ounces. Everything was fair game.

Further up the track, Filile pointed out a blind he had built high in a tree. He indicated that the colorful lorikeets would visit the flowering *Schefflera* vine that grew in the adjacent tree. Filile had built the blind in anticipation of this year's flowering, during which time he would perch in the little blind for a number of days, shooting any and all birds that came to take nectar. The Yali people knew the habits of the birds and the seasons of the plants. With this information they could crop the forest's available protein supply in a remarkably effective manner. This was good for their livelihood, but it was unfortunate for me, the bird-watcher.

The nets I set captured no birds of interest. My walks in the forest were frustrating. I decided to head back down to Holuwon. After a night in the luxury of the mission station (fresh bread baked by Sahaliek, stacks of *National Geographic* to read), I regrouped and led our party southward from the airstrip to examine the forest below the mission station.

This decision was a mistake. We hiked into a "barren," an impoverished, scrubby forest dominated by casuarina and pandanus. Epiphytic *Freycinetia* was abundant, as were *Nepenthes* pitcher plants and a lovely peach-colored rhododendron (*R. zoelleri*). In five hours, I recorded only three species of birds: a tiny myzomela, a whistler, and a robin. We were in a white-sand barren, a peculiar ecological formation that appears in various parts of the southern scarp of the central ranges. It is an ornithological desert because of botanical impoverishment. Bird populations are so low that doing a census is akin to pulling teeth. I spent a single night in this god-forsaken site before returning to Holuwon. I had discovered that the good forest, up the hill, was apparently overhunted, and the poor forest below Holuwon, rarely visited by the Yali people, was almost devoid of birdlife because of a quirk in the geology and botany of the area.

Thus, the trip down into Yali territory was an ornithological disappointment, but I had a glimpse of what much of New Guinea had been like in earlier times. I could also see, graphically, the struggle these Yali people faced every day of the year. In the battle to subdue nature and create an environment benign and fruitful, the Yali people were only marginally successful. These were a people fighting for survival. I was not sad to leave Yali territory, a land resistant to human settlement.

Lake Habbema

Upon my return to Wamena from Holuwon, I spent a day cleaning up and getting reorganized, and then I hired three field assistants who had a knowledge of the high country southwest of town. I was headed to Lake Habbema, the site, in 1938, of the most important field camp of the Archbold Expedition to the Snow Mountains.

In 1974, while visiting the American Museum of Natural History in New York, I closely examined the wonderful diorama of a Lake Habbema vista. All of the plant and bird specimens shown in the exhibit were collected and preserved by the scientific staff of the Archbold Expedition in October 1938. I spent several minutes scrutinizing the encapsulated version of the spectacular natural features and exotic birdlife. I never dreamed that in 1980 I would be the first ornithologist to return to the lake since the Archbold team departed, forty-two years earlier.

My visit to Lake Habbema was a product of chance. I had no plans to make the trek, but an MAF staff member mentioned that the teenaged children of some of the missionaries would occasionally hike up to the lake just for fun. If they could do it, then I could, as well. I pressed the man for as many details as possible. He told me that there were two ways of approaching the lake, one from the west and one from the east. I decided that I would make a loop, hiking up by the eastern route, via Wamena Creek, Illare, and Wellesi. I would return by heading due north to the head of the Ibele (Bele) valley, which would lead back to the Grand Valley, and thence back to Wamena.

I was chafing to get up to Habbema, especially after my disappointment with the birdlife around Holuwon. Three mountain men were assigned to the job of guiding me. They were associated with the mission station in Sinatma. After stopping at the market to purchase onions and rice, we made our way up the Wamena Creek, and by late afternoon were at Sinatma Mission. Here I pitched my tent, in anticipation of a very early departure for the mountains the next morning.

===

Our first few hours of walking were very pleasant, with a gradual ascent through tribal lands. We followed a narrowing stream valley and crossed the white-water river twice, where it was spanned by remarkable suspension bridges, hand constructed of vines by the villagers. I was hard pressed to imagine how they accomplished this until, outside of the last village, we found a group of men in the process of making a new bridge. We ate lunch and watched them form a human chain to carry the heavy, twisted canes across the torrent in order to suspend them from several large streamside trees. The men shouted lustily as they resisted the chilling cold of the water and the force of the stream. All were dressed without a trace of western clothing. Looking around, I felt a thrill of excitement at being here, surrounded by scenery and culture that must have looked little different in 1938 or even 1838.

We rested briefly at Wellesi, and it was here that Ernis, the self-appointed leader of our group, made a request from the villagers for a

Rope Bridge, near Wamena, Balim valley

week's worth of *ubi* (sweet potato). My guides had sagely realized that it would have been silly to pay a premium price at the Wamena market when, at a lower price, *ubi* could be had, garden fresh, at the last outpost of human settlement before our ascent into the mountain forest.

I was feeling good at this last village. Before long, however, I was gasping for air and cursing under my breath. The track that led into the forest began to climb steeply, but my men kept up their pace as they struggled toward Uli Guli, our afternoon's destination. The track, already treacherous and slick from previous rains, worsened as new precipitation began to fall, first as a mist, then as steady rain.

By four o'clock I was ready to give up. In English, I asked my men whether we should stop and make a shelter from the rain. I was angry and tired. Politely, they signaled that we go on, for everyone's good. My anger rose, but an hour later, when we broke out of the forest at Uli Guli, I could understand why they had wished to press onward, in spite of the hardship. Uli Guli was a small, marshy, frost-pocket at about eight thousand feet above sea level. Surrounded by forested hills, the bottom of this depression was entirely grassy, like a miniature alpine basin. In the middle of the sump stood five low huts, one of which we would use for our night's camp. There were clear water, plenty of firewood, and a beautiful open vista in all directions—an improvement over the dank forest where the myriad roots and saplings would have made setting a camp well-nigh impossible.

Nothing is so pleasurable as dropping one's pack and knowing it can be left until the next day. The smell of a wood fire and the metallic gurgling of water boiling for hot tea all gave a sense of elation and freedom—the reward of a hard day's exertion. I was rewarded ornithologically by the abundant and conspicuous birdlife that moved through the habitat around me. First, a Grass Owl coursed over the marshy vegetation, in much the manner that a Short-eared Owl hunts the winter marshes of the eastern United States. I will never become accustomed to seeing an owl foraging during the afternoon. Then, a crisply plumaged Western Alpine Mannikin, a small black-faced finch, flitted above the grass, carrying nesting material. A second species new to me, and one of my first Snow Mountain endemics! I flushed an unidentified snipe from one of the wet spots, while several Island Thrushes, calling discordantly, moved warily through the shrubbery of the hillside. Things were improving. Dinner tasted ever so sweet as the dark closed in on Uli Guli.

Early the next morning our packs were filled and the four of us began the march to the lake. We moved through tracts of stunted forest and expanses of grassland as we ascended to the great upland valley that parallels the northern scarp of the mighty Trikora Range. Grasslands dominated the broad floor of the valley, whereas the remnant forest prospered only on the hillsides that surrounded the upland basin through which we hiked. By late morning we could see the lake, and I was impressed by its size. It was hemmed in by low hills cloaked in scrubby forest, and to the south rose the great granite mass of Mount Wilhelmina (now called Mount Trikora)—at 15,558 feet, the island's second highest mountain. This vista called to mind the diorama of the museum in New York—here was nature's model for the lovely painted background of that display.

Seeing the lake before me, I assumed we were near our destination; but it was late in the afternoon before we arrived at a campsite that satisfied my guides. I found that we had to hike from the southeast end of the lake to the northwest end, and all the while, of course, in my ignorance I complained about what seemed to me a needless waste of effort, and of course, the men knew exactly what they were doing. One of them had been to the lake and knew of a hunter's hut that would be warm and dry—an ideal place for them to pass the cold nights while I slept in my tent.

We spent six days at the lakeside camp, and during this time I explored the finest alpine environment that New Guinea has to offer. The weather, remarkably, was rainless, with frosty mornings and warm, sunny, blue-sky afternoons. Each day I could gaze across the broad lake to the summit of Trikora. I wanted to climb that peak, but I realized that it was much farther than it looked. There was plenty for me to do right where I was.

=====

The plant life was remarkable, in part for its oddity, and also for its relative poverty of species. Fewer species inhabit the higher altitudes, but many of these are peculiar, little-known forms, confined to the high ranges, many endemic to the Snow Mountains. The most prominent components of the flora were two species of coniferous trees, several large shrubs, a *Schefflera*, a large ant plant, and some rhododendrons and their allies. Though the flora was not as diverse as the botanical riches in the lowland forest, everything, being novel, was of interest.

Rhododendrons flourished here, and every one was new to me. The common shrublike species (*R. versteeghi*) displayed hanging clusters of red-and-yellow, bell-shaped flowers. On the slopes of the rocky lateral moraine south of the lake grew the delicate *R. revolutum*, one of the deep "reds" with a short, flaring corolla. Most remarkable of all was tiny *R. saxifragoides*, which formed a ground-level herbaceous mat in boggy parts of the lakeside grasslands. The leaves of this species stood no more than an inch or two above the duff, and the most prominent feature of the plant was the single red flower that rose from a slight stalk from the mat of leaves.

The most peculiar plant around, and the most obvious to the visitor, was the huge, tuberous ant plant of the genus *Myrmecodia*. This grew like a barrel cactus on the ground and also epiphytically in the upper parts of the conifers. The plant is mostly a bulbous stem about two feet high that is bristling with sharp spines; it is topped by a few green leaves. The entire plant looks like a bloated and oversized porcupine fish planted head down into the ground. The fat stem (as much as a foot in diameter) is full of hollow chambers—no ants here, though, since we were above the altitude that ants can survive in New Guinea.

I saw not a mammal in this habitat. That is, I suppose, typical of New Guinea. Most mammal species, being nocturnal, are difficult to find. The annual depredation of hunters also has its effect. We had settled at a hunters' camp, so it was not surprising that the tree kangaroos and wallabies were scarce. The repeated culling, year after year, can greatly reduce the population levels of any large vertebrates.

Of course, I had not hiked to Lake Habbema to observe mammals. I was here for birds, and I was not disappointed. I watched, netted, and handled some species, such as the Orange-cheeked Honeyeater, Short-bearded Melidectes, and Snow Mountain Quail, that have been observed by only a handful of western naturalists in the decades since their discovery. The honeyeater was a big, unwary creature that moved along the forest's edge and often visited small patches of shrubby vegetation far from the forest proper. The melidectes did not differ much in habits, except that it was more wary. The quail was perhaps the prize of the trip, having been encountered by naturalists only once or twice since the turn of the century. I spent five days walking the grasslands around camp before seeing it. I was beginning to wonder whether the bird existed, when I flushed a single individual from some woody scrub. It rocketed up from the thick vegetation, giving a loud, squealing double note. Once I got over the initial fright and the excitement of finding the bird, I was impressed by the size of what I had seen—this bobwhite-sized bird dwarfs the other puny quail species that inhabit New Guinea.

I described the bird to my assistants, and they told me it was an edible treat that they hunted when up in these grasslands. I asked how they would procure such a secretive and agile beast, and they told me that it would be shot down in flight with an arrow, which I found hard to believe until a few days later, when we scared up six of the birds in the open grasslands. Elias, who had an arrow in his bow, quickly shot into the group of birds, just missing one.

Lake Habbema is a big, beautiful montane lake that is roughly the shape of a kidney. Its deep blue waters reflect the surrounding ridges and grey granite peaks, as well as the rich colors of the sky. I never tired of sitting and looking at this pristine body of water. It was a haven for water birds. Repeatedly I watched a single Great Egret wing its way across the lake. Was this a resident or a wandering migrant? I assume that the Eurasian Coots and Salvadori's Teal that paddled about near the shore were breeders. Little Pied Cormorants dived for fish and moved across the water like low-riding submarines. This was their peaceful corner of the world.

———

Since I was spending nearly a week around the lake I was determined to focus my attention on some particular bird species. The choice of topic was settled when we found that a confiding pair of Macgregor's Bird of Paradise inhabited the copse of trees just below our campsite. Velvety black, crowlike, with an ochre wing patch and orange eye wattle, the species was striking. This bird is rarely observed, not because it is elusive, but because it inhabits a high mountain environment that few naturalists visit.

Each morning I would get up at dawn and walk down to the grove of stately *Dacrycarpus* trees where the pair roosted. Snug in my down parka, I would sit in the frost-covered grass and watch the birds' coming and going. They would sit for hours in this copse and never left it for very long. It was obvious that they had a real attachment to this site. Such a sedentariness and faithfulness to a small patch of habitat is unusual for a bird of paradise, but this species is unlike any other.

I assumed there were more of these birds around, but I had not seen any. I decided to try to census the population in the forest on the northwestern side of the lake and spent several mornings in search of other pairs. I found that they were habitat specialists. I never encountered pairs in the large expanses of scrubby *Libocedrus*, the dominant tree around the lake. Instead, they were invariably associated with small groves of *Dacrycarpus*.

Rand had noted this close relationship between Macgregor's Bird of Paradise and the *Dacrycarpus* tree. He found that this plant produced fruit that was a favorite component of the bird's diet. My census showed that the birds were scattered in small numbers through the habitat, basing their centers of activity on patches of *Dacrycarpus*. It was evident that Macgregor's Bird of Paradise is a specialist, with an important dependence on a single species of woody plant.

My three assistants enjoyed themselves during our stay beside the lake. They had plenty of food, good weather, and a cozy house for sleeping out of the cold. The hunter's house was built for warmth. A fire smoldered in the center of the earthen floor all day and night. This meant that the house was perpetually filled with thick smoke, which could escape only by slowly seeping through the thatch. The only way I could remain in the house without becoming asphyxiated was to lie down with my head close to the floor. The assistants were immune to this pollution and were amused at my suffering. Since I had my tent, I was not forced to sleep in these conditions.

For me, my guides' most startling habit was their devotion to ebullient Christian worship. They delivered a loud prayer before each meal, in Indonesian. One of the three would speak the prayer, and the other two would chime in at key points with what sounded like particular refrains. The prayer's delivery, punctuated by exuberant shouts of O *Tuhan* (O Lord), would carry a great distance. I was impressed by the vigor of their declared faith and felt uncomfortable for not joining in these frequent services. The men seemed to take my absence with equanimity, however, and generally held forth inside the house, while I was outside, guiltily enjoying my portion of our camp meal.

The Christian religion is an important part of Irianese culture and society. The Christian missions continue to maintain a large presence in western New Guinea, in spite of the fact that Indonesia is a Muslim state. Any visitor to Papua New Guinea knows the mission influence there, yet it seems that the missions are even more important in the West. The reason for this may be that the level of village development is generally lower in Irian, and the available government resources for regional development are fewer. Along with the religion, the missions provide a critical source of expert and dedicated personnel who often have access to the best of western technology.

Education, literacy, and health programs are the most obvious practical contributions that missions make to the people of New

Guinea. These alone have a significant impact on the diverse societies on this island. Purists criticize the missions for their deleterious effect on the maintenance of indigenous traditions, yet this criticism is based on the unreasonable assumption that, in the absence of missions, no other equally strong outside influences would take their place. Change in the southwest Pacific is a fact of life. The missions give the people clear benefits, and in some cases actually help to slow the loss of many aspects of traditional culture that are worth preserving.

———

Lake Habbema's environment was free of unwanted distractions. The sun shone every day. The frosty mornings were as bracing and invigorating as an October day in New England. Mount Trikora was always in view. The sun, blue sky, the lake, and the grasslands made for such an open, cheerful habitat, that it bore no resemblance to the dark, dank, closed-in forest that dominated so much of New Guinea's land area.

On our last day, we visited the site of the base camp of the Archbold Expedition, where many exciting zoological and botanical discoveries had been made, thanks to the adventurous spirit of the members of that pioneering expedition.

Richard Archbold, a son of heirs to the Standard Oil fortune, grew up in the twenties when "adventure" was a favored career of those well-to-do young gentlemen who did not "fit in." He became a pilot and amateur mammalogist and financed, in conjunction with New York's American Museum of Natural History, seven daring and exceedingly productive biological field expeditions to the New Guinea region. Three of these he led himself, often piloting personnel and supplies under adverse conditions. These were, indeed, heroic exploits in the heady days before World War II.

The Archbold camp clearing was still evident, after more than forty years. A few rusting food containers marked the spot on the south side of the lake. In lowland forest, all signs of a campsite are gone within a few years. In the high mountains, the return to the natural state is very slow, and every disturbance leaves a mark that can be seen decades later.

After a week, we packed up and began our trek out. That morning the fog was thick on the grasslands and lake, and as we moved along the lake's edge we could see a pair of Salvadori's Teal making small wakes on the still water. A myriad of spiders' webs caught the mist and shimmered in the weak sunlight. The air was chill and damp. This was our first morning of fog, and we were now ready to be heading down to a warmer clime.

Our hike back by way of Ibele allowed me to see another part of the country. I realized it would take me down the route of the Archbold Expedition's walking track between the lake and their Bele River Camp. It was along this route that they had collected the first specimens of *Archboldia papuensis*—the nearly mythical Archbold's Bowerbird.

The track that led down to Ibele was well marked. We climbed up a low morainal ridge, and after cresting this we were in damp subalpine forest. The trail abruptly dropped off the high plateau into a deep, forested valley. Our knees took a brutal punishing as we had to ease our way down this steep decline. When we encountered our first tiny settlement, after about five hours of walking, I begged the men to stop for a rest and some *ubi*. We talked with some people in their gardens, and they handed us some fresh-dug potatoes and pointed out their hut. Once inside, my eyes burned from the smoke, but I was glad to be off my feet and aching legs. We had been without sweet potatoes for several days; we roasted a dozen, and I watched in amazement as Ernis happily wolfed down three of them in what seemed like less than a minute. A fire-blackened sweet potato is a marvelous treat after a long morning on the road.

In spite of the rest, the afternoon march was painful. We were no longer dropping steeply, but instead were weaving around the side of a rugged river valley in wild, but populated country. Even by New Guinean standards, this was the boondocks. We continued to walk on, and I was fading fast when finally the shout of the men announced our arrival at the Ibele mission station. There stood a small western-style homestead and tiny airstrip. I walked to the front door, knocked, and was greeted by an American missionary in his late twenties. Sporting a football jersey and bright smile, he welcomed me to Ibele. I was bearded, unwashed, and hungry. The missionary and his wife took me in, heated water for a long, soaking, hot bath, and revived me with a cup of hot tea and some fresh-cooked doughnuts. That day I had hiked from a little-visited subalpine plateau, down through muddy montane forest, and into a dream of comfort at the mission homestead. My guides had friends here at Ibele and were able to celebrate their return to civilization with a feast of fresh food, which we had sorely missed up top. I slept in clean sheets after a delicious supper.

My physical trials were not over; the next morning, after departing the hospitality of the Ibele mission, the four of us had to make our way back to Wamena—about twelve miles on foot. As we dropped lower into the Ibele valley, the vista opened, the valley floor broadened, and the sun rose higher and hotter. Once we reached the junction of the Ibele and Grand valleys, the sun was atop the sky, the wide expanses of grasslands shimmered, and the heated air began to catch thickly in my throat. The march had only begun. At this point, there was nothing more to look at, the adventure was over, and it was simply a matter of making our way home to Wamena. I learned, the hard way, that the Ibele route was considerably longer than the Sinatma route. This was the inglorious end of my first adventure to Irian.

My return to Papua New Guinea was not uneventful. Initially I was refused entry into Papua New Guinea because I did not hold a vaccination card with a recent cholera shot. I was told that I would have to charter a small plane and return to Irian immediately. Thank heavens that, at times, the rules in Papua New Guinea can be bent. After much hand-wringing and pleading, I was allowed to quarantine myself for three days in Wewak, my port of entry, before traveling back to Wau. I was not, by the way, carrying cholera, and all was well back in Wau.

I have twice returned to Irian to look for birds, but in neither instance could I recapture the wonder of that first visit. Things are changing fast there, so it is with a sense of anxiousness that I admit that I long to spend another week in western New Guinea that might equal my stay at Lake Habbema—with the deep blue cloudless sky; the early morning sun melting the frost from the brown tufted grass; the green of shrubbery lit here and there by the crimson of flowering rhododendrons and fruiting *Scheffleras*; a blurred reflection of Mount Trikora in the dark waters of the lake; and the high, sweet, whining sound of air ripping through the flight feathers of Macgregor's Bird of Paradise as it glides across an alpine clearing.

Opposite: Honeymoon Camp vista, Kakoro

8   Jungle Camps

I spent more than two years in New Guinea before I decided to do some fieldwork in lowland rainforest. I had long been put off by stories of the heat, the humidity, the swarming mosquitoes, and the general unhealthiness of the lowland environment. Few of my associates had spent any amount of time in the lowland forest, but after all this time, I needed to broaden my horizons and learn something of the birdlife of this great unknown—New Guinea's jungle habitats.

Ninga's Camp

In 1979 I chose to set up a field camp in the Lakekamu basin, across the central range almost due south of Wau. This basin supports a large expanse of lowland alluvial rainforest. The closest airfield was the tiny grass strip at Kakoro village, on the Biaru River. This site was only a twenty-minute flight from Wau, and it supported a very small human population, so the forests would be relatively undisturbed. I was accompanied on the trip to Kakoro by Ninga Kawa, my chief field assistant.

Our pilot flew us over the Ekuti Divide and down into the Lakekamu lowlands. My gut filled with butterflies as we circled the riverside landing ground in the flat terrain before us. In the hills around Wau we could catch a fresh breeze and have the cool refreshment of a tumbling brook, but I was sure this would not be so in the sumpy alluvial forest, which I dreaded. The strip was very rough, and the twin-engine Norman-Britten Islander bounced and jumped to a stop. As usual, a crowd of ever-curious children surrounded the plane, and before long our bags were hefted and carried to Kakoro village. The cool air of the Wau valley had been traded for dense, soggy, warm air of a near sea-level village clearing. Here we arranged for porters and a guide to take us into the forest.

By early afternoon Ninga and I had begun to clear a dry and uncluttered patch of ground beside a beautiful stony stream filled with perfectly clear, cool water. Our Kakoro guide had led us to an ideal camping spot at the base of the hills, just above the flat alluvial plain that stretched southward without relief. Once our camp was established I was ready to begin learning the lowland forest birdlife. I started by setting some mist nets. Most of the avian voices I heard that first day were unfamiliar. The birdlife at two hundred feet above sea level is quite distinct from that at five thousand. Our nets were productive, and almost immediately we were encountering birds new to us.

The Hooded Pitohui we knew in Wau was replaced with the very sociable Rusty Pitohui, a larger and nasty-tempered creature that travels in vocal flocks. The Slaty-chinned Longbill so common on Mount Missim was absent, and in its place was its relative, the Yellow-bellied Longbill, nearly identical, except that it had a sweeter call. Here we found the low-altitude relatives of the montane species that were so familiar to us in the Wau valley.

———

After a few days, we cut a new net lane down toward the swamp forest. Ninga and I worked for several hours to clear an open path through the jungle. Although the air temperature in the forest interior was not much above eighty degrees Fahrenheit, we were soaked with sweat and grime when we completed this trail. The humidity is near saturation point in this sort of closed forest, and this is never so apparent as when swing-

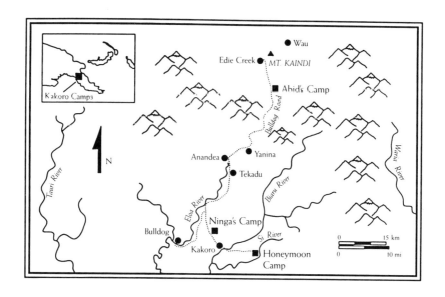

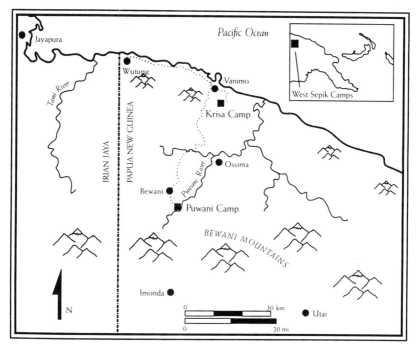

Jungle camps near Kakoro (Ninga's Camp, Honeymoon Camp)
and in the West Sepik (Puwani Camp, Krisa Camp)

ing a bush knife. Our trail led all the way down to the swamp edge, and it was a stark change from the forest where I had first set the nets. Here in the low zone the ground was flat, dark with decaying vegetation. Tiny blackwater streams threaded through the forest. Big *Orania* palms were scattered about in the middle story, mixed with the abundant pandanus that were virtually absent in the dry areas above our camp. I was mesmerized by the swamp forest itself: the ground dropped another several feet, and instead of sumpy ground, there was dark, standing water. Pandanus, unidentified water-loving, broad-leaved species, and tall Sago Palms dominated this menacing-looking environment.

At this swampy edge I came upon a most interesting observation spot. I found a fruiting tree of the genus *Glochidion* (family Euphorbiaceae) whose orange capsular fruit attracted an array of frugivorous birds. A fallen log provided a convenient seat for me, and over the next several days I learned the subtle art of "sit-and-wait" natural history. In the lowland rainforest this is a technique that requires patience and forbearance, but which often pays off in valuable observations. I prepared by wearing a long-sleeved shirt and long pants, socks, hat, and a powerful insect repellent. I then simply waited and watched.

The first wildlife to arrive were the day-flying mosquitoes. They made for the ears, tip of the nose, and neck. It was then that forbearance was required. One must not jerk about, swatting insects, for this would frighten away the animals one had come to observe.

I sat and sat. A miniscule, jewellike Little Kingfisher came and perched on a twig in the low understory. It called *tseet!* and then the blue-and-white pixie zipped off when I swatted a mosquito. Next, a flock of Metallic Starlings hurled themselves into the fruiting tree. They noisily gamboled from clump to clump and shortly were joined by a small flock of Orange-breasted Fig-Parrots. Were these little gems after fruit pulp or seeds? I had assumed fig-parrots visited only fig trees.

I heard a loud rustling of leaves. Cassowary? Wallaby? The sound continued, out-of-sight, from a point behind my back. I waited breathlessly as the mosquitoes continued to feast through my cotton shirt. The noisy creature marched around the fallen log and, failing to notice my motionless form, zigzagged right past me. It was a Thick-billed Ground-Pigeon. Crow sized, this little-seen forest bird sports a small crest, ivory bill, and gray tail that is held folded, tentlike, and which is rhythmically jerked downward.

When waiting expectantly for wildlife, the rustling of a creature's footsteps on the forest floor always sounds like those of something much larger. I had supposed the ground-pigeon might be a young cassowary. Such an illusion is further enhanced at night, when a small bandicoot can sound like a wallaby, something ten times its size.

The pigeon was gone when my attention was drawn to the fruiting tree by the sound of heavy wings. I glimpsed a bright pink pair of legs, attached to a weird-looking bird with a long black bill, red eye, black cap, and cinnamon back and wings—a female Twelve-wired Bird of Paradise. She flushed when I lifted my binoculars. A few minutes of silence passed when my ears were confused by a sharp *tss tss tss tss tss tss* as another large bird entered the tree. I very slowly scanned the tree. Through the thick foliage I could make out a form that showed yellow and black. Before gaining a full view, I heard the sharp *tss* sound of the wings and the creature was gone. An adult male Twelve-wired Bird of Paradise had left the tree for the refuge of the palm-studded swamp forest. I heard its loud *babr!* notes and the rich, deep *Koi, koi koi koi koi* call from about two hundred yards off. This was the first time I was able to associate that prominent vocalization with a species name. This bird of paradise was remarkably elusive and wary, but learning the call was a coup, for it meant that in subsequent field work I could census the bird vocally, without actually having to see the individuals. For this alone, my time sitting on the fallen log was well spent.

Rainforest

What makes a tropical rainforest? In New Guinea, the classic forms of this forest habitat develop on flat and well-drained alluvial soils deposited by the abundant rivers that rush out of the mountains. Tumbling down from the uplands, a river travels at high speed and can carry great quantities of silt, rock, and soil. As the river flushes out onto a flat plain, its water loses speed and can no longer carry its heavy burden of sediment, which is deposited along the river banks, actually reshaping the river's course in the process. Periodic flooding forces the river over these banks and spreads the lightest sediments far out into the forest.

On these nutrient-rich beds of riverine sediments grow New Guinea's finest rainforests.

There is no single "true rainforest." Different forest botanists will disagree about use of the term. I confine my usage here to tall lowland humid forest that develops great structural and floristic complexity under conditions of high humidity and constant benign temperatures. Rainforest is typified by a complete and regular canopy, usually more than one hundred feet high. Much of the available sunlight is captured by this upper stratum. Thus, the building block of a rainforest is a tall canopy tree, dozens of which stand, side by side, on each acre of forest. While they are tall, these typically are not as great in girth as the larger temperate forest trees, and this may be because of the fierce competition for sunlight and the lessened need for protection against strong winds. The trees have devoted more energy to grow tall rather than robust.

Rainforest trees differ from temperate trees in other ways. Often the root systems are shallow, and physical support is, in many species, provided by basal buttressing or stilt roots. Most rainforest trees are smooth barked, perhaps an evolutionary attempt (often unsuccessful) to avoid the burden of vines, the larger lianas, and stranglers. The last three are a common feature of lowland rainforest, and they are the primary component of the "green wall" at the forest's edge.

A well-developed lowland rainforest in New Guinea is quite unlike the thick and tangled "jungle" of popular movies. The interior is often quite open. Ferns, small palms, and gingers grow near the ground, but it is easy to walk about relatively unhindered except at light gaps created by the fall of a canopy tree. In the finest rainforests, the big trees are widely spaced, and in many instances their green canopies are remarkably broad. Between these giants grow an array of understory palms with sprays of dark green leaves, spiny rattans, and young broadleaved trees of various ages, from tiny saplings to decades-old, submature individuals, waiting for a light gap to open in the canopy.

The palms, ferns, and gingers are perfectly suited to inhabit the dim underworld near the forest floor. Their oversized leaves, many bizarrely shaped, are adapted to this habitat. Such is not the case for the offspring of canopy trees, rattans, and vines. These all share a fate begun when the seed from which they sprout hits the ground. The sapling must struggle up toward the light until an opening breaks.

While hiking through a mature forest in New England, one's feet will rustle through a deep deposit of leaf litter, something one normally does not hear in a lowland rainforest. On sites close to a watercourse, it is common to have a muddy forest floor devoid of leaves, detritus, and humus. On higher sites there may be a light covering of litter over a net of fine rootlets that many of the smaller plants put out in search of nutrients.

One finds familiar "house plants" in the Papuan rainforest understory. Air plants (Araceae) with large floppy leaves hanging off thick succulent vines creep up large tree trunks. Prickly begonias cover wet spots on the forest floor. Geometric palms of various sizes and shapes abound in swampy spots. All of these prosper in low light situations, and that is why they succeed in offices and homes that rarely see a direct shaft of sunlight.

The lowland rainforest is often frustrating to the inquisitive zoologist or botanist. For both, much of the natural life dwells in the canopy. To identify tree species, one may require a sample of the leaves, flowers, and fruit. The nearest sample may be waving in the breeze ninety or more feet overhead. Some botanists in Malaysia have employed pet monkeys to clamber up into the trees to pluck these botanical samples. The New Guinea naturalist often must use a high-powered rifle with a telescopic sight.

———

New Guinea is one of the wettest areas on earth, receiving, on average, more than eighty inches a year. Some of the wetter sites receive three or four times this average. The abundance of water fosters rich growth of vegetation, and it is this plant life that provides the gross physical structure of the environment to which the animal life must adapt.

One of the marvels of the rainforest, though, is the remarkably high level of interactions between plant and animal. *Predation, parasitism, hyperparasitism, symbiosis,* and *mutualism* are terms that describe interactions that are commonplace in the rainforest. Some biologists believe the level of plant-animal interaction is a major factor that promotes the remarkable diversity of life in the rainforest. This notion requires testing but is certainly a possibility. Birds pollinating flowers; bats transporting seeds; figs pollinated by tiny wasps; strangler figs stealing sunlight and support from an established canopy tree—all of these interactions seem to promote specialization and diversification. These interactions constitute some of the most interesting topics for study in the rainforest and may be a major cause of its remarkable luxuriance.

Honeymoon Camp

After my first trip to the lowland rainforest, the horrors I had imagined were proven to be exaggeration and illusion, and I was eager to return. My next opportunity to do this did not come until July 1982. I worked out the details over several months while back in the United States. I chose a new field site on a detailed topographic map of the region, selecting a flat tract of unsettled forest a distance east of Kakoro village, only ten miles as the crow flies from my first jungle camp. I also began the complicated process of obtaining permission for the research from the government of Papua New Guinea.

Once the papers were in order, I had to deal with a novel complication: a wife. During the considerable period between applying for a visa and obtaining it, I courted and married a co-worker at the Smithsonian Institution. She agreed to accompany me on the field trip, making it a sort of jungle honeymoon.

Our planned research site was about six miles east of the village. We followed our porters along a muddy path of orange earth that led us up and down over some low hills that bordered the river. Carol and I became separated in the long string of our walking team. Within a few minutes we were in rainforest. We continued, slowly, for about two-and-a-half hours without a break before we struck out of the forest interior and down onto a gravelly sandbar of the Si River. Here we wended our way upstream several hundred yards and found the fastest of the group resting on their pack loads at a large gravel bar. This was it—our home for the next two weeks.

We were in "pure bush"—beautiful Papuan rainforest. Here was a lovely, small river that flowed clear from the uninhabited mountains above us. The river bend was wide and the gravel bar gave us a nice opening from which to escape the dampness of the forest interior. Arriving at a site like this, chosen in the cold of a northern winter many months before, was, for a naturalist, like hitting a home run in a World Series game. The effort required to get to this spot made the relief of finally standing there all the more exhilarating. Still, in spite of my triumph, Carol was, if anything, anxious and unsure of what was to come. She had never camped in lowland jungle.

Carol squealed when she saw a leech on her ankle just above her canvas boot top. This forest was leech heaven, not a pleasant discovery either to Carol or our assistants. Carol simply did not like the concept of "leech," whereas the men, who were barefoot and barelegged, were constantly being preyed upon by the diminutive bloodsuckers. Because I wore boots and long pants, I was usually safe from attack.

The common leech in the lowland forest of New Guinea is about an inch long and very slim before a blood meal. This leech has one enemy—desiccation. The leeches that inhabited the Si River forests had little worry about drying out, especially in the shaded jungle interior where the humidity remained high because of incessant afternoon rains.

The forest leech hunts by an ingenious method involving touch and taste. It first locates a pathway regularly used by vertebrates (pigs, cassowaries, wallabies, humans). It then ascends into the low vegetation, perches on the top of a leaf, and waits, waving its sensitive, grasping "tail." When a large animal brushes against the vegetation, quick as lightening the leech throws itself at the prey item, grasping hold of any surface. Once aboard, the leech begins its search for a skin surface with a good net of capillaries. For the western field-worker, this usually is at the top of the boot, where the socks have sagged. The leech will often work its way down into the sock and begin its meal in the warm protection of the boot. For the New Guinean, the most vulnerable leech feeding zone is between the toes.

The remarkable thing about the leech is that it has such a terrible reputation. In reality, it is one of the most benign ectoparasites. These leeches rarely transmit disease, and their bite is entirely painless. The only unpleasantness comes after the leech departs. The little creature deposits an enzyme in the wound to prevent blood clotting; this enzyme continues to work long after departure. Leech bites bleed for several hours, making a mess of socks.

Carol's first leech had not yet made an incision, and I was able to pluck it off without complications. This did not altogether allay Carol's sense of discomfort. Leeches were just one of the unsavory pests that haunted Carol's first few days in the jungle.

———

Having Carol there helped me to see the wonder of being in the forest with these New Guineans. Little things that I had become insensitive to were of intense interest to Carol; and in watching her, I saw how curious our situation was. Carol and I were eleven thousand miles from our home, in a forest that had rarely or never been visited by a white man (or woman), and we had brought with us many accouterments of our culture that were entirely novel to our field assistants here in camp. Muinai, the youngest, developed an attachment to a multicolored bungee cord that was used to attach a sleeping bag to a backpack. He wore it around his neck like a choker, and it looked quite stylish on him. Carol was fascinated by the way Zagai prepared a river fish he had caught the second day. After gutting it, he wrapped it in a large palm leaf, tied this with vine (*busrop* in Pidgin), soaked it in water, then placed it in the fire to cook. It was taken out of its wrapper perfectly poached.

Muinai was amazed by the microcassette recorder I was using to record observations. He was especially pleased when we taped his voice and played it back to him. Carol was delighted when, in my absence, she, Ray, and Zagai took it upon themselves to organize the camp, and the men, using only forest materials, quickly and masterfully constructed a series of benches and shelves to keep the food, plates, equipment, and utensils off the ground.

I was here to study and map the distribution of the five species of birds of paradise inhabiting this forest. Carol, here as an observer, could focus on her new surroundings while I plowed off into the forest with our assistants. From what she jotted down in her diary, it is clear that she viewed this world with different eyes: "I am sitting on the beach now. The sky behind the clouds is a cerulean blue. The air is fresh and hot. The insects' racket is audible, invisible. Thousands of anonymous insects. The sweat bees and flies are nagging—I curse and slap at them. The forest is a shimmering green. Butterflies flash blue.

HOT!! no breeze."

Insects were to become a dominant theme of her experience: "The incessant hum of flies, gnats and mosquitoes really bothers me. Also sweat bees and flies crawling all over the food. . . . Tomorrow I will go into the bush to collect some specimens to draw. I thought I might try some landscapes, but all I see is a big intimidating wall of vegetation."

The climate was another focus for Carol: "16 July 1982. Still no change in the weather. Rained most of the night, and this morning the sky was overcast. Everything—all our clothes, tent, etc.—has an odor of mildew. . . . Nothing can dry in this weather. This is supposed to be the dry season! Anyway, I spent most of the morning in the tent, away from the flies and bees, reading."

Denizens of the Rainforest

Our "honeymoon" in Kakoro was hardly that. Camping for two weeks in the rainforest is more work than play. The tent was always wet, and we woke up stiff and sore from the uneven ground. The food became monotonous. Insect and leech bites became infected. Successive days of rain and cloud weighed on the spirits, yet there were always payoffs. The field work went well and I was happy with that. But there were more personal joys of coming to know our private square kilometer of jungle. When I first started cutting census trails, the forest was a blur of green—monotonous and unrecognizable. After walking and watching for two weeks, the forest grew to be a well-known neighborhood; individual trees became favored landmarks. Certain unknown birdsongs that we now had identified became pleasing morning serenades that proved we were learning the lowland birdlife.

Then there were the big bonuses that a jungle occasionally offers. Carol will never forget the sight of the pair of great, dusky Palm Cockatoos in the dead tree next to camp, nimbly climbing around the leafless branches with a total lack of wariness, their frilled black crests erected to a comical angle. For Steve Pruett-Jones, a co-worker who joined our camp for the second week of field work, it was the face-to-face encounter with a five-foot-tall Southern Cassowary, New Guinea's largest and wariest bird. Its presence is usually known only from its dinosaurlike footprints in the mud of the forest floor. In spite of my efforts, I still have not observed this species in the Papuan rainforest.

My payoff came in the form of a flock of Southern Crowned Pigeons, the world's largest. Three species of crowned pigeons inhabit the lowland forests of New Guinea and a few satellite islands. All are rare except in the absence of hunting of any kind. These turkey-sized pigeons spend much of their time on the ground and are easy prey for the ever-patient Papuan hunter. Crowned pigeon populations within a day's walk of a village are usually wiped out if shotguns are available. Camping a few hours east of Kakoro, I had not been optimistic about observing any of these birds, but I had hoped for luck, especially when Zagai said scattered birds continued to survive in small numbers in the forest around the Si River.

New Guinea's three species of crowned pigeon are natural treasures of the southwest Pacific. Their only apparent relative, the Choiseul Crowned Pigeon of the Solomon Islands group, is apparently extinct, having never been observed alive by western naturalists (the few known specimens were brought to field collectors by indigenous hunters). To see a crowned pigeon of any sort is a feat of perseverance and some luck. On my first trip to Kakoro the only evidence of crowned pigeon was handed to me by a passing Papuan, on his way from Anandea to Kakoro for the Independence Day celebrations. What he handed me was the lovely, lacelike crown plume of a freshly killed individual. The day before, the men had dined on the bird and saved the crown feathers. Ninga Kawa bought this ornament for a Kina (a dollar).

I encountered a party of four crowned pigeons on my seventh day of walking our census trails. Late in the afternoon, all alone, I was on a small rise when I heard a very low-pitched hooing sound. I froze in my tracks. Gradually the notes grew louder, and I began to make out ghostly shapes moving through the obscure light of the forest floor. I fixed on a single bird and with aid of my binoculars picked out the creamy-colored, filamentous crown plume, rising like the arched ornament atop a Roman helmet, but much more delicate. The bird's deep red iris was set against a small black mask. The plumage was a rich gray blue, except for the large maroon patch covering the breast, the gray

Southern Crowned Pigeons

tip to the tail, and the broad, dove gray wing bar, edged in purple.

Most remarkable about the bird's behavior was its apparent nervousness. It walked about, zigging and zagging, all the while rapidly flicking downward its large broad tail. One can understand that a species that is so heavily persecuted would be a bit nervous. I do not know whether it suffers from any natural predation. But it was obvious that the four birds, probably a remnant population only, were not at all tame; the four took flight before they got within thirty feet of me. Their wings clapped together loudly and crashed against vegetation as they labored to gain altitude. Upon settling clumsily on small branches about forty feet above the ground, they nervously peered about as I savored the sight. The fieldwork I had been doing was very satisfying, yet it lacked the intensity of finding such a bird, one I had long wished to see. Observing a new and elusive creature of the rainforest brought me closer to that environment. The time I had spent thinking about the pigeon and the effort expended actually searching for it all added to the intense pleasure of finally seeing the bird, a real moment of joy. It was like a deep secret finally shared, making it all the more treasured.

Crowned pigeons are a natural wonder. It is sad they are so difficult to find, and becoming rarer each day, because of the continuing toll taken by hunters. The three species are protected by law, and thus, taking them with a shotgun is illegal. Unfortunately, the law is virtually unenforceable, for who patrols the forest to check a villager's "bag" from a hunting excursion? Perhaps the evidence has already been eaten, and who can prove that the lovely crown feathers that now adorn the man's hair were taken by gun and not by bow and arrow?

Jungle Watching

I learned, and relearned, a lot about the Papuan forest by having Carol with me at Kakoro. As a field-worker intent on studying difficult-to-observe birds, I tended to overlook some of the inconveniences involved in getting this job accomplished. The swarm of tiny mosquitoes that quickly assembled around us in the wet lowland forest was virtually blocked out from my consciousness. I applied bug repellent and then went about my business. If the mosquitoes continued to hover, they were accepted as a part of the job. Carol could not understand how I could block them out, and her main desire was to escape this menacing plague.

The breathless claustrophobia of rainforest interior was palpable to Carol when she accompanied me on the trail system I set up. In search of a bird in the canopy, I barely noticed the forest and had no sense of being closed in. Carol, standing beside me, could not see the bird for the layers of greenery, and she started breathing freely again only after she got back out on the gravel bar, with open sky above.

Did those birds actually exist? Carol made me understand that my interaction with the birds I was studying was often based on little that was evident to an outsider. The King Bird of Paradise would vocally signal its whereabouts to me, as I knew its scolding advertisement call. This was often lost to Carol among the other noises of the morning—drones of a thousand cicadas, shrieks of a Sulphur-crested Cockatoo, *hoo* notes of a tree full of fruit-droves, and metallic complaints of a drongo, not to mention a dozen other bird sounds. I already knew well the appearance of the King Bird of Paradise. I knew its shape in flight and its tendency to remain hidden in a tangle of vines. I was aware that the ruby coloration of the bird can change to a dark brown in the failing light of the forest interior. By the time I had gotten what I would consider a great look at a male King Bird of Paradise, it would have escaped to another hiding place, and Carol would be straining her eyes to pick up some sign of movement of a bird that had already disappeared.

Making observations in the rainforest can be difficult, frustrating, and at times, impossible. It is an acquired skill that requires a taste for the demands of the environment. Idealized representations of the jungle filled with color and activity are misleading. The real jungle, most of the time, appears dull and dark. Much of each day the forest is silent and there is not a bird to be seen for love or money. Perhaps that is why for so many decades the rainforest has received little attention from the world at large. The rewards are hard-won. But how many will be able to savor the memory of a crowned pigeon at thirty paces, or know the satisfaction of having discovered one of the secrets of a bird's behavior? These encounters are what make it worthwhile.

The Pale-Billed Sicklebill

In 1983, the least known of the forty-two species of birds of paradise was the Pale-billed Sicklebill, then known to inhabit a small expanse of lowland rainforest in northern Irian Jaya. The only ornithologist to have made field observations on this elusive bird was Dillon Ripley, who had encountered it near Bodim in 1960. Little was known of the Pale-billed Sicklebill's ecology or behavior. Why was its range so circumscribed? Was it monogamous or polygynous? The mate's nuptial plumes are much reduced, and so the answer to the latter question was not obvious.

One of the reasons the Pale-billed Sicklebill was so little understood was because it was known only from Irian Jaya, where permission for western biologists to study wildlife was not generally available. But in August 1983, Bret Whitney, a very keen field ornithologist from Austin, Texas, visited the westernmost part of Papua New Guinea's West Sepik Province and located a widespread and vocal population of this sicklebill. Whitney's discovery kindled my desire to study Papua New Guinea's population of the bird. Carol and I traveled to the lowland jungles of the West Sepik in 1984. We set a camp in the forest beside the Puwani River, about thirty miles south of the small coastal town of Vanimo, quite near Papua New Guinea's border with Irian Jaya.

Puwani Camp

I have mentioned the remarkable stature of the lowland rainforest, and here we found our jungle environment as grand as any I have seen in the tropics. It would have been unthinkable to camp anywhere else in the forest except near the opening created by the river. The forest was too dark, too damp. By contrast, the broad opening of the river's floodway was more than four hundred feet across. The river comprised two narrow channels of swift-flowing water, amid an uneven and rock- and log-strewn swath of sand, mud, and regenerating riverine vegetation. The river gave us access to the sky, the sunlight, a place to dry wet clothing, a deep channel for bathing—and a most interesting natural nonforest habitat.

From the short entrance trail to the camp we could look across the floodway to a high cliff that was the last outlier of the Bewani Mountains. Several other, higher ridges were visible behind this prominent topographic feature. We gained great comfort from these hills, because with the oft-shifting weather the view of them provided us with an ever-changing panorama.

During the hike to our camp, Simon, one of our guides, had pointed out the cry of the Pale-billed Sicklebill. Remarkably, among the three men we had hired at the Vanimo police station, Simon happened to be a local expert on the forest wildlife. When we showed him a painting of the Pale-billed Sicklebill, Simon told us he knew the bird well from his home at Utai! This was doubly remarkable, because the bird is very elusive, and most local people do not know it. In addition, Utai is in the Sepik drainage, and this species was thought not to occur in that vast lowland area to the southeast.

The first task of our study was to locate the singing males near our camp. We sent Simon and Jack out the second morning, and they returned having found one male Pale-billed Sicklebill about a half-mile away. This lone male, the only male we found in proximity to the camp, became the focus of our study at Puwani. We next began laying out a trail system for our research work.

Our first trail led from camp out to the focal male. Simon pointed out the "song," which can only be described as a bizarre series of mournful, slurred, hoarse notes in a minor key. It was very peculiar,

Pale-billed Sicklebill

yet it had components reminiscent of the calls of the Magnificent Riflebird and of the Lesser Bird of Paradise, birds that shared this Puwani rainforest.

I marked about four miles of trails. All attention was focused on the single male that inhabited the forest enclosed in this network of trails.

———

Studying the Pale-billed Sicklebill in the Puwani forest was humbling. Only after seven days did I actually observe the bird with my binoculars. Up to then, I had had no more than a brief glimpse of a dark shape flying through the forest canopy.

In the initial days I marked out trails and also kept track of the movements of the male, which could be done without having to see him, because he called with metronomic consistency. I could even get foraging records without seeing the male. He regularly visited and called from a tall *Sloanea* tree. While he was hidden high in the canopy leaves, I could collect seeds that he regurgitated, one by one, down through the vegetation. The seeds he dropped, by the way, were not

Sloanea seeds, but instead belonged to another tree, presumably one he had visited earlier that morning.

The male is both weird and beautiful, a fact that rarely is apparent from the illustrations of this species. My first encounter was typical. Sitting quietly in the shaded middle story of the forest, on a small horizontal branch, was a slim, small-headed bird about the size of a Gray Jay. Like that jay, it was generally dull colored, except for the prominent rich russet tail and the very long and deeply decurved, ivory-colored bill. The chin and cheek were blackish; the breast and belly were smoky gray, and the back was dull brown. Short, copper-tipped pectoral plumes protruded out from each shoulder. What caught my attention was the face: the dark eye was surrounded by a patch of maroon skin, devoid of any feathers. This bare patch extended well above the eyebrow so that the blackish feathering of the crown was no more than a narrow, mohawklike strip of short plumage that extended from its bill back to the more extensive feathering on the nape. This gave the bird an almost reptilian look, but it was the four-and-a-half inch, decurved bill that held my eye. What special feeding methods did he use this for?

I had hopes of radio-tracking some Pale-billed Sicklebills in order to learn more of their habits. To catch them I set up a series of mist nets on thirty-foot poles in places where the singing male was spending much of his time. We caught lots of birds, but not a single Pale-billed Sicklebill.

Still, I made progress. The focal male was quite cooperative in all things besides netting. I began to make regular foraging observations and discovered that this bird was spending a significant amount of time feeding on fruit. The male was regular in its habits and kept a fixed home range that I came to know well. I followed the bird each day for more than eight hours, mapping its movements and recording its activities.

After the first week I was able to answer the initial question that had been posed. The Pale-billed Sicklebill differed little in behavior or ecology from its closest relatives and acted like the typical polygamous bird of paradise. Like the Buff-tailed Sicklebill and the Brown Sicklebill, the species was sedentary, territorial, and very vocal. Like the Black Sicklebill, its diet included nearly equal portions of fruit and insects. The male devoted most of each day to patrolling and singing on his thirty-acre territory, and there seemed to be no pair-bonding between the male and the rarely seen, mute female.

What is remarkable about doing fieldwork on an unknown species is that as soon as one question is answered, the new knowledge is immediately taken for granted, and the next question looms up as the critical one. The researcher is never satisfied with the data at hand. With the Pale-billed Sicklebill, I wanted more information on its diet, its display, and relations between adult males. I attacked these questions by continuing to shadow my focal male. I slowly garnered more about the bird's diet of capsular fruit and arthropods, but at Puwani I saw no interactions between sicklebills, male or female.

———

Doing fieldwork in the flat floodplain forest required patience and care. In the mountain forest, keeping track of my location was simpler—a matter of ridgelines and well-defined watersheds. On the flats, there is nothing to guide you except the sun, which near the equator stays high overhead for much of each day. With the open understory it was most helpful for me to set out the colored plastic survey lines. These saved me from having to blaze trails by cutting and marking the sparse vegetation at ground level. However, even with the colored lines and a compass strung about my neck, I lost my way at times. This happened because I couldn't stay along the lines all of the time. I had to follow my mobile subjects. A few days before departing from Puwani, I came upon a big mixed flock of foraging birds that included Lesser and Twelve-wired birds of paradise, Variable Pitohuis, Rufous Babblers, and a male and female Pale-billed Sicklebill. I followed the party for twenty minutes, all the while keeping track of the direction of its movement by referring to my compass. When I was finished observing, I began moving quickly through the featureless forest on a bearing that I assumed would bring me back to my transect line, but after following this course for about ten minutes I began to have doubts. The doubts made my heart flutter and brain spin. Was I following the correct course, or was I 180 degrees off? I tried to gather my wits, but this was difficult against a rising flush of fear. In fact, I was standing only a few dozen yards from one of my colored trail lines, which I stumbled upon after a few minutes' more wandering.

Another potential disadvantage of working in a floodplain is flooding. After several nights of heavy rain, we found that our sandy playground was gradually being converted to river. The once-clear water turned steel gray and began to overrun the channels that seemed so well defined the week before. Since this water was all we had to drink, it had to be collected and allowed to settle before we could use it. My forest plot, likewise, was inundated. The flat expanse had insufficient drainage to accommodate the quantity of water it was receiving. I found myself slogging through ankle-deep water along many of my trails. I'm glad I wasn't there during the rainy season!

Life in a Rainforest

New Guineans who inhabit lowland rainforests like that at Puwani face several challenges. One is that sources of nutritional protein are limited. In the villages, a few pigs and chickens are raised, but these are consumed only irregularly. Young cassowaries, often captured when their parent has been killed, are also raised, but these, too, are consumed only on special occasions. The most regular sources of protein come from the forest and rivers. The villagers around Bewani regularly tapped these natural resources. Children searched the river for fish. The men hunted the forest for cassowaries, wallabies, wild pigs, and birds. Needless to say, our three assistants kept their eyes open for forest edibles. One day, Carol saw a fire quite a distance upstream and guessed it might have been made by some Irianese border crossers. It turned out to be a fire made by our assistants. They had encountered some feral dogs that had killed a wallaby. The men drove off the dogs and roasted the wallaby remains for an afternoon snack.

Several days later, Carol and I were awoken at 3 A.M. to the sounds of excited talk and crashing noises from the vegetation. I rose to investigate and found our assistants excitedly discussing possible means of capturing a small ring-tailed possum that they had treed in a sapling. The crashing sound came from their hurling pieces of firewood at the terrified beast, smaller than a house cat. It was only with the greatest reluctance that they gave up the chase at my insistence. Their desire to kill and roast the little creature could only be likened to a powerful bloodlust. Both Carol and I had noticed that the men had gained weight in the ten days since they had been here. And only a few hours before, they had dined on a meal of corned beef, potatoes, onions, and rice, topped off with a dessert of hot cocoa and gingernut cookies. Still, that meal had not satisfied the craving for fresh-killed possum.

Our assistants were eager to consume anything that was captured in the mist nets. This was a source of some contention, as they could not see the sense of releasing edible birds and bats after their capture. Carol and I prevailed, and our assistants had to satisfy themselves largely with rice and the tinned corned beef. For much of our stay the fishing was poor because of the turbidity of the river, and the men had no weapons for hunting forest game. On one occasion, they did bring in six large ready-to-hatch eggs of a brush-turkey, one of the chicken-like mound builders. These were consumed before nightfall.

We had been told that crowned pigeons were entirely eliminated from the forests near the river and that cassowaries and wallabies were present only in low numbers. What appeared to be pristine forest, without discernible hunting tracks, was, in fact, regularly visited by hunters in search of game and by children in search of edible nuts (mostly okari—the large nut of a Terminalia). I found this out when we were visited by a large troop of villagers from Bewani. On departing, the children simply took off into the forest and followed barely discernible traces that I had not even noticed. They moved easily through the habitat, acting as if it was their backyard, as I suppose it was. Often, the villagers' activities in the forest leave little visible evidence, but their influence is probably considerable. Removing many of the important dispersers of seeds, as well as many of the larger, edible, seeds themselves, may influence the dynamics of forest regeneration, especially over the long run.

The most important influence that lowland villagers have on the forest is their slash-and-burn agriculture. Typical families own gardens in several stages of development. Virtually every year, the gardeners of each family will clear a new patch by felling a small tract of forest. At the same time, they abandon an old garden whose soil has been depleted by several years of crops. This means that in a large lowland village, much of the land within a half-hour's walk (a mile or more) has been disturbed in the not-so-distant past, assuming the village has been stationed in this vicinity for that period of time.

It is not uncommon for villages to be resituated every decade or so. The reasons given often relate to the desire to escape from evil spirits that come to dominate the area, but this more likely can be translated into the diminished quality of the environment brought about by human exploitation. There is probably a reduction in crop productivity and also increased sanitation problems that can create periodic outbreaks of a host of diseases, the most palpable of the evil spirits. Much of the habitable lowland areas have been colonized at one time or another during the last millennium. Much of what looks like "virgin" rainforest is probably old secondary growth.

The actual level of long-term interaction between humans and lowland rainforest in New Guinea is still a matter of speculation. Often, indigenous people have been looked upon as living in some sort of ecological harmony with the forest. In most instances this paradigm is probably the exception to the rule. The so-called "hunter-gatherers" are a rarity in Melanesia. Subsistence agriculture, supplemented by hunting and gathering, can place considerable stresses on forest ecosystems. This problem has been examined by anthropologists with a special focus on the human adaptations to this way of life. The nature of these stresses, and the manner in which the forest adapts (or fails to adapt) to them, would be an interesting research problem for future tropical ecologists.

━━

At Puwani I spent most of the daylight hours in the dank forest interior. Fortunately, relief from this tedium was available along the banks of the Puwani River. The rocky floodway created a wonderful open path for bird-watching and for escaping from the claustrophobic, breathless humidity of the jungle interior. The green wall of the forest's edge often throbbed with avian activity. Towering *Eucalyptus* formed stands in the old riverbeds. In full flower, their canopies were home for several pairs of tiny, green Papuan Hanging-Parrots. Golden Mynas spent each afternoon in viny tangles, and a resident Yellow-breasted Bowerbird perched and growled from atop a lone casuarina. White-breasted

Wood-swallows and Rainbow Bee-eaters sallied for insects in the riverine scrub. Every evening, solitary Eclectus Parrots would wing high overhead, traveling in a straight line for some distant night roost. Parrot movements in New Guinea add to the joy of watching the day come to an end—one sees the cockatoos, lories, lorikeets, and parrots, each with its own style and look, heading for their inaccessible sleeping places.

Krisa Camp

After two weeks at our Puwani camp, we took a brief rest at Vanimo, where we spent some time lying in the sun and snorkling on the reef. We then searched for a second camp where we could study the Pale-billed Sicklebill. This we located south of Waterstone village, on the walking track to Krisa. With the permission of the headmaster of the local high school, we employed ten students on a Saturday to carry our supplies in to the campsite. The students returned to school and Anton Balo, a father of one of them, volunteered to look after us and help with the work. Both for Carol and myself, the shift from Puwani to the Krisa camp was for the better. Here the forest was low and relatively open. The birds were easier to observe. Still, life here had its own demands. It was difficult to keep clean because our only source of water was a tiny stream about a quarter of a mile from the house. We were camped on a limestone tableland, and in spite of regular rain, there were no big creeks. Being in the forest interior, we never had a chance to dry our clothing. Worst of all, Carol began to suffer the scourge of tropical ulcers. These are small sores that usually develop on the legs and feet, and if left unattended, become serious and debilitating infections.

A tropical ulcer usually develops at the site of a blister or insect bite. The site is attacked by staph germs and begins to flush and swell. Before long, an infection is seated down under the skin, and the area becomes very tender. These made it difficult for Carol to walk, so she had to spend most of her time at the camp. New Guinean villagers, especially children, suffer from these ulcers with some regularity. Since their households universally lack antibiotics, villagers usually delay until an ulcer has burrowed deep into the flesh before seeking medical help. At this point, the lymph glands must struggle to handle the illness, and a fever develops. Usually it is a painful hike to a local first-aid station or town hospital, followed by repeated injections of penicillin, before these are brought under control. Most villagers bear the scars of serious tropical ulcers—deep indentations in the flesh where the infection has eaten away the muscle. In our case, a timely treatment of antibiotics solved Carol's problem before it got out of hand.

On the first evening at our Krisa camp we heard the low booming and popping notes of the New Guinea Harpy-Eagle, a sound that can be likened to nothing avian, but instead sounds like a gigantic beast belching or clearing its throat. The species calls most regularly at dusk and just before dawn. Commonly, two birds—presumably a male and female—call back and forth to one another. The Harpy-Eagle is a mysterious crepuscular creature. Although considerably smaller than its two closest relatives, the South American Harpy and the Philippine Eagle, it is New Guinea's largest endemic forest raptor. And it is the only one known to search for its prey at dawn and dusk.

Although widespread through the lowlands and mountains of New Guinea, the Harpy-Eagle rarely strays from the seclusion of undisturbed forest. It forages in canopy vegetation for arboreal possums but also takes terrestrial prey, especially the giant rats of the genus *Uromys*. The eagle uses its long legs to reach into large knotholes where possums roost, and also to run down its terrestrial prey. Anton told us that this great bird even raids the nests of bees. At the Krisa camp, Carol and Anton together flushed a Harpy from a low perch in the forest. Since the species does not soar, it is remarkably difficult to observe except when the adults are active in bringing food to the nest. Although the general location of nests has been confirmed by ornithologists, remarkably, no observations have been made at an active nest of this species as of this writing. This, certainly, is one of the major lacunae in Papuan ornithology. Despite its great size, it is a ghostlike presence in the forests of New Guinea.

Ghosts and New Guinea are two very compatible subjects. Called *masalai*, Papuan spirits inhabit both highland and lowland regions of New

Guinea, according to the people who should know, the villagers, big men, and hunters. Anton Balo, a very intelligent man, as well as a practicing Christian, assured us that ghosts inhabited the very forest where we were camped. For most New Guineans, ghosts are an important, but hidden, part of everyday life. Some are simply spirits that control nature, make good weather for planting and harvesting, or good winds for sailing. Anton told Carol that he traditionally sang certain songs to placate the *masalai* of the forest in order to have a successful hunt. Other ghosts are evil and bring disease and pestilence to a village, causing the people to flee for their lives.

All of the New Guinean informants I have worked with believe in spirits and manage to reconcile these beliefs with their faith in Christianity. I have found this remarkable, but I suppose it is no more unusual than a practicing Christian also believing in Darwin's explanation for the evolution of life. For many New Guineans, most misfortunes that befall a village are blamed on an enemy, often from another village or another tribe, working some form of magic. In fact, certain tribal groups have the reputation of having the power to work potent magic from afar. An ailing uncle or a death in childbirth is rarely explained as bad luck, or disease, but instead is thought of as the end product of some evil intervention. There are ways of profitably harnessing the power of these beliefs. When Anton showed us his Sago patch in a small clearing not far from our camp, he pointed out a *tambu* post that he had erected there. This small sign, woven of palm leaves and posted atop a walking stick thrust into the ground near the Sago work site, warned everyone that this area was protected and that any attempt to steal or damage the things there would be compensated by misfortune. This sort of *tambu* protection remains respected in many parts of the island.

———

Anton was a marvelous storyteller, and both Carol and I enjoyed sitting around the fire at night and listening to him. One of the most remarkable stories, which he insisted was true, dealt with the great Palm Cockatoo, second largest parrot on earth. This bird uses its massive bill to crack the *galip* nut, a huge and nearly impenetrable seed of the incense tree *Canarium indicum*. This nut is popular among New Guineans for the rich, edible nutmeat that lies hidden inside the massive *Canarium* seed. Anton told us that when the *galip* fruit fall, the Palm Cockatoos arrive in numbers to creep around on the ground, foraging for the nuts. More remarkable is Anton's claim that the great physical exertion required to break the seed coat of the *galip* nut not only produces a far-carrying *crack* like a rifle shot, but also can cause the bird to "faint" for as long as a minute.

Anton told us how one of his aunts, while walking along a forest path, came upon a Palm Cockatoo sprawled lifeless under a *galip* tree. Surprised, she picked up the bird, placed it into her string *bilum*, and reset the bag on her back. Anton chuckled and recounted that there was quite a commotion when the cockatoo recovered from its faint and attempted to escape from the string bag.

Anton also reported that during the *galip* season, hunters shoot Palm Cockatoos from a small blind placed on the ground under a *galip* tree. Papuan hunters rely upon knowledge of the habits of their prey species to gain an advantage over the species they pursue. Hunters regularly "sit and wait" rather than stalking, simply because the latter method rarely produces positive results except for the largest prey—pigs and cassowaries. In the sit-and-wait technique, the hunter builds a hiding place of vines, branches, and palm fronds, situated close to a regular drinking or feeding place. Then the hunter waits, motionless and silent, until prey arrives.

During the dry season, a hunter will go for forest birds by setting a blind near a favored drinking spot. He builds his blind near a small pool or drip along a nearly dry stream. The hunter then cuts lots of brush and covers all of the other watering spots for a hundred yards on either side of the blind. At the selected spot, he also limits the number of potential drinking perches to only one or two, with the prime perch being the spot on which he focuses. With the blind practically abutting the drinking perch, the hunter extends a long cane arrow out of a small peephole, and the multipronged bamboo head of the arrow is adjusted so that it rests only a few inches from the prospective drinking perch. Any bird that alights at the drinking spot is instantly dispatched. When food acquisition is concerned, the New Guineans leave nothing to chance—this is not sport, after all.

Palm Cockatoo

Our reason for camping on the Krisa track was to learn more about the Pale-billed Sicklebill. This we were able to do, in part because of Anton's knowledge of the forest, and in part, because the bird was more abundant here than it was at Puwani. We awoke to the mournful cries of this species every morning. Observing the Pale-billed Sicklebill was a simpler process, as well, because the forest permitted better visibility. Choosing this site as a second camp was a stroke of great luck.

Here, I was able to document, for the first time, the display of the male Pale-billed Sicklebill. Displays normally given to woo a female were here given to dominate a rival male. The male perched upright, opened his bill, erected his short, iridescent pectoral plumes over his shoulders, and puffed out his skirt of longer flank plumes into a striking pose much like what I had seen given by the montane Brown Sicklebill.

For a field biologist, one of the great treats is to observe a display behavior never before recorded by western naturalists. Here, I was learning three fascinating facts in one encounter: first, the details of the stereotyped display posture of the Pale-billed Sicklebill; second, the fact that the display posture was used in male-male territorial interactions; and third, that the males of this species are territorial creatures that defend their home range with border interactions involving voice and display. We also found that the male was an important member of the remarkable mixed-species bird flocks in this forest.

———

Mixed bird flocks are a common occurrence in many parts of the humid tropics, and New Guinea is no exception. The Krisa camp was a good place to observe flock behavior. For some reason, the flocks were bigger, noisier, and easier to observe than those of any other part of New Guinea I have worked.

What is so remarkable about a bird flock? After all, the chickadees, titmice, kinglets, and Downy Woodpeckers in my neighborhood in the suburbs of Washington, D.C., form mixed flocks each winter, moving through the vines and tangles in search of insects and other edible tidbits. In New Guinea, the flocks are bigger, more complex, and probably more important to the ecological structuring of the forest avifauna in all seasons. In fact, to have much success observing birds in the lowland forest, it is usually necessary to find a flock, for that is where most of the birds are.

In the Krisa forests, the most prominent bird flock was one dominated by birds of paradise. A flock that I observed daily comprised a male Pale-billed Sicklebill, a male Twelve-wired Bird of Paradise, a male Magnificent Riflebird, one or more female-plumaged Lesser Birds of Paradise, a female-plumaged King Bird of Paradise, two species of the jaylike pitohuis, a Spangled Drongo, and a family party of Rufous Babblers. These birds moved noisily through the middle and lower levels of the forest. The pitohuis and babblers kept up a relatively quiet conversation of notes, and the riflebird and sicklebill irregularly gave their loud whistled calls. In addition, each time the male riflebird or Twelve-wire flew to a new perch, its wings produced the distinctive rustling or hissing sound, discernible from a distance of more than fifty meters.

This mixed flock was a bit atypical of most Papuan mixed flocks because it contained birds that regularly forage on fruit as well as arthropods. Thus the birds of paradise stopped to take fruit from a variety of plants while moving in the group. Most tropical bird flocks are predominately insectivorous. The fact that these frugivores joined a mixed flock argues that an adaptive advantage to joining may relate to the protection afforded from attack by predators rather than the oft-cited advantage of having other birds "beating" the vegetation for insect prey. Of course, the birds of paradise could take advantage of that phenomenon, as well.

At Krisa, the appearance of a bird flock was exciting. Suddenly, the forest would awaken to the whistles of the sicklebill. Then came the three-note *whoop* of the riflebird, not too far off. And then the hoots of a group of Rufous Babblers and the bright scolding notes of a Spangled Drongo. It was then evident that a foraging flock was forming, even in the heat of the afternoon. Hearing these telltale signals, I would rush off with binoculars and notebook and soon was amidst the foraging birds, with colors flashing, and wings whistling, and birds scolding. The Rufous Babblers would clamber through the vines, ripping at dead leaves in search of hiding prey. The wraithlike Rusty Pitohuis would travel higher up, moving like brownish ghosts through the limbs of the upper forest strata, always on the move, always skittish, rarely permitting a clear look. The Spangled Drongo perched erect, at the edge of a tiny forest opening, wagging its tail and looking for any stray insect flushed by the activity of the other birds. The big, black riflebird would chip at a dead stub, in search of a fat white grub of a longhorn beetle, while the sicklebill hung on an erect, green, corncoblike fruit of an aroid climber and delicately plucked the little fruitlets from the cob. Before long, the group would move on with a flurry of wings and call notes.

Jared Diamond has studied the composition of these bird flocks in New Guinea, and he has found that the birds all tend to be either brown or black. This flock at the Krisa camp was almost entirely composed of brown or black birds, except for the adult male Twelve-wired Bird of Paradise. What is the advantage to being brown or black? Diamond believes that there is advantage in uniformity. Looking like a bunch of fellow foragers makes for added confusion for a potential predator and makes it more difficult for the predator to focus on a single individual. The uniformity may also reduce aggressive encounters among flock mates. For the flockers, anonymity may spell increased chance of survival.

Tropical flocks exhibit yet another more fascinating trait. Studying the extremely complex flocks of ant-shrikes and ant-wrens in Amazonian Peru, Charles Munn discovered that certain species acted as sentinels for the group. They do this by virtue of their foraging habits. Instead of creeping through tangles and vines, taking stationary prey, the sentinel species perch on a branch, sallying out for prey flushed by the leaf- and vine-gleaners. These sentinel species, then, benefit from the flock association by the free prey scared up by the other flock members. In a neat evolutionary return on this favor, the sentinel species provide enhanced detection of predators and give an alarm call whenever they sight a potential predator. This alarm call is recognized by all the species of the flock, who respond by taking cover. Munn's discovery cleverly explained both the foraging-enhancement and predator-avoidance sides of the flock story.

For the black-and-brown bird flocks of New Guinea, a similar dynamic may exist. The Spangled Drongo is clearly a sentinel species, benefiting from the prey driven up by the fellow foragers. It remains to be proven whether the drongo provides the concomitant benefit of alarm calls for the vulnerable foliage-gleaning species. This system deserves additional study. It would be exciting to show that these same flocking roles have developed independently among entirely unrelated bird families on both sides of the Pacific.

Opposite: View of Lake Omha Camp, English Peaks

9   *Tropical Tundra*

eighing about a half-pound, and some fourteen inches long, Macgregor's Bird of Paradise is a handsome bird that looks like an ornamented crow. I say crow because the bird is mostly black and has the general shape of its well-known relative. It is ornamented in three ways: the body feathers are thick, fluffy, and velvety black; the flight feathers are brightened by a large, ochre yellow patch that practically fills the outer wing when the bird is in flight; finally, there is the glowing, half-moon-shaped orange eye wattle that covers the cheek. This last, in tandem with the bright wing patch, neatly offsets the basic black plumage and gives the species a particularly striking look. Nothing garish and overdone—just naturally beautiful.

Macgregoria was described by William De Vis in 1897, from specimens collected on an 1896 expedition of William Macgregor, the adventurous first governor of British New Guinea. Macgregor and field collector Amedeo Giulianetti were the first westerners to ascend into the high country of the Owen Stanley Range, which rises like a great dark wall behind the coastal hills of Port Moresby. This is the high central cordillera that exceeds thirteen thousand feet in a number of places. Macgregor and his party crossed the range over the high country where I would be working in 1986. Theirs was a remarkable feat in nineteenth century New Guinea.

Macgregor's Bird of Paradise inhabits only a scattering of sites in the highest reaches of New Guinea's central cordillera. Its favored habitat is the subalpine forests at the verge of the alpine grasslands that cap the high peaks. Virtually nothing was known of the bird's habits until ornithologist Austin L. Rand twice visited the bird's habitat in the 1930s. In 1933, Rand found *Macgregoria* on Mount Albert Edward, the great alpine massif that dominates the Wharton Range, a northern spur of the Owen Stanleys. Rand found that the black bird, which the natives called Mo, was highly frugivorous, and that it favored the fruit of a single species of alpine gymnosperm in the family Podocarpaceae.

In 1938, Rand spent several months at Lake Habbema in the Snow Mountains, as ornithologist for the Third Archbold Expedition. He somehow managed to make significant field observations on *Macgregoria* in the time not taken with overseeing the collection and preparation of the more than 4,800 bird specimens.

Rand clearly had a special interest in the birds of paradise. His field records on Macgregor's Bird of Paradise in the Snow Mountains are evidence of his talent for clear and insightful observation. The two take-home points of his published report were that this alpine bird of paradise is monogamous, with both parents helping raise their offspring, and that the diet of the birds seems to consist mainly of the fruit of *Dacrycarpus compactus*, the handsome tree that is a prominent component of the subalpine forest of New Guinea's central ranges.

In its habitat *Macgregoria* is remarkably visible and approachable. Pairs regularly roost on open perches at the verge of alpine grasslands. The birds are conspicuous because of their patterned plumage and the remarkable rustling or zipping sound their wings produce in flight. This is a far cry from the typical, forest-dwelling birds of paradise that, although vocal, can be very difficult to observe.

So what more did we need to know about this mountaintop bird of paradise? At least two questions begged for answers. First, the academic query: what was the nature of the relationship between Macgregor's Bird of Paradise and its food-plant *Dacrycarpus compactus*? Was it a tight, coadapted mutualism, as I suspected? Was the bird the primary disperser of the plant's seeds? Was the plant the diet of choice for the bird?

The world distribution of the bird neatly corresponded with world distribution of the tree (both occur only in the high mountains of New Guinea's central cordillera). Was this more than a coincidence, and is this an example of the type of bird-plant cooperation that is theoretically possible, but rarely observed in nature?

The second general question related to the bird's future. Was, in fact, Macgregor's Bird of Paradise one of New Guinea's rarest and most threatened species? Could the large gap in its range (through the central highlands of Papua New Guinea) be explained by hunting pressures? What made this species, which inhabited such a remote environment, so vulnerable, and what might be done to ensure its continued survival?

The Climb to Lake Omha

In the winter of 1985, I decided I would study Macgregor's Bird of Paradise in eastern Papua New Guinea. Scouring the Papua New Guinea

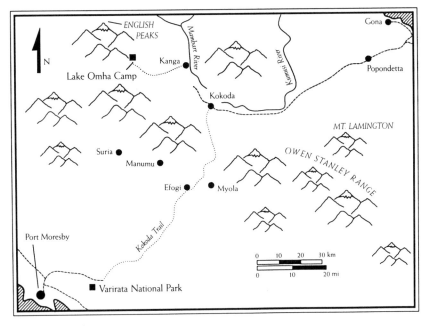

English Peaks and environs

vegetation map, my eye fell on an alpine plateau between the summits of Victoria and Albert Edward. This plateau was known variously as the English Peaks or Mount Scratchley. The broad grassland plateau was dotted with small alpine lakes and a scattering of rocky peaks. The area was isolated from local settlement and offered what seemed to be a perfect site to study an undisturbed population of *Macgregoria pulchra*.

For a study site I chose a tiny lake on the northeastern verge of this highlands massif, about a fifteen-mile walk up a prominent ridge from the village of Kanga, in the Yodda valley of the Mambare River. The environs around the alpine lake looked to be a likely spot for the bird because of the altitude (twelve thousand feet) and the evident mix of grassland and forest. I decided I would make my way to the lakeside study site by way of Kanga village.

———

After assembling provisions and equipment for the expedition in Port Moresby, I stored the bulk of this at a helicopter charter company. They would ferry these stores up to my camp after I had hiked there from Kanga. I wished to hike up for two reasons. I needed the support of the local landowners from Kanga, and I wanted a ready exit trail in case of an emergency. I would have no radio to contact the helicopter company, so I allowed myself ten days to get to the high camp, thinking this would leave generous leeway in my plans.

From Port Moresby I made my way to Kanga by plane, jeep, and finally on foot the final five miles. There I was received warmly and told that all was ready for the planned trek into the high country. They had received my letter from the United States and had even arranged for the village youth group to clear a walking track up the mountain. I was told that they had managed to cut the trail to the summit of the peak they called Manoro. They assured me that this was quite close to the lakeside study site I had selected.

The next day broke fair, with pale sunlight illuminating the high peaks looming up behind the small village. Accompanied by eleven men who carried our supplies, I first traversed their small holdings of rubber and cacao, then followed a trail up a very steep ridge in old forest. The first day we climbed from thirteen hundred feet altitude to about four thousand feet and camped atop the ridge at a traditional hunting camp in submontane forest.

Robert, one of the village elders, was leading our party. He was the owner of this vast tract of forest that extended to the alpine heights. He told me that the hike to the lake would take two or three days. He then astounded me by saying that he was curious to go along with us, since he, himself, had never seen the lake—that *no* living Kanga villager had been up to the alpine grasslands, even though it was acknowledged that they were the tribal owners of this vast domain!

Robert assured me that his forebears had visited the lake area to hunt game and to collect the special grass (called *omba*) that grew around its marshy verges. The *omba* grass was used to make the skirts worn by the women of the village (a tradition long-since abandoned). Robert told me that it was several generations since a Kangan had been up top, but that he knew quite a bit about it from the stories he had been told as a boy. The oral tradition was still strong among these people.

The northern slope of the English Peaks is a pristine private reserve for a few dozen men who are the hunters of Kanga. It was here that I observed my first wild tree kangaroo, a long-tailed, arboreal relative of the terrestrial species so well-known in Australia. Tree kangaroos in New Guinea are considered big game and are hunted with dogs. As a result, the six species that inhabit the island are exceedingly shy and difficult to observe. In many areas they have been eliminated. Ask any naturalist working in New Guinea how easy it is to observe tree kangaroos in the forest, and you will be told that it's not worth the effort. Between 1975 and 1986 I had spent more than four years in New Guinea and had never seen a wild tree kangaroo, nor had my field assistants even spotted one, even though they commonly encountered wildlife that I never had the luck to see.

When Robert told me that one of his dogs had a tree kangaroo "treed" down off the track, I followed him with anticipation. There, perched foolishly in a small sapling, staring dumbly down at the scrawny but feisty dog, was a big "mountain bear"—the frosty brown Doria's Tree Kangaroo. It was immediately apparent that these tree kangaroos are not terribly bright and that their inability to elude the hunting dogs has spelled their doom in much of New Guinea.

The presence of tree kangaroos was a signal that this forest was rarely visited. Robert told me that Kangan hunters came up here only once or twice a year. That night the men dined on "big game." They rewarded the dog with the less-desirable components of the poor creature's viscera. I, myself, had my standard rice and stew.

———

Never trust a topographic map in the tropics. It always makes ascent routes look so easy, so straightforward, so close. The 1:100,000 scale map we had as reference was a lovely piece of art, and I examined it closely (along with my compass and altimeter) at least a dozen times a day, in order to mark our progress. I had chosen this route to the English Peaks because it looked so *good* on the map—a single, well-defined ridge, leading fifteen miles from Kanga to the lake—foolproof, mistakeproof. Well, we made no mistakes over the ensuing six days, but the route tested our will and stretched our resolve to the limits.

Fifteen miles doesn't sound like much, but over that stretch we were required to ascend more than two vertical miles. In order to accomplish this we had to cut more than a dozen miles of trail through some of the most unforgiving vegetation in New Guinea. Here's the catch: in New Guinea, the vegetation between sea level and six thousand feet is friendly. The canopy is high and the undergrowth is relatively thin. Above six thousand feet, the forest changes, and in places the understory fills with tangles of pandanus, bamboo, or a thick growth of saplings, so that every step forward requires several swings of a bush knife. The climb to the lake was not so much a battle with altitude as a battle with vegetation.

Days One and Two were relatively easy. To save our food rations, we sent back five men on the third day. We stored a large heap of supplies at the campsite and then lurched forward into a pandanus jungle that allowed us just two miles of progress that day. Mount Manoro and the track cut by the youth group were far to the rear at this point. Everyone took turns at the lead, swinging the big knife. A chilling rain fell steadily, and the men suffered because their bare feet were no match for the thick carpet of many-spined pandanus leaves that fell from our trail-clearing efforts. After passing the zone of pandanus we met thickets of the wirelike *Nastus* bamboo, and this stuff hindered our

Doria's Tree Kangaroo

progress for another day. At the end of Day Four, we camped in a tiny ridgetop patch of grassland. In the clear, sharp evening air we could gaze out to the forbidding mountain ridges that cascaded down off the main cordillera. We were thick among them now. With a black, cloudless night sky, the temperature dropped almost to freezing.

We were cold but satisfied. We had escaped from the pandanus and bamboo, and the next morning we entered the first tracts of the elfin forest that has a fairyland look because of the soft, multihued moss that coats trunks, branches, rocks, and ground. A pair of Macgregor's Birds of Paradise perched over our heads as we took lunch in a small col on the ridgeline. I was happy to see the birds but wondered what they were doing down here in the thick forest at 9,200 feet. After dusk, a Rufous Woodcock serenaded us with its croaking and buzzing aerial courtship song. We assumed we were fast approaching our alpine destination. But each day's progress was measured on the map in millimeters, not inches.

The fifth day, we found ourselves in the doldrums. We were high up, but the ridge flattened out and most of our movement was lateral, with little ascent, which was frustrating. We walked through soggy, misty, dwarf forest all day long and suffered from lack of water, because we did not find a single stream or spring until afternoon. After a fretful lunch without water, our morale sagged, and our bodies were drained of energy. The novelty of exploration was replaced with worry about making it to the lake before the helicopter. We would arrive at the lake with food to keep us going for no more than a couple of days. If the helicopter did not find us, the pilot would return without dropping the supplies. That would be disaster.

On Day Six I decided that we should make a reconnaissance without packs. Four of us continued cutting a trail, while three stayed back at the camp to rest. We broke out into a patch of grassland on the ridge. This was encouraging. But after a few minutes we had to cut our way back into the stunted elfin woodland, and we hacked and hacked to get to the next grassland patch. Fortunately, I had an aerial photograph of the lake environs, and by afternoon I saw that we had made our way into an identifiable clearing that lay less than a mile east of the lake. We were all but there! We raced back to camp in high spirits, knowing we could reach the lake the next morning. The only worrisome thing was that we had seen not a single *Macgregoria* that day.

A woodcock's flight song woke us before dawn, and we were off early to make for the lake. With the aerial photo as a guide, we picked our way through the myriad patches of forest and grassland, and just before noon we cut our way through a tangle of vegetation and walked out onto a small lip of grassland overlooking the alpine lake that Robert named "Omha." We were mesmerized by the sight—a deep green jewel set in a narrow rift valley, surrounded by stands of stately *Dacrycarpus* trees and low thickets of *Rhododendron*, *Pittosporum*, *Styphelia*, and *Dimorphanthera*. From the tiny outlet of the lake we could look down a broad meadow to a mat of clouds ten thousand feet below, blanketing the Solomon Sea. We were on top of the world.

Tree Line

Instead of climbing above the tree line into an alpine "tundra," we camped on a rugged plateau *at* the tree line. If you looked one direction you saw low grasslands, and by turning slightly you could see a thick stand of subalpine forest. This illustrates the fact that the boundary between forest and grassland is rarely uniform except on very steep slopes or where there has been some sort of recent disturbance.

It may be that at twelve thousand feet we were seeing a false tree line. Botanists have written that the natural tree line in New Guinea lies at thirteen thousand feet. Below that one finds grassland growing in areas that are poorly drained (boggy), subject to heavy frost (the floors of closed valleys), or where hunters have burned in search of game. Natural or not, the captivating environment we found around our little lake was wonderful—a reward for all our recent suffering.

The reader may wonder why there would be a tree line in the tropics in the first place? Imagine the difficulties plants face with increasing altitude: burning rays of the sun, followed by fog and chill; frost throughout the year; heavy waterlogging rains; and rarefied air blown by the strong winds to desiccate every leaf and blade of grass when the clouds are gone and the sky is clear. The weather here rapidly changes from extreme to extreme. It's a wonder anything can survive this unpredictable and stressful regimen.

Lakeside Camp

Upon arriving at the little lake, we built a big fire to warm ourselves. Mist and rain swirled around us as we began building a hut—one closed in on all sides, and with a door that could be shut. The men's construction was low and sturdy—we did not know what weather to expect, but it was better to prepare for the worst.

That night, six Kanga men, their two hunting dogs, and I huddled by an outdoor fire beneath the Southern Cross and talked quietly. We gazed up in amazement at a sky filled with stars. The Milky Way was a prominent band of hazy white across the sky. Robert pointed to a slowly moving satellite that cut through the thickets of stars. Michael,

Robert's nephew, and leader of the youth group, spoke of Neil Armstrong and the Apollo mission to the moon. This, to him, was an event read about in a school text, an important bit of modern history. Such are the icons that have been adopted by the culture of that isolated corner of the globe.

My memory of that first night at Lake Omha burns through the mist of passing years. It is for memories of nights like that, in places like that, that I keep returning to New Guinea. The research is important, but the memories that stand in sharp focus are images of an instant in time when one sees a perfect natural world, and warm thoughts of friendships bonded by shared experience and discovery. Doing fieldwork produces these memories in ways that may be rarely known to the white-coated lab-worker.

———

It was difficult to sleep because the air was so thin and dry. The cloudless night sucked every drop of humidity from the air. I awoke with chapped lips and dried sinuses. The men rose early to stir the fires and restore some warmth to their chilled bones. These were lowland people who were seeing, for the first time, thick glassy crystals of ice in the brown grass around the hut. Their bare feet rebelled at the cold of the frosty ground. These people were stunned by this environment; amazed that they had come so far; amazed that this strange land belonged to their uncle Robert!

The lake itself is no more than two hundred yards long, and about eighty across. Its water we measured to be chilled to fifty degrees. Behind the camp was a small, protective ridge, topped with dwarf forest. The other side of the ridge led downward all the way to the Mambare Valley and gave lovely views of the sea when it was clear. Across the lake were rocky heights, the continuation of the very ridge we had ascended from Kanga village. These heights hid the lake from the rest of the world and cast a chilly shadow on us in the late afternoon.

That morning some of us decided to climb atop the nearest summit. From there we looked down to the bottle-green lake waters, our smoke-veiled camp, and the rugged, conical crags to the southwest, the English Peaks. Further off were the two great alpine massifs, Victoria to the south and Albert Edward to the north. Stark wilderness surrounded us.

The first full day at our lakeside camp was blessed with blue sky and hot sun. On a fair day at this altitude the air is cool but the direct sun is strong, barely filtered by the thin layer of atmosphere. At midday I could strip to shorts and bare feet and feel comfortable, as long as the sun was out. In a matter of minutes, though, a breeze from down the mountain could bring a pile of soggy clouds up from the Solomon Sea and dump them into our little rift valley. This happened on most days, especially in the afternoons. The temperature would plummet, the lights would go out, the wind would swirl, and the drizzle would begin. Thus, the usual Lake Omha forecast was afternoon rain and temperatures in the high forties.

———

The Lake Omha environment is a rarefied subset of the island's biota. Not much lives up at this altitude, especially if compared to an acre of forest near Kanga village, which probably supports more than seventy species of trees and another hundred or more species of lesser vascular plants (vines, shrubs, herbs, ferns). An acre of forest at Lake Omha supports no more than 25 or 30 species of plants of all categories. The forest at Kanga is home to more than 130 species of birds. At Lake Omha, only fifteen miles from Kanga, fewer than 40 species are resident. This is New Guinea's toughest environment. A few species eke out a living here, and only a tiny subset prospers.

For the field-worker, the advantage is many fewer variables to deal with. The canopy of the forest is dominated by a single species of tree—*Dacrycarpus compactus*—the tree that was supposed to be the key to our understanding the life of Macgregor's Bird of Paradise. Nowhere else in New Guinea can you find a forest so dominated by a single tree. This species of *Dacrycarpus* seems to be one of the specially adapted alpine plants that has learned the secret of success in this rigorous habitat.

Only a handful of birds were common around camp: the Crested Berrypecker, New Guinea Pipit, New Guinea Thornbill, and Sooty Melidectes. And, of course, Macgregor's Bird of Paradise.

A pair of *Macgregoria* zipped by our campsite the first afternoon.

The next morning a pair appeared across the lake, and, of all things, flew down to the ground and began foraging in some very low, woody ground plants. I sat by the fire, watched the birds with my binoculars, and eagerly took notes as they hopped about in an ungainly fashion, searching for and picking at what I assumed were fruits. This was the first record of this species visiting the ground.

I would have ample opportunity to get to know something about this big black bird once the helicopter arrived with the two hundred pounds of provisions. It was due our second morning at the lake. We then discovered one of the disadvantages of camping in a hidden valley: fog. I awoke at 6:30 and looked out my tiny tent to see nothing but gray obscurity. It had been a clear night, but for some reason fog settled in before dawn. I assumed there was no hope for the chopper that day, so I rolled back to sleep, only to be awoken a few minutes later to the heavy thudding sound of its rotors. We all scrambled to life, but we were in pea soup, and we could only stamp our feet in frustration. The sound drifted off and our shoulders slumped.

About twenty minutes later we heard the thudding of the chopper blades again, and I quickly organized our men, each with a brightly colored piece of clothing to use as a signal flag. We waited nervously as the sound came and went in the fog from different directions. It was clear, now, that the pilot was brave enough to make the full effort. I had run the length of the lake to the open grassland at its southwestern end. There I could see that the fog lay just at our level and that it was clear just a few yards down the hill. I knew that each minute the machine was aloft cost me seven dollars. It was excruciating to think that the pilot might have to relent and return to the base.

I finally saw the black-and-yellow whirlybird in the grassland down the slope, below the fog. I waved madly, but it passed on to the east. A few minutes later, the pilot brought it back and I caught his eye, at last. He slowly brought the craft up the hill and ever so gently brought it to rest in the grass where I had been standing. The rotors spun in a high idle as I hastily unloaded the tightly packed cabin. I then shouted for Robert and two others to pile in. The pilot agreed to take them back to Kanga, saving them a difficult hike down. In about seven minutes he covered the ground it had taken us seven days to ascend.

Now we could proceed with the work at hand, an ecological study of *Macgregoria pulchra*. First, we attempted to mist net the species. This proved fairly easy, mainly because the birds were spending a lot of time foraging near the ground. We placed nets where we observed birds feeding, and we caught nine individuals. These we color-tagged. We also attached radio transmitters to four birds in order to keep better track of their movements. Most of each day, I was out in search of active birds.

We also needed to properly document the distribution of food-plants. Our first discovery was that virtually none of the thousands of *Dacrycarpus* trees around the camp was producing ripe fruit. In any event, we marked a hundred mature trees of this species in order to keep long-term reproductive records of these individuals. We also mapped quarter-hectare plots of forest to document the flora and to determine the availability of alternate fruit resources for the bird.

We found that the birds commonly associated in pairs, and these pairs foraged together day after day. In some instances, pairs were associated with a third individual, which by behavior and plumage we identified as an offspring of the last nesting. These youthful hangers-on were noisy, complaining individuals that tagged along after the two parents, continually giving annoying distress calls and otherwise pestering the adults.

By radio-tracking, it was possible to determine the extent of daily movements of pairs of birds. Residents occupied ranges of about thirty acres, and it was a simple matter to keep in touch with them. They spent most of their time moving about at the verges of the subalpine forest. Although the birds tended to retreat when they saw me, they were easy to observe and required no special caution in tracking. The only oddity was that, of the four radio-tracked individuals, three remained resident, and the fourth disappeared the same day the radio was applied. At the time, I assumed that the radio had been removed by the bird and was no longer transmitting. But once or twice I did make brief contact with the signal, apparently far off down the mountain. I would later see this as significant.

The immediate mystery concerned the diet of the birds. *Macgregoria* spent lots of time in the *Dacrycarpus* trees and even consumed the fruit at the few trees with remnants of the last crop. We found the distinctive seeds in the excreta of netted birds, as well. Still, it was clear the birds were subsisting on something else. We found that they were foraging for virtually any fruit that was available, and much of the edible stuff was being produced by the tiny shrublets that grew in low mats at the edge of the forest. Time and again we saw the big black birds drop to the ground and clamber among these little prostrate shrubs in search of the tiny berries being produced. I interpreted this unnatural-looking behavior as a response to the absence of *Dacrycarpus*. After all, this bird was not built for terrestrial life, and no one had previously observed the birds foraging on the ground.

I had designed the project on the assumption that at least a decent proportion of the *Dacrycarpus* would be fruiting at any time in the year and that *Macgregoria* would be subsisting, at least largely, on the fruit of this tree. What was I to make of what I now found? The plant was not "behaving" as it should if there were a tight mutualism established with the bird. If, in fact, the bird *was* dependent upon the fruit, then, clearly, it was a one-way street, and the plant was not cooperating.

A partial modification of my hypothesis was in order: Macgregor's Bird of Paradise was a specialized frugivore that depended heavily upon the fruit of *Dacrycarpus*; I postulated that the bird would breed only when *Dacrycarpus* fruited; the plant, on the other hand, followed no special fruiting cycle that was beneficial to the bird. This scenario sounds much like that for the monogamous Trumpet Manucode and its favored fig fruit. The manucodes are fig specialists, yet the fig plants seemed to make no special allowances to benefit these birds. Thus, this bird-plant interaction was not a mutually beneficial interdependency as I had hoped to prove.

———

We were not cut out for the environment in which Macgregor's Bird of Paradise thrives. On my last day of radio tracking I sat huddled under the protection of a broad, sloping trunk of a nearly recumbent *Dimorphanthera*. Rain sheeted down, and the dark gray clouds continued to boil up over the lip of the plateau scarp. Two *Macgregoria* I was watching sat placidly in the open branches of a tall, forest-edge *Dacrycarpus*, preening each other. The rain beaded off the backs of these hardy, high-altitude specialists. I had found out enough in this stay to be satisfied that we were on the right track and that, indeed, there was something interesting going on up here in the English Peaks. Now it was time to close up camp and march back down the mountain to the comfort of the balmy climes of Kanga village.

Return to English Peaks

I had scheduled a return to Lake Omha in July 1987, one year after establishing the field study. In late 1986 Helen Hopkins and Ian Burrows, biologists at the University of Papua New Guinea, visited Lake Omha and found that *Macgregoria* had disappeared from the site. The birds I had color marked were gone, and there was no indication that the *Dacrycarpus* trees would be fruiting any time soon. These findings were a shock and threw into doubt the usefulness of my planned trip, but I had no flexibility in my schedule, so I proceeded. Michael Lucas and Rodney Goga, of Kanga village, joined me and my father-in-law on the mountain. My father-in-law had volunteered to serve as a field assistant in order to find out what, exactly, I did when I went off to the South Seas.

Getting to Lake Omha by helicopter was a marvel, but it took a while for our bodies to acclimate to the rarefied air. It was not long, though, before we were observing interesting things.

We first discovered that the vast population of *Dacrycarpus compactus* was in the midst of a synchronous mass flowering. The canopy was patterned with the colors of the flowering trees. In this orgy of reproductive activity, the male trees gave off a pale yellow-green glow, the females a pale blue-green glow. The phenomenon was obvious from the helicopter and from the ground as well. The male plants were releasing large quantities of pollen into the wind to fertilize the female cones, which resembled miniature fruit.

We were, of course, excited by this remarkable biological event, but it did not bode well for our study of Macgregor's Bird of Paradise, assuming the bird depended in some way on the fruit of *Dacrycarpus*. For there were certainly no ripe *Dacrycarpus* fruit to be seen around Lake Omha.

Although in August 1986 the study site supported a good non-

Dacrycarpus *tree and fruit*

breeding population of *Macgregoria*, we found that in August 1987, the Lake Omha study site supported none at all. With no ripe *Dacrycarpus* fruit for more than a year, there was no sign of Macgregor's Bird of Paradise.

We had labored to get to our study site, and now we found the focal species was not here. This was a disappointment, yet the remarkable disappearance of the bird did correspond with the disappearance of the fruit crop. We had documented the first example of a Papuan songbird that shows significant movement in relationship to a major environmental cycle—the periodic reproductive activities of *Dacrycarpus compactus*.

Where do the birds go when they depart Lake Omha? We searched the forest far below the plateau scarp without encountering a single *Macgregoria*. Daily reconnaissances were made of the other tracts of grassland and forest within half-a-day's walk from the camp, without success. The birds were gone.

Gone, but to where? This now becomes one of the mysteries of Macgregor's Bird of Paradise. Do groups of the birds migrate to other subalpine areas where the *Dacrycarpus* is fruiting? Possibly the birds simply descend to a lower altitude and subsist on whatever fruit is there until some presently unknown signal lets them know that the *Dacrycarpus* is ripe again. Might there be a significant local die-off of the species when this occurs?

Why would Macgregor's Bird of Paradise evolve to specialize on a food-plant that fruits unpredictably over a long cycle? We obtained a plausible answer in this season's fieldwork. It related to the remarkable abundance of the fruit crop. We censused *Dacrycarpus* cone production on selected forest plots. We found that, on average, at least fifteen million fruit would be produced per hectare of forest—certainly the richest single-species fruit crop known in the tropics. What a potential bonanza for a bird that can exploit it!

Theoretical ecologists for years have told us that tropical humid forest environments are predictable and benign. This notion has been used to explain the remarkable richness of the tropical forest biota. However, each subsequent season of study in New Guinea reinforced for me the opposite notion. Our observations during August 1987 at Lake Omha further strengthened the counterargument.

August 1986 was a month of rain, mist, and westerly winds. August 1987 was a month of sun and cloudless sky. All of eastern New Guinea was caught in a deep drought, and gardens were wilting, villagers hungry. In 1986, the three most common resident birds at Lake Omha were New Guinea Thornbill, Crested Berrypecker, and Macgregor's Bird of Paradise. In 1987, the three most common species were Red-collared Myzomela, Plum-faced Lorikeet, and Sooty Melidectes. The seasonally resident bird community changed drastically from one August to the next. This sort of change in community dynamics has not previously been exhibited in New Guinea. But it is obvious that major events are happening on an irregular schedule, and predictability is probably not a significant feature of some Papuan habitats. It just so happens this was easier to document in an impoverished, high-altitude environment, where the changes were not masked by environmental complexity.

The Future

One objective of the study of Macgregor's Bird of Paradise was to develop a practical plan for the bird's long-term protection. We discovered that Macgregor's Bird of Paradise would be difficult to protect in a single habitat reserve, for at this time we do not know the extent of the bird's movements. Add to this the knowledge that New Guinean hunters shoot the species for consumption whenever they encounter it, and it is clear that the bird faces an uncertain future.

Macgregor's Bird of Paradise inhabits small segments of New Guinea's central cordillera in western, central, and southeastern New Guinea. Why is it absent from the seemingly suitable high-mountain habitats in Papua New Guinea's central highlands? The intermediate populations disappeared either because of natural or human-caused pressures. Either way, it indicates that the bird is vulnerable. The species has not been seen for decades on Mount Albert Edward, just north of Lake Omha. Has this isolated subpopulation been wiped out by the growing number of hunters carrying firearms into this subalpine habitat?

For a species like Macgregor's Bird of Paradise, no simple remedy exists for its protection. The species is naturally protected by virtue of its mountaintop distribution, but this very same trait means the species is broken up into a series of small, islandlike populations. Do colonists move from one mountaintop to the next? This is unknown. If not, then the demise of this species can occur, mountaintop by mountaintop, and it could even occur because of natural population fluctuations, with or without the added influence of hunting.

The example of Macgregor's Bird of Paradise shows that tropical nature is often complex and unpredictable. Clearly, we have only the sketchiest understanding of the workings of New Guinea's forest environments at this point.

———

Some 75 percent of New Guinea's original forests remain undisturbed. This is as large a percentage as for any humid, equatorial region. However, this expanse of forest is small by tropical standards; it is dwarfed by those of the continental masses of Africa or South America. The entirety of New Guinea's prime lowland forests could be clearfelled in a blink of the evolutionary time scale, a single human lifetime.

Although New Guinea still supports vast tracts of original forest, it is never too early to make efforts to set aside representative areas of habitat that support the natural riches of the island. The Indonesian government has sponsored the development of a remarkable system of natural reserves in Irian Jaya, created with the aid of the World Wildlife Fund and the International Union for Conservation of Nature. Yet Indonesia is a very populous and a very poor country, and its bureaucracy is not noted for its ability to resist the pressures of development and short-term economic incentive. Will the vast reserves in Irian, today relatively pristine by virtue of their isolation and economic insignificance, remain inviolate decades from now? What can be done to insure their long-term preservation?

In Papua New Guinea, the problem is quite different. Virtually all of the lands are traditionally owned, and the village elders (like Robert of Kanga) have direct say over the preservation or exploitation of these lands. In general, this has a conservative effect. It is more difficult for large timber and mining companies to gain easy access to land for exploitation. But this is not to say it is impossible. And what match is a village elder against some clever businessman, offering visions of cash, cars, and luxury? Fortunately, the Papua New Guinea government has been protective of village interests in such schemes, yet it increasingly faces the need to reduce foreign debt. Of late, there is evidence that the timber concerns have begun to gain an upper hand.

The national park and reserve system of Papua New Guinea is in its infancy, mainly because of the tribal land tenure system. Certainly the national government should actively pursue some means of accommodating the needs of its local landowners, while attempting to set aside significant blocks of land for internationally recognized habitat reserves. At present, a system of locally administered wildlife management areas is being established, but this is not adequate, considering the future pressures from a growing world hunger for raw materials.

Change is coming fast to New Guinea. Before long it will be too late to carry out the ecological studies necessary to determine a proper and prudent course of action with regard to development of the island. At what price is a logging concession granted to an aggressive multinational timber concern? What is lost, and is it significantly outweighed by the local economic and cultural gain?

Over the longer term, human population growth can effect a similar environmental degradation. New Guineans obtain a majority of their foods from family gardens. These are cropped on patches of land that have been cleared from forest. The garden plot is exploited for several years and then replaced with a new plot of recently cleared ground. More people require more gardens, with more annual clearing of forest. Although forest can regenerate on old garden plots, this takes decades; as population grows, the cycle of regeneration may be broken, so that clearing outstrips the pace of regrowth. This has happened at a devastating level in the overpopulated Indian region. It may one day happen in New Guinea. Certainly, a national government cannot ban forest clearance for new gardens in the same manner that it can limit the number of multinational timber concerns exploiting local forests. Instead, family planning and land-use planning are required, but these sorts of social programs are not quickly accepted by village societies that value large families and traditional land tenure.

The question of gardens, overpopulation, and forest destruction is as complex in Papua New Guinea as it is for other tropical regions. It involves the interplay of culture, religion, government policy, economics, and education. Ultimately, any robust solution to the threat of widespread forest degradation is one that must include elements of these variables—and hence will be a long-term developmental solution.

―――――

Today, biologists working in the humid tropics have an obligation to make some sort of contribution to the preservation of habitat, diversity, and rare species. This can be accomplished without forsaking academic or theoretical research. Indeed, it is from the literature of academic science that many new practical applications arise, to be borrowed and subsequently adapted by environmental managers and conservation biologists.

One of the points that I have raised in the preceding chapters is the level of our ignorance of the workings of New Guinea's tropical

New Guinea Harpy-Eagle

forest. Certainly, this is the main lesson of my initial studies of the "simple" relationship between Macgregor's Bird of Paradise and the food-plant *Dacrycarpus compactus*.

The first sustained, field-based doctoral project on an ecological topic in New Guinea was conducted by Allen Allison during the years 1973 to 1975. That's only yesterday. How many more doctoral field projects must be conducted before we have even a vague understanding of the annual and supraannual dynamics of a Papuan rainforest? What physical or biotic factors trigger fruiting cycles in important canopy trees? How is the nesting seasonality of birds tied to the rhythm of the forest? How can these cycles become attuned to the major, unpredictable weather perturbations allied to the South Oscillation (El Niño)? To what extent are long-distance (province-wide) migrations a regular phenomenon in Papuan forest birds?

These and other questions may sound esoteric, but answers to them are needed if we are to have sufficient information to make responsible decisions on conservation of habitats and threatened species. Take Macgregor's Bird of Paradise—a conservation plan would have to recognize the importance of periodic movements of the birds. It would be useless to design a small reserve encompassing a few dozen square miles, if the major threatened species regularly migrates out of the area's boundaries.

The mysterious life history of Macgregor's Bird of Paradise emphasizes the importance of ecological relationships that span major forms of life. Both Papua New Guinea and Indonesia have banned the hunting of all species of birds of paradise, but this legislation fails to accommodate the potential problems related to habitat alteration and loss of food-plants. To ban hunting is irrelevant if a bird's populations are dwindling because of habitat degradation. What food-plants are important to the most threatened birds of paradise?

Papua New Guinea's population of Archbold's Bowerbird may exemplify this problem. This species is known only from a few high altitude localities in the western and southern highlands, areas that have seen significant disturbance from timber extraction. The bowerbird, a habitat specialist, and uncommon even in ideal conditions, is a fruit-eater, yet not a single plant species in its fruit diet has been identified, to date. It may be that preservation by loggers of selected trees of a few key species can ensure the long-term preservation of Archbold's Bowerbird in Papua New Guinea. At this time, ignorance prevents our developing any sort of specific conservation hypothesis that can accommodate the pressures of the timber industry.

There is yet another side of this conservation problem. Fruit-eating bird species are often important dispersers of forest seeds. How many species of trees will disappear from Papuan forests if important seed-dispersing bird species are extirpated? In an earlier chapter, I mentioned that there are specialized forest trees whose seeds are dispersed *only* by birds of paradise. Certainly there are hundreds of other ecological examples in which the livelihood of one forest inhabitant is dependent upon another. These relationships must be studied by the future students of the rainforest. And why should this work depend solely on the interests of foreign scientists? Let's hope that in the near future, New Guinea's forests can benefit from study by not only a new generation of footloose and adventurous students from the West, but also by a whole cohort of New Guineans, who deserve the right to share in these exciting discoveries being made in the forests owned by their village elders. This will happen only with increased international support for education and technical training of promising indigenous natu-ralists; little such effort has been made to date. It is now time to share the excitement and responsibilities of studying these tropical forests with those who will ultimately have to decide their fate.

References

Archbold, R., A. L. Rand, and L. J. Brass. 1942. Summary of the 1938–1939 New Guinea expedition. *Bull. Amer. Mus. Nat. Hist.* 79:197–288.

Beehler, B. M. 1980. A comparison of avian foraging at flowering trees in Panama and New Guinea. *Wilson Bull.* 92:513–519.

———. 1983. Frugivory and polygamy in birds of paradise. *Auk* 100:1–12.

———. 1983. Lek behavior of the Lesser Bird of Paradise. *Auk* 100:992–996.

———. 1983. Notes on the behaviour and ecology of Macgregor's Bird of Paradise. *Emu* 83:28–30.

———. 1985. "Adaptive significance of monogamy in the Trumpet Manucode (Aves: Paradisaeidae)." In *Avian monogamy*, ed. P. Gowaty and D. Mock, 83–99. *Ornith. Monogr.* 38.

———. 1987. Birds of paradise and mating system theory—predictions and observations. *Emu* 87:78–89.

———. 1988. Lek behavior of the Raggiana Bird of Paradise. *Natl. Geogr. Research* 4:343–358.

———. 1989. The birds of paradise. *Scientific American*, Dec., 117–123.

Beehler, B. M., and C. H. Beehler. 1986. Observations on the ecology and behavior of the Pale-billed Sicklebill. *Wilson Bull.* 98:505–515.

Beehler, B. M., and M. S. Foster. 1988. Hotshots, hotspots, and female preference in the organization of lek mating systems. *Amer. Nat.* 131:203–219.

Beehler, B. M., T. K. Pratt, and D. A. Zimmerman. 1986. *Birds of New Guinea*. Princeton: Princeton University Press.

Beehler, B. M., and S. G. Pruett-Jones. 1983. Display dispersion and diet of eight birds of paradise. *Behav. Ecol. Sociobio.* 13:229–238.

Bell, H. L. 1980. Foraging ecology, territoriality and seasonality of the Common Paradise Kingfisher at Brown River, Papua New Guinea. *Corella* 4:113–126.

———. 1983. A bird community of lowland rainforest in New Guinea. 5. Mixed-species feeding flocks. *Emu* 82:7–11.

Brass, L. J. 1956. Summary of the' Fourth Archbold Expedition to New Guinea (1953). *Bull. Amer. Mus. Nat. Hist.* 111:83–152.

Coates, B. J. 1985. *Birds of Papua New Guinea.* Vol. 1. *Non-Passerines.* Alderley, Queensland: Dove Publications.

Diamond, J. M. 1970. Ecological consequences of island colonization by southwest Pacific birds. II. The effect of species diversity on total population density. *Proc. Natl. Acad. Sci.* (U.S.A.) 67:1715–1721.

Diamond, J. M. 1972. *Avifauna of the eastern highlands of New Guinea.* Publication no. 12. Cambridge, Mass.: Nuttall Ornithological Club.

———. 1982. Mimicry of friarbirds by orioles. *Auk* 100:187–196.

———. 1987. Flocks of brown and black New Guinean birds: a bicolored mixed species foraging association. *Emu* 87:201–211.

Flynn, E. 1960. *My wicked, wicked ways.* New York: Putnam.

Frodin, D. G., and J. L. Gressitt. 1982. "Biological exploration of New Guinea." In *Biogeography and Ecology of New Guinea,* ed. J. L. Gressitt, 87–130.

The Hague: W. Junk Publishers.

Gardner, R., and K. Heider. 1969. *Gardens of war.* London: Andre Deutch.

Gash, N., and J. Whittaker. 1975. *A pictorial history of New Guinea.* Milton, Queensland: Jacaranda Press.

Gilliard, E. T. 1969. *Birds of paradise and bower birds.* Garden City, N.Y.: Natural History Press.

Goff, M. L. 1982. "New Guinea chiggers (Acari: Trombiculidae)." In *Biogeography and Ecology of New Guinea,* ed. J. L. Gressitt, 545–556. The Hague: W. Junk Publishers.

Greenway, J. C. 1935. Birds from the coastal range between the Markham and Waria rivers, northeastern New Guinea. *Proc. New Engl. Zool. Club* 14:15–106.

Gressitt, J. L., ed. 1982. *Biogeography and ecology of New Guinea.* The Hague: W. Junk Publishers.

Gressitt, J. L. and N. Nadkarni. 1978. *Guide to Mount Kaindi.* Handbook no. 5. Wau, Papua New Guinea: Wau Ecology Institute.

Hall, T. 1981. *New Guinea 1942–44.* Sydney: Methuen Australia.

Hides, J. *Papuan wonderland.* London: Blackie.

Hoy, B. D. 1987. Amelia Earhart remembered. *Paradise* no. 63:11–17.

Johns, R. J. 1977. The vegetation of Papua New Guinea. Part 1: An introduction to the vegetation. Bulolo, Papua New Guinea: Forestry College of Papua New Guinea.

Lawrence, P. 1964. *Road belong cargo.* Manchester, England: Manchester University Press.

Löffler, E. 1977. *Geomorphology of Papua New Guinea.* Canberra: Australian National Univ.

MacArthur, R. 1972. *Geographical ecology.* New York: Harper and Row.

MacArthur, R. H., and E. O. Wilson. 1967. *The theory of island biogeography.* Princeton: Princeton Univ. Press.

Majnep, I. S., and R. Bulmer. *Birds of my Kalam country.* Auckland, New Zealand: Auckland Univ. Press.

Mayr, E., and E. T. Gilliard. 1952. The ribbon-tailed bird of paradise (*Astrapia mayeri*) and its allies. *Amer. Mus. Novit.* no. 1551.

McAlpine, J. R., G. Kieg, and R. Falls. 1983. *Climate of Papua New Guinea.* Canberra: Australian National Univ.

Menzies, J. I. 1975. *Handbook of common New Guinea frogs.* Handbook no. 1. Wau, Papua New Guinea: Wau Ecology Institute.

Miller, A. 1978. *Orchids of Papua New Guinea.* Canberra: Australian National Univ.

Miller, A. H. 1964. A new species of warbler from New Guinea. *Auk* 81:1–4.

Mitton, R. 1980. *The lost world of Irian Jaya.* Melbourne: Oxford Univ. Press.

Munn, C. A. 1985. Permanent canopy and understory flocks in Amazonia: Species composition and population density. In *Neotropical ornithology,* eds. P. A. Buckley, et al., 683–710. *Ornith. Monogr.* 36.

Paijmans, K., ed. 1976. *New Guinea vegetation.* New York: Elsevier Scientific Publishing Co.

Paull, R. 1983. *Retreat from Kokoda.* Richmond, Victoria: William Heinemann Australia.

Peckover, W., and L. W. C. Filewood. 1976. *Birds of New Guinea and tropical Australia.* Sydney: A. H. and A. W. Reed.

Pieters, P. E. 1982. "Geology of New Guinea." In *Biogeography and ecology of New Guinea,* ed. J. L. Gressitt, 15–38. The Hague: W. Junk Publishers.

Pratt, T. K. 1983. *Seed dispersal in a montane forest in Papua New Guinea.* Ph.D. diss., Rutgers University.

Pratt, T. K., and E. W. Stiles. 1983. How long fruit-eating birds stay in plants where they feed: Implications for seed dispersal. *Amer. Nat.* 122:797–805.

Rand, A. L. 1940. Breeding habits of the birds of paradise *Macgregoria* and *Diphyllodes. Amer. Mus. Novit.* no. 1073:1–14.

Rand, A. L., and E. T. Gilliard. 1968. *Handbook of New Guinea birds.* Garden City, N.Y.: Natural History Press.

Richardson, D. 1979. *Lords of the earth.* Glendale, Calif.: Regal Books.

Ripley, S. D. 1964. A systematic and ecological study of birds of New Guinea. *Bull. Peabody Mus. Nat. Hist. (Yale Univ.)* 19:1–87.

Robinson, M. H., and B. Robinson. The ecology and behavior of the giant wood spider *Nephila maculata* (Fabricius) in New Guinea. *Smithson. Contrib. Zool.* 149:1–76.

Royen, P. van, and P. Kores. 1982. *The Ericaceae of the high mountains of New Guinea.* Vaduz, Netherlands: J. Cramer.

Ryan, P., ed. 1972. *Encyclopaedia of Papua and New Guinea.* Carlton, Victoria: Melbourne Univ. Press.

Simon, M. 1983. The ecology of parental care in a terrestrial frog. *Behav. Ecol. Sociobio.* 14:61–67.

Sinclair, J. 1978. *Wings of gold*. Bathurst, New South Wales: Robert Brown and Associates.

Sleumer, H. 1966–67. Ericaceae. *Flora Malesiana.* 1(6)4:469–668; 5:669–914.

Steinberg, R. *Island fighting*. Alexandria, Va.: Time-Life Books.

Stevens, P. H. 1976. The altitudinal and geographical distribution of flower types in *Rhododendron* section Vireya, especially the Papuasian species. *J. Linn. Soc. Bot.* 72:1–33.

Wallace, A. R. 1869. *The Malay Archipelago*. New York: Harper Brothers.

Whitney, B. 1987. Pale-billed Sicklebill in Papua New Guinea. *Emu* 87:244–246.

Index